T0237891

Communications
in Computer and Information Science   29

Haeng-kon Kim   Tai-hoon Kim
Akingbehin Kiumi (Eds.)

Advances in Security Technology

International Conference
SecTech 2008, and Its Special Sessions
Sanya, Hainan Island, China, December 13-15, 2008
Revised Selected Papers

 Springer

Volume Editors

Haeng-kon Kim
Catholic University of Daegu
South Korea
E-mail: hangkon@cu.ac.kr

Tai-hoon Kim
Hannam University, Daejeon
South Korea
E-mail: taihoonn@empal.com

Akingbehin Kiumi
University of Michigan-Dearborn
Dearborn, MI, USA
E-mail: kiumi@umich.edu

Library of Congress Control Number: Applied for

CR Subject Classification (1998): E.3, D.4.6, K.6.5, D.2, C.2

ISSN 1865-0929

ISBN 978-3-642-10239-4 Springer Berlin Heidelberg New York

springer.com

© Springer-Verlag Berlin Heidelberg 2009

Typesetting: Camera-ready by author, data conversion by Scientific Publishing Services, Chennai, India
Printed on acid-free paper   SPIN: 12792863   06/3180   5 4 3 2 1 0

Preface

As security technology (ST) becomes specialized and fragmented, it is easy to lose sight that many topics in ST have common threads and because of this, advances in one sub-discipline may transmit to another. The presentation of results between different sub-disciplines of ST encourages this interchange for the advancement of ST as a whole. Of particular interest is the hybrid approach of combining ideas from one discipline with those of another to achieve a result that is more significant than the sum of the individual parts. Through this hybrid philosophy, a new or common principle can be discovered which has the propensity to propagate throughout this multi-faceted discipline.

This volume comprises the selection of extended versions of papers that were presented in their shortened form at the 2008 International Conference on Security Technology (http://www.sersc.org/SECTECH2008/) and 2009 Advanced Science and Technology (http://www.sersc.org/AST2009/).

We would like to acknowledge the great effort of all in the SecTech 2008 and AST 2009 International Advisory Board and members of the International Program Committee, as well as all the organizations and individuals who supported the idea of publishing these advances in security technology, including SERSC (http://www.sersc.org/) and Springer.

We would like to give special thanks to Rosslin John Robles, Maricel O. Balitanas, Farkhod Alisherov Alisherovish, Feruza Sattarova Yusfovna. These graduate school students of Hannam University attended to the editing process of this volume with great passion.

We strongly believe in the need for continuing this undertaking in the future, in the form of a conference, journal, or book series. In this respect we welcome any feedback.

April 2009
Haeng-kon Kim
Tai-hoon Kim
Akingbehin Kiumi

Organization

General Co-chairs

Tai-hoon Kim Hannam University, Korea
Wai Chi Fang NASA JPL, USA

Program Co-chairs

Changhoon Lee Korea University, Korea
Kirk P. Arnett Mississippi State University, USA

Publicity Co-chairs

Hai Jin Huazhong University of Science and Technology, China
Antonio Coronato ICAR-CNR, Italy
Damien Sauveron Université de Limoges/CNRS, France
Hua Liu Xerox Corporation, USA
Kevin Raymond Boyce Butler Pennsylvania State University, USA
Guojun Wang Central South University, China
Tao Jiang Huazhong University of Science and Technology, China
Gang Wu UESTC, China
Yoshiaki Hori Kyushu University, Japan

Publication Chair

Yong-ik Yoon Sookmyung Women's University, Korea

System Management Chair

Sang-Soo Yeo Kyushu University, Japan

International Advisory Board

Dominik Slezak Inforbright, Poland
Edwin H-M. Sha University of Texas at Dallas, USA
Jong Hyuk Park Kyungnam University, Korea
Justin Zhan CMU, USA

Kouich Sakurai   Kyushu University, Japan
Laurence T. Yang   St. Francis Xavier University, Canada
Byeong-Ho KANG   University of Tasmania, Australia

Program Committee

Abdelwahab Hamou-Lhadj   Concordia University, Canada
Ajay Kumar   Indian Institute of Technology Deihi, India
Bin Xiao   The Hong Kong Polytechnic University, China
ByungRae Cha   Honam University, Korea
C. Lambrinoudakis   University of the Aegean, Greece
Chin-Laung Lei   Taiwan
Chun-Yang Chen   Institute of Information Science, Academia Sinica,
                               Taiwan
Damien Sauveron   UMR 6172 University of Limoges / CNRS, France
E. Konstantinou   University of the Aegean, Greece
Edwin H-M. Sha   University of Texas at Dallas, USA
Eul Gyu Im   Hanyang University, Korea
Gerald Schaefer   Aston University, UK
Hsiang-Cheh Huang   National University of Kaohsiung, Taiwan
Hyun-Sung Kim   Kyungil University, Korea
J. H. Abbawajy   Deakin University, Australia
Jaechul Sung   University of Seoul, Korea
Jan deMeer   University of Applied Sciences TFH Berlin, Germany
Javier Garcia Villalba   Complutense University of Madrid, Spain
Jiang (Leo) Li   Howard University, USA
Jin Kwak   Soonchunhyang University, Korea
Jongmoon Baik   Information and Communications University, Korea
Jordi Castella-Roca   Rovira i Virgili University, Spain
Jordi Forne   Universitat Politecnica de Catalunya, Spain
Jung-Taek Seo   The Attached Institute of ETRI, Korea
Justin Zhan   CMU, USA
Kyungjun Kim   Honam University, Korea
Larbi Esmahi   Athabasca University, Canada
Luigi Buglione   Atos Origin, Italy
MalRey Lee   Chonbuk University, Korea
Martin Drahansky   University of Technology, Czech Republic
Michael Tunstall   University College Cork, Ireland
Qi Shi   Liverpool John Moores University, UK
Radu G. Andrei   PluraTech, USA
Rodrigo Mello   University of Sao Paulo, Brazil
Seokhie Hong   Korea University, Korea
Serge Chaumette   University Bordeaux 1, France
Stan Kurkovsky   Central Connecticut State University, USA
Stan Matwin   University of Ottawa, Canada
Stefanos Gritzalis   University of the Aegean, Greece

Tanya Vladimirova	University of Surrey, UK
Tony Shan	University of Phoenix, USA
Tughrul Arslan	University of Edinburgh, UK
Vincent Hsu	L1-Identity Solutions, USA
Wen-Shenq Juang	National Kaohsiung First University of Science & Tech., Taiwan
Yeong Deok Kim	Woosong University
Yong Man Ro	Information and Communication University, Korea
Young Ik Eom	Sungkyunkwan University, Korea

Table of Contents

Security Analysis of "A Novel Elliptic Curve Dynamic Access Control System"

Wen-Chung Kuo

Department of Computer Science and Information Engineering,
National Formosa University, Taiwan, R.O.C.
simonkuo@nfu.edu.tw

Abstract. In 2007, Wen *et al.* proposed a novel elliptic curve dynamic access control system. In this paper, we will show that the scheme is vulnerable to various attacks.

Keywords: Elliptic Curve Cryptosystem, Hierarchy, Access Control.

1 Introduction

As the development of information data and networking technology increase rapidly, various digital multimedia can be transmitted over the Internet. In order to manage the accessing priority, many computer communication systems often employ user hierarchies to solve access control problems. A user hierarchy structure is constructed by dividing users into a number of disjoint classes $SC_1, SC_2, \ldots, SC_n$ are n disjointed classes with a binary partially ordered relation $\leq$. The meaning of $SC_i \leq SC_j$ denotes that the security class SC_j have a security clearance higher than or equal to the security class SC_i, while the opposite is not allowed. This form of access control mechanism has many proven operational and security benefits, and has therefore been widely applied for a diverse range of governmental, diplomatic, military and business systems applications[13].

Fig.1 shows the poset in a user hierarchy and the arrowhead represents a relationship that the higher-level security class is authorized with the security clearance higher than the lower-level one. For example, there is an arrow from SC_3 to SC_6, i.e. the statement $SC_6 \leq SC_3$, means that SC_3 is the predecessor of SC_6 and SC_6 the successor of SC_3. In other words, users in SC_3 can derive the secret key in SC_6 and access information held by users in SC_6, but the users in SC_6 cannot access the information held by the users in SC_3. Furthermore, if there is no other security class SC_2 in SC so that $SC_5 \leq SC_2 \leq SC_1$, then SC_1 is called the immediate predecessor of SC_5, and SC_5 the immediate successor to SC_1. [2]

Akl and Taylor [1](AT-scheme for short) first proposed a simple cryptographic key assignment scheme to solve the access control problems in 1983. However, there is a serious drawback in AT-scheme, i.e., it fails to provide the user with a convenient way to change his/her secret key under the secure considerations. In

T.-k. Kim, T.-h. Kim, and A. Kiumi (Eds.): SecTech 2008, CCIS 29, pp. 1–14, 2009.

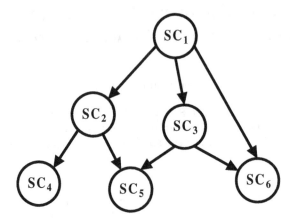

Fig. 1. Poset in a user hierarchy

order to solve this drawback, a dynamic access control scheme is proposed with the following characteristics: (1)the key generation and derivation algorithms are as simple as possible; (2)the re-updating key problem can be efficiently solved; (3)the users can change theine secret keys anytime and anywhere for the sake of security; (4)the system can withstand the collusive attacks[2]. Until now, there are several key management schemes [5,11,14,15] were forwarded for improving dynamic access control. In 1997, a novel cryptographic key assignment scheme for dynamic access control in a hierarchy based on Rabin's public key system[10] and Chinese remainder theorem[3] was proposed by (SCL-scheme for brevity). They stated that the SCL-scheme is much simpler to implement than other cryptographic key assignment schemes for access control in a hierarchy. In fact, Shen *et al.* used the Rabin's scheme to hide the user's secret key K_i. Furthermore, reducing the computation time for key assignment and the storage size for public parameters in the SCL-scheme, Hwang used the exclusive-or operation to replace the main function of Rabin's scheme[5].

Lately, a hierarchical access control scheme based on the secure filter method was proposed by K. P. Wu *et al.*[15] (WRTL-scheme for short) in 2001. They used the exponential operation formula $Sf_i(x) = \prod_{k=0}^{n-1}(x - g_i^{s_k}) + k_i \bmod p$ to construct a secure filter, in which p is a large prime; s_k represents a secure code, with $0 \geq s_k \geq p-1$; g_i is the primitive root, with $1 \geq g_i \geq p-1$; and k_i is the secret key. Afterward this secure filter had been applied to the dynamic access control system[15]. However, Wen *et al.*[14] pointed out the secure filter has the following two faults. One is the secure filter employs exponential operation which takes a longer time than the simple multiplication does and the other is the exponential operation takes up a much larger storage space than the simple multiplication does.

Recently, a novel access control in user hierarchy based on elliptic curve cryptosystem was proposed by Wen *et al.*(WWC-scheme for short)[14]. According to the WWC-scheme, the special feature of this scheme can not only solve dynamic access problems in a user hierarchy but also perform in terms of both security and efficiency is quite commendable. However, the security of WWC-scheme is also insecure under the dynamic exterior attack. In other words, the security of WWC-scheme is not guaranteed when a new security class joins or a new ordered relationship is added into this scheme. In this paper, we will show that the attacker can easily recover the user's secret key without knowledge of the CA's private key.

The rest of the paper is organized as follows: In Section 2, we briefly introduce the WWC-scheme. In Section 3, we discuss the security of WWC-scheme. Conclusions are drawn in last section.

2 Review the WWC-Scheme

2.1 The Operations of the Elliptic Curve

We assume that the general form of elliptic curve $E_p(a, b) : y^2 = x^3 + ax + b \mod p$, where p is a prime and the values of a, b satisfy the discriminant condition, $D = 4a^3 + 27b^2 \neq 0 \mod p$, is used in this scheme. From this definition, we can define the rules of addition over an elliptic curve $E_p(a, b)$:[7,9,12]

1. $\mathcal{O}$ serves as the additive identity. Thus $-\mathcal{O} = \mathcal{O}$ and $P + \mathcal{O} = P$.

2. $-P$ is the negative of a point P; that is, if $P = (x, y)$, then $-P = (x, -y)$. Note that $P + (-P) = \mathcal{O}$.

3. If $P \neq \mathcal{O}, Q \neq \mathcal{O}$, and $Q \neq -P$, then $P + Q = -R$. Here, R is the intersection point of $E_p(a, b)$ and the line segment $\bar{PQ}$.

Let $P = (x_1, y_1) \in E_p(a, b)$, $Q = (x_2, y_2) \in E_p(a, b)$, then $P + Q = (x_3, y_3)$, where

$$x_3 = \begin{cases} (\frac{y_2 - y_1}{x_2 - x_1})^2 - x_1 - x_2, & \text{if } x_1 \neq x_2, \\ (\frac{3x_1^2 + a}{2y_1})^2 - 2x_1, & \text{if } x_1 = x_2. \end{cases}$$

$$y_3 = \begin{cases} -y_1 + \frac{y_2 - y_1}{x_2 - x_1}(x_1 - x_3), & \text{if } x_1 \neq x_2, \\ -y_1 + \frac{3x_1^2 + a}{2y_1}(x_1 - x_3), & \text{if } x_1 = x_2. \end{cases}$$

Therefore, if a point G is taken as the base point over the elliptic curve $E_p(a, b)$, then the operation on nG has the following properties. $1G = G$, $2G = G + G$, $3G = 2G + G$, ..., $(n-1)G = (n-2)G + G$, $nG = (n-1)G + G = O$ and $(n+1)G = G$.[7]

The Table 1 lists the elements of the elliptic groups with $p = 23$[8].

Example 1. Let $P = (3, 10)$ and $Q = (9, 7)$ be in $E_{23}(1, 1)$, then we can find out $P + Q = (17, 20)$ as the following operations.

Step 1. Compute $\frac{y_2 - y_1}{x_2 - x_1} = \frac{7 - 10}{9 - 3} = (-3) \times 6^{-1} = 11 \mod 23$.

Table 1. The Elliptic Group $E_{23}(1,1)$

(0,1)	(0,22)	(1,7)	(1,16)
(3,10)	(3,13)	(4,0)	
(5,4)	(5,19)	(6,4)	(6,19)
(7,11)	(7,12)	(9,7)	(9,16)
(11,3)	(11,20)	(12,4)	(12,19)
(13,7)	(13,16)	(17,3)	(17,20)
(18,3)	(18,20)	(19,5)	(19,18)

Step 2. Calculate $x_3 = (\frac{y_2-y_1}{x_2-x_1})^2 - x_1 - x_2 = 11^2 - 9 - 3 = 17 \bmod 23$.

Step 3. Compute $y_3 = -y_1 + \frac{y_2-y_1}{x_2-x_1}(x_1 - x_3) = 11 - \times(3 - (-6)) - 10 = 20 \bmod 23$.

2.2   The WWC-Scheme

The WWC-scheme based on elliptic curve cryptosystem [14]. We assume that a Central Authority(CA) exists and the set $SC = \{SC_1, SC_2, \ldots, SC_n\}$, where $SC_1, SC_2, \ldots, SC_n$ are n disjointed security classes with a binary partially ordered relationship $\leq$ in WWC-scheme. Therefore, $SC_i \leq SC_j$ denotes that the security class SC_j have a security clearance higher than or equal to the security class SC_i. SC_j is classified as a predecessor of SC_i, and SC_i as a successor of SC_j. The predecessors SC_j have the accessibility to information belonging to their successors SC_i, but not vice versa. Here, the WWC-scheme is summarized as follows:

Key generation. To complete the key generation phase, CA executes the algorithm below.

Step 1. Choose select an elliptic curve $E_p(a, b) : y^2 = x^3 + ax + b \bmod p$, where a, b such that $D = 4a^3 + 27b^2 \neq 0 \bmod p$, and the point G_i on $E_p(a, b)$ as the base point for SC_i.

Step 2. The CA chooses user secret codes n_j for all j satisfying $SC_i \leq SC_j$ and $j \neq i$, where n_j is a prime, and performs elliptic curve multiplication with the base point G_i to get $n_j G_i = (x_j, y_j)$ and $f(n_j G_i) = x_j \oplus y_j$.

Step 3. The CA constructs a public elliptic curve polynomial(ECP) $E_i(x)$ as follows:

$$E_i(x) = \prod_j [x - f(n_j G_i)] + k_i \bmod p, \tag{1}$$

where k_i is the secret key of the user u_i and $\prod_j$ is performed for all j such that $SC_i \leq SC_j$ and $j \neq i$.

Step 4. The CA distributes $E_i(x)$ and G_i to the user u_i of security class SC_i and publishes them.

Example 2. There are six users, i.e., $U = \{u_1, u_2, \ldots, u_6\}$ in the poset diagram shown as Fig.2. According to Eq.(1), the CA can construct the public ECP for each user. Here, we suppose the ECP of user u_1 is 0, and then we can obtain

$$u_1 : E_1(x) = 0 \bmod p,$$
$$u_2 : E_2(x) = [x - f(n_1 G_2)] + k_2 \bmod p,$$
$$u_3 : E_3(x) = [x - f(n_1 G_3)] + k_3 \bmod p,$$
$$u_4 : E_4(x) = [x - f(n_1 G_4)][x - f(n_2 G_4)] + k_4 \bmod p,$$
$$u_5 : E_5(x) = [x - f(n_2 G_5)][x - f(n_3 G_5)] + k_5 \bmod p,$$
$$u_6 : E_6(x) = [x - f(n_1 G_6)][x - f(n_3 G_6)] + k_6 \bmod p.$$

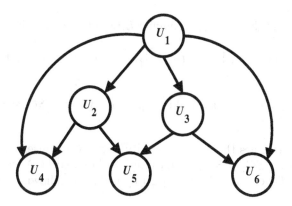

Fig. 2. Dynamic access control system for six users

Retrieval of Secret Key. Assume that $SC_i \leq SC_j$, i.e., the predecessor SC_j can recover the secret keys k_i by using their secret code n_j. However, users in the lower class SC_i cannot access the secret key k_j of users in the upper class SC_j. Here, SC_j calculates k_i by the following steps,

Step 1. A user in the upper class SC_j uses his secret code n_j, he can compute $n_j G_i = (x_j, y_j)$.

Step 2. Calculate $f(n_j G_i) = x_j \oplus y_j$.

Step 3. Substitute $f(n_j G_i)$ into the Eq.(1) to obtain the secret key k_i.

For example, in the $SC_4 \leq SC_2$ poset user hierarchy shown in Fig.2, user u_2 in the upper class uses his secret code n_2 in accordance with the ECP secret key retrieval method to discover the secret key k_4 of user u_4.

2.3   Inserting New Security Class

Apply the above structure to the dynamic access control scheme, we suppose that a new security class SC_a is inserted into the hierarchy such that $SC_i \leq SC_a \leq SC_j$. CA will do the following process to update the partial relationship to manage the accessing priority when SC_a joins the hierarchy.

Step 1. The CA randomly selects user's secret code n_a and the secret key k_a both of which are prime. He sends n_a and k_a to user u_a by a secure channel.

Step 2. The CA adds $E_a(x)$ to the $SC_a \leq SC_j$ poset with

$$E_a(x) = \prod_j [x - f(n_j G_a)] + k_a \bmod p.$$

where $\prod_j$ is performed for all j satisfying $SC_a \leq SC_j$ and $j \neq a$.

Step 3. Determine the public polynomial $E_i'(x)$ by the following equation,

$$E_i'(x) = \{\prod_j [x - f(n_j G_i)]\}[x - f(n_a G_i)] + k_i' \bmod p, \tag{2}$$

where $\prod_j$ is performed identical to Eq.(1) and for each SC_i such that $SC_i \leq SC_a$.

Example 3. It assumes that a new security class SC_7 is inserted into the user hierarchy such that $SC_6 \leq SC_7 \leq SC_1$ in Fig.3. Afterward CA will generate the information n_7, k_7, G_7, $E_7(x)$, and $E_6'(x)$ by using the following steps,

Step 1: Randomly selects two primes n_7, k_7 and the base point $G_7 \in E_p(a, b)$ for user U_7.
Step 2: Calculate $E_6'(x)$ and $E_7(x)$ such that

$$u_7 : E_7(x) = [x - f(n_1 G_7)] + k_7 \bmod p, \tag{3}$$
$$u_6 : E_6'(x) = [(x - f(n_1 G_6))(x - f(n_3 G_6))][x - f(n_7 G_6)] + k_6' \bmod p. \tag{4}$$

Step 3: Use the $E_6'(x)$ to replace $E_6(x)$ as the public polynomial.

Finally, CA transmits n_7 and k_7 to user u_7 via a secret channel and announces G_7, $E_7(x)$, and $E_6'(x)$.

2.4   Adding Ordered Relationships

Suppose a new ordered relationship $SC_i \leq SC_b \leq SC_a \leq SC_j$ to replace the original relationship $SC_i \leq SC_a \leq SC_j$. CA will do the following process to setup this new ordered relationship $SC_i \leq SC_b \leq SC_a \leq SC_j$.

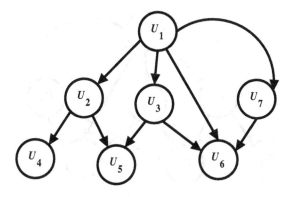

Fig. 3. The consequent poset after inserting u_7

Step 1. When $SC_b \leq SC_a$ is added to the original relationship $SC_a \leq SC_j$, the CA needs to modify the public polynomial $E_b(x)$ of SC_b to $E'_b(x)$ as follows:

$$E'_b(x) = \{\prod_j [x - f(n_j G_b)]\}[x - f(n_a G_b)] + k'_b \bmod p.$$

where $\prod_j$ is performed identical to the original $E_b(x)$.

Step 2. The CA also use the following polynomial $E'_i(x)$ to replace the original public polynomial $E_i(x)$ such that the new relationship $SC_i \leq SC_b \leq SC_a$.

$$E'_i(x) = \{\prod_j [x - f(n_j G_i)]\}[x - f(n_a G_i)] + k'_i \bmod p.$$

where $\prod_j$ is performed identical to the original $E_i(x)$.

Example 4. We assume that there is a new ordered relationship $SC_5 \leq SC_7$ is added and the new hierarchy structure is shown as Fig.4. Therefore, CA will reconstruct a new E'_5 as follows:

$$u_5 : E'_5(x) = [(x - f(n_2 G_5))(x - f(n_3 G_5))][x - f(n_7 G_5)] + k'_5 \bmod p. \quad (5)$$

Then, CA transmits k'_5 to user u_5 via a secret channel and publishes E'_5 and G_5.

2.5   Deleting Relationships

Suppose, in an ordered relationship $SC_i \leq SC_b \leq SC_a \leq SC_j$ system, the $SC_b \leq SC_a$ poset will be deleted. Then, CA will do the following process to delete this relationship.

Step 1. From the original $SC_b \leq SC_a \leq SC_j$ ordered relationship, delete the $SC_b \leq SC_a$ relationship, forming an $SC_a \leq SC_j$. The $E_b(x)$ polynomial in

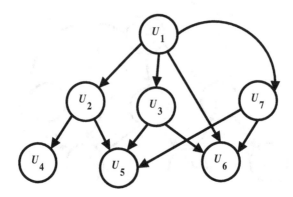

Fig. 4. Adding a relationship between U_7 and U_5

SC_b will be changed to $E'_b(x)$ as follows:

$$E'_b(x) = \prod_j [x - f(n_j G'_b)] + k'_b \bmod p.$$

where $\prod_j$ is performed for all j such that $SC_b \leq SC_j$ and $j \neq b$ after the deletion.

Step 2. From the original $SC_i \leq SC_b \leq SC_a$ ordered relationship, delete the $SC_b \leq SC_a$ relationship, forming an $SC_i \leq SC_b$. The $E_i(x)$ polynomial in $SC_i b$ will be changed to $E'_i(x)$ as follows:

$$E'_i(x) = \prod_j [x - f(n_j G'_i)] + k'_i \bmod p.$$

where $\prod_j$ is performed for all j such that $SC_i \leq SC_j$ and $j \neq b$ after the deletion.

Example 5. We assume that there is an ordered relationship $SC_6 \leq SC_3$ in Fig.4 is deleted and the new hierarchy structure is shown as Fig.5. Therefore, CA needs to reconstruct a new ECP:E'_6 of user u_6 as follows:

$$u_6 : E'_6(x) = [(x - f(n_1 G'_6))(x - f(n_7 G'_6))] + k'_6 \bmod p. \tag{6}$$

Then, CA transmits k'_6 and G'_6 to user u_6 via a secret channel and publishes E'_6 and G'_6.

2.6 The Security Analysis and Discussion

In [14], Wen *et al.* discuss the security of WWC-scheme from two parts, the secret code and the secret key.

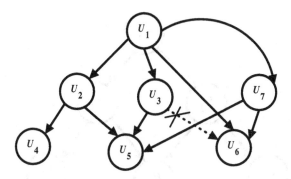

Fig. 5. Deleting a relationship between U_3 and U_6

2.6.1 Secret Analysis for Secret Code

In this subsection, they proposed the following five attacks such as contrary attack, interior collecting attack, interior mutual attack, exterior attack and collaborative attack to analyze the security of WWC-scheme. Now, we take the collaborative attack for an example.

Collaborative attack: It is defined as m successors have a common predecessor and they collaboratively want to obtain the secret code of their predecessor in WWC-scheme. In this attack, for convenience, u_2 and u_3 have the common predecessor u_1 and they collaboratively attempt to obtain the secret code n_1 in Fig.6. The ECP's of u_2 and u_2 are generated as following,

$$E_2(x) = [x - f(n_1 G_2)] + k_2 \bmod p, \tag{7}$$
$$E_3(x) = [x - f(n_1 G_3)] + k_3 \bmod p. \tag{8}$$

By setting $x = 0$ in the Eqs.(7) and (8), we can obtain Eqs.(9) and (10).

$$e_1 = [k_2 - E_2(0)] = f(n_1 G_2) \bmod p, \tag{9}$$
$$e_2 = [k_3 - E_3(0)] = f(n_1 G_3) \bmod p. \tag{10}$$

With collaboration, users u_2 and u_3 can discover e_1 and e_2 through the known values k_2, k_3, $E_2(0)$ and $E_3(0)$. Obviously, it is very difficult to determine n_1 from both Eqs.(9) and (10) based on the known values e_1, e_2, G_2 and G_3. Therefore, Wen *et al.* claim that WWC-scheme provides qualified secure tolerance for resisting the above attacks on secret code.

2.6.2 Secret Analysis for the Secret Key

For the secret key attacks, there possible attacks such as exterior attack, sibling attack, and ordered relationship changing attack are discussed in [14]. Here, we will roughly review the exterior attack was proposed by Wen *et al.* in 2007. For a more detailed discussion on other attacks, the reader can refer to [14].

Exterior attack: It is defined as an unauthorized user w wishes to access the secret key k_i of some user u_i in the WWC-scheme through the related public

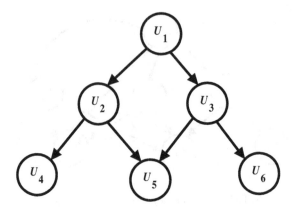

Fig. 6. Dynamic access control system for six users

information. Wen *et al.* pointed out two possible ways to acquire k_i when user w is not a member of this hierarchy.

The Way 1: The illegal user w recovers the secret key k_i directly from the ECP. The ECP of u_i is generated as Eq.(1). Hence, the illegal user w can only obtain k_i by substituting $x = 0$ into Eq.(1), i.e.,

$$E_i(x) = \prod_j [-f(n_j G_i)] + k_i \bmod p. \tag{11}$$

Obviously, it is infeasible for the illegal user w to obtain k_i without knowing the values $f(n_j G_i)$ for all considered j.

The Way 2: The illegal user w collects the secret code $n_{j'}$ of some predecessor of u_i and then computes $E_i(f(n_{j'} G_i))$ to obtain k_i. Obviously, this issue is similar to the Way 1. In other words, it is also infeasible to obtain k_i without knowing the values $f(n_{j'} G_i)$ for all considered j. Hence, the security of WWC-scheme about the exterior attack on secret key is guaranteed[14].

Finally, Wen *et al.* concluded that the WWC-scheme is practical after they analyze the security of secret keys and secret codes by using the possible attack such as contrary attack, interior collecting attack, interior mutual attack, exterior attack and collaborative attack, exterior attack, sibling attack, and ordered relationship changing attack.

3   On the Security of WWC-Scheme

However, the WWC-scheme still cannot resist another case of the exterior attack which is not discussed in [14]. Before we introducing this novel exterior attack, we must review the result of product $(X - r_1)(X - r_2) \cdots (X - r_n)$ by the following theorem:

Theorem 1. *[4] The product* $(X - r_1)(X - r_2) \cdots (X - r_n)$ *can be expanded as follows.*

$$(X - r_1)(X - r_2) \cdots (X - r_n) = \sum_{0 \le k \le n} (-1)^k s_k X^{n-k}, \qquad (12)$$

where

$$s_k = s_k(r_1, r_2, \ldots, r_n) = \sum_{1 \le i_1 < i_2 < \cdots < i_k \le n} r_{i_1} r_{i_2} \cdots r_{i_k}.$$

For instance, $s_0 = 1$, $s_1 = r_1 + r_2 + \cdots + r_n$, $s_2 = \sum_{1 \le i < j \le n} r_i r_j$ *and* $s_n = r_1 r_2 \cdots r_n$.

3.1 The Novel Exterior Attack

In this section, we will define the modified exterior attack as following,

Dynamic Exterior Attack: an illegal user w wishes to access the secret key k_i of some user u_i through the related public information when a new class joins this hierarchy or a new ordered relationship is setup.

Consider the example shown in Fig.7. The public ECP of user u_6 is formed $E_6(x) = [(x - f(n_1 G_6))(x - f(n_3 G_6))] + k_6 \bmod p$ before user u_7 joins the hierarchy. After u_7 joins the hierarchy, the public polynomials $E_6'(x)$ and $E_7(x)$ is defined as the Eqs.(3) and (4).

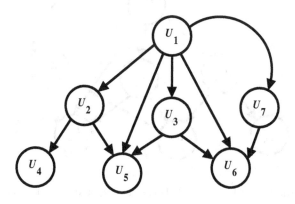

Fig. 7. The consequent poset after inserting u_7

In fact, anyone can obtain the public information $E_6(x)$ before the new class SC_7 joins and also obtain $E_6'(x)$ after he joins this scheme, respectively. Therefore, anyone can discover the secret key k_6' from the public information $E_6(x)$

and $E_6'(x)$ by the following equations.

$$E_6(x) = [(x - f(n_1G_6))(x - f(n_3G_6))] + k_6 \bmod p$$
$$= x^2 - (f(n_1G_6) + f(n_3G_6))x + (f(n_1G_6)f(n_3G_6) + k_6) \bmod p. \text{ (13)}$$
$$E_6'(x) = \{[(x - f(n_1G_6))(x - f(n_3G_6))]\}[x - f(n_7G_6)] + k_6' \bmod p.$$
$$= x^3 - (f(n_1G_6) + f(n_3G_6) + f(n_7G_6))x^2 + (f(n_1G_6)f(n_3G_6)$$
$$+ f(n_1G_6)f(n_7G_6) + f(n_3G_6)f(n_7G_6))x - (f(n_1G_6)f(n_3G_6)$$
$$f(n_7G_6) - k_6') \bmod p. \tag{14}$$

Therefore, from the Eqs.(13) and (14), we can find out the coefficient a of x in $E_6(x)$ is $-(f(n_1G_6) + f(n_3G_6)) \bmod p$ and the coefficient b of x^2 in $-(f(n_1G_6) + f(n_3G_6) + f(n_7G_6)) \bmod p$, respectively. Therefore, we can recover the information $f(n_7G_6)$ by $a - b \bmod p$. Furthermore, we can find out the secret key k_6' from Eq.(14). Hence, this proposed scheme is insecure when a new class joins this hierarchy.

3.2 On the Security of Adding Ordered Relationships in WWC-Scheme

Similarly, the attacker can get the public information $E_5(x)$ before the new ordered relationship $SC_5 \leq SC_7$ is added. In order to explain the novel exterior attack when adding ordered relationships in WWC-scheme, we redraw the poset diagram as following figure.

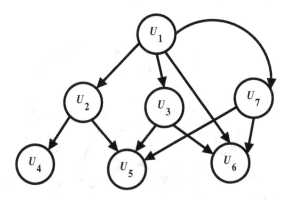

Fig. 8. Adding a relationship between user u_7 and u_5 to the hierarchy

In Fig.8, the attacker w_a can find out the public information $E_5(x)$ from Eq.(15) before the new ordered relationship $SC_5 \leq SC_7$ is added.

$$E_5(x) = [(x - f(n_2G_5))(x - f(n_3G_5))] + k_5 \bmod p.$$
$$= x^2 - (f(n_2G_5) + f(n_3G_5))x + (f(n_2G_5)f(n_3G_5) + k_5) \bmod p. \text{ (15)}$$

The attacker w_a also obtains this public information $E_5'(x)$ after this new hierarchy, including this ordered relationship $SC_5 \leq SC_7$, is setup.

$$E_5'(x) = \{[(x - f(n_2G_5))(x - f(n_3G_5))]\}(x - f(n_7G_5)) + k_5' \bmod p.$$
$$= x^3 - (f(n_2G_5) + f(n_3G_5) + f(n_7G_5))x^2$$
$$+ (f(n_2G_5)f(n_3G_5) + f(n_2G_5)f(n_7G_5) + f(n_3G_5)f(n_7G_5))x$$
$$+ (f(n_2G_5)f(n_3G_5)f(n_7G_5) + k_5') \bmod p. \tag{16}$$

By dynamic exterior attack, the attacker w_a can easily obtain $f(n_7G_5) = a_1 - b_1$. Where $a_1 (= -(f(n_2G_5) + f(n_3G_5)) \bmod p)$ is the coefficient of x in Eq.(15) and $b_1 (= -(f(n_2G_5) + f(n_3G_5) + f(n_7G_5)) \bmod p)$ is the coefficient of x^2 in Eq.(16), respectively. Therefore, it is feasible for the attacker w_1 to obtain the secret key k_5' with knowing the value $f(n_7G_5)$. As a result, the security for the dynamic exterior attack on secret key is not guaranteed in WWC-scheme[14].

4 Conclusions

In this paper, we have shown that an illegal user can find out the secret key when a new class joins or a new ordered relationship is added into the WWC-scheme. In other words, the security of WWC-scheme about the dynamic exterior attack on secret key is not guaranteed.

Acknowledgments. This work was supported by National Science Council NSC 97-2221-E-150-038.

References

1. Akl, S.G., Taylor, P.D.: Cryptographic solution to a problem of access control in a hierarchy. ACM Transactions on Computer System 3(1), 239–247 (1983)
2. Chen, T.S., Huang, J.Y.: A novel key management scheme for dynamic access control in a user hierarchy. Applied Mathematics and Computation 162(1(4)), 339–351 (2005)
3. Denning, D.E.: Cryptographic and Data Security, pp. 39–48. Addison-Wesley, Reading (1982)
4. Grillet, P.: Algebra. John Wiley & Sons, Inc., Chichester (1999)
5. Hwang, M.S.: An Improvement of Novel Cryptographic Key Assignment Scheme for Dynamic Access Control in a Hierarchy. IEICE Trans. Funda. E82-A(3), 548–550 (1999)
6. Horng, G.B., Liu, C.L., Hwang, Y.T.: Security Analysis of a Threshold Access Control Scheme Based on Smart Cards. IEICE Trans. Funda. E87-A(8), 2177–2179 (2004)
7. Koblitz, N.: Elliptic Curve Cryptosystems. Mathematics of Computation 48, 203–209 (1987)
8. Konheim, A.G.: Computer Security and Cryptography. John Wiley & Sons, Inc., Chichester (2007)
9. Miller, V.: Uses of Elliptic Curves in Cryptography. In: Williams, H.C. (ed.) CRYPTO 1985. LNCS, vol. 218, pp. 417–426. Springer, Heidelberg (1986)

10. Rabin, M.O.: Digitalized Signatures and Public-Key Function as Intractable as Factorization, Technical Report, Computer Science, MIT/LCS/TR-212, MIT Lab., vol.1, pp. 100–123 (1979)
11. Shen, V.R.L., Chen, T.S., Lai, F.: Novel Cryptographic Key Assignment Scheme for Dynamic Access Control in a Hierarchy. IEICE Trans. Funda. E80-A(10), 2035–2037 (1997)
12. Stallings, W.: Cryptography and network security Principles and Practices, 4th version. Pearson Education, Inc., London (2006)
13. Tzeng, W.G.: A Time-Bound Cryptographic Key Assignment Scheme for Access Control in a Hierarchy. IEEE Trans. on Knowledge and Data Engineering 14(1), 182–188 (2002)
14. Wen, J.H., Wu, M.C., Chen, T.S.: A Novel Elliptic Curve Dynamic Access Control System. IEICE Trans. Commun. E90-B(8), 1979–1987 (2007)
15. Wu, K.P., Ruan, S.J., Tseng, C.K., Lai, F.: Hierarchical access control using the secure filter. IEICE Trans. Information & System E84-D(6), 700–708 (2001)

VoIP SPAM Response System Adopting Multi-leveled Anti-SPIT Solutions*

Jongil Jeong, Seokung Yoon, Taijin Lee, Hyuncheol Jeong, and Yoojae Won

IT Infrastructure Protection Division, Korea Information Security Agency
IT Venture Tower, Jungdaero 135, Songpa-Gu, Seoul, Korea 138-950
{jijeong,seokung,tjlee,hcjung,yjwon}@kisa.or.kr

Abstract. VoIP spam will become severe problem preventing from generalization of VoIP service. For comprehensive response against spam, this paper implemented VoIP SPAM response system adopting multi-leveled anti-spam solutions. To adopt them, we divided VoIP service domains into three domains as outbound, intermediary, and inbound. The main goal of anti-spam solution in outbound domain is to prevent spam by monitoring and detecting call traffic of registered users. In intermediary domain, we focused on blocking SIP message forgery spam using SIP-based sender policy framework. Inbound domain has the "easy spam reporter". This module enables victims to report spam contents to the administrator directly. The reported contents and information, of course, are shared with other domains as a black list. Through the experimental result, we showed this system is enough to prevent, detect, and block VoIP spam.

Keywords: VoIP, SPIT, SPIM, ANTI-SPIT, VoIP SPAM.

1 Introduction

According to the *"Hype Cycle for Consumer Technologies in 2007"* [1], the residential Voice over Internet Protocol (VoIP) service has already reached the stage of *"Slope of Enlightenment"*. This means the residential VoIP service became the practical technology and its technical process can be accepted as the actual service model for achieving commercial business goals. The cycle expected the residential VoIP service will reach the *"Plateau of productivity"* stage within 2 years. At this stage, the related technologies are commercialized and market also grows up based on its technical maturity. In advancing to the next stage, VoIP spam also will become a severe issue like email spam problems. VoIP spam may cause social problems increasing stress at home and in office, and deteriorate performance at work. Since these problems will bring down the value of VoIP service, customers will hesitate to use VoIP service consequently; therefore, providing secure solutions against VoIP spam is required for continuing growth of VoIP business.

---

* This work was supported by the IT R&D program of MKE/IITA. [2008-S-028-02, The Development of SIP-Aware Intrusion Prevention Technique for protecting SIP-base Application Services]

T.-k. Kim, T.-h. Kim, and A. Kiumi (Eds.): SecTech 2008, CCIS 29, pp. 15–30, 2009.
© Springer-Verlag Berlin Heidelberg 2009

This paper divides VoIP service scope into three domains as the outbound, the intermediary, and the inbound domain respectively. We implemented modules for countering spam attacks in each domain. In the outbound domain, we focus on preventing spam and detecting callers who generate abnormal call traffic similar with that of spammers. In the intermediary domains, we focus on preventing from abusing intermediary domain name as the originator of the forged SIP messages. In the inbound domain, we focus on handling spam information immediately as well as the prevention and detection of spam.

This paper is organized as follows: In section 2, we introduce VoIP and SIP features and we present types of VoIP spam attack scenarios and current anti-spit solutions. In section 3, we briefly discus the requirements for VoIP spam response system and we design a phased anti-spit framework architecture. In section 4, we implement anti-spit modules and deployed them in the outbound, intermediary, and inbound domain respectively. In section 5, we experiment and evaluate the proposed framework. Finally, we conclude this paper in section 6.

2 Background Study

VoIP communication between a caller and a callee is established by two phases: the session establishment and the media exchange. The caller initiates a session with the callee. After completing this phase, two parties can exchange media traffic. Session Initiation Protocol (SIP) is used in the first phase and Real-time Transport Protocol (RTP) is used in the second phase. This means two parties cannot exchange media traffic without establishing the session between them; so detecting and blocking SPIT calls at the first phase can take advantage in terms of bandwidth and computational resources [2]. This section introduces anti-spit solutions which can be used for detecting and blocking SPIT calls at the initial handshake stage.

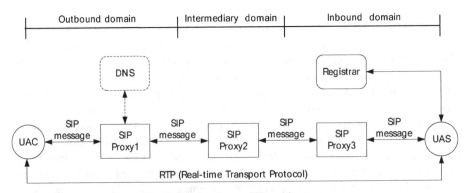

Fig. 1. The barebones SIP architecture

2.1 Session Initiation Protocol (SIP)

Session Initiation Protocol (SIP) [3] facilitates to create, delete, and modify multimedia sessions among devices that want to communicate with others over the Internet.

Figure 1 shows the barebones architecture consisted of several SIP components. User Agent Client (UAC) is a logical component generating SIP request messages. It begins SIP transactions. User Agent Server (UAS) is a logical component generating response messages corresponding to the SIP request messages requested by UAC. SIP proxy routes the SIP messages between UAC and UAS. Registrar is a server to offer personal mobility of SIP. It gives UAC specific information about UAS's connection address.

2.2 Types of VoIP SPAM

In the *"Threat Taxonomy"*, which was published by VOIPSA (Voice Over IP Security Association) in 2005 [4], VoIP spam was classified into the "unwanted lawful contents". This includes that a seller solicits consumers to purchase lawful contents or goods for adults. Most users, however, strongly want to screen such solicitation. Types of VoIP spam can be assorted as call spam, IM spam, and presence spam.

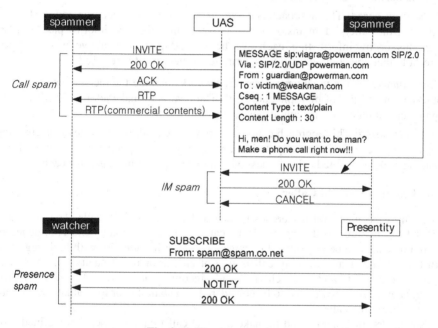

Fig. 2. VoIP spam scenarios

Call spam: spammers attempt to send a bulk unsolicited set of SIP messages in order to establish a multimedia session. *IM spam:* spammers send bulk unsolicited set of instant messages. Mainly this spam is sent via the extended SIP message for IM such as *MESSAGE*, but it is also sent via the *"Subject"* field of SIP Request message such as *INVITE*, *OPTION*, and *SUBSCRIBE*. *Presence spam:* using the *"SUBSCRIBE"* message of SIP, spammers send bulk unsolicited set of presence requests to become a member of the *'whitelist'* or *'buddy list'* of a user.

2.3 Adapting Anti-spam Solutions for Email Field to VoIP Service

Blacklist/Whitelist: Black lists generally include users that are considered as spitters. These lists are usually used to block calls being initiated by the enlisted users. On the other hand, white lists contain trusted users, either to the domain or the end-user. Calls made by white-listed users are never blocked.

Content filtering: These frameworks incorporate filters that analyze the contents of messages, characterizing them as spam or not. This technique could be used for the detection of instance messaging SPIT (similarly with email spam), but it appears to be inappropriate for SPIT calls due to its processing requirements.

Challenge-response: The communication is established if the caller can prove that she is a human and not a bot. This proof is provided if the caller correctly answers a challenge sent by the callee.

Consent-based: These frameworks require the explicit consent of the callee for the communication to be established.

Reputation-based: This approach is based on the notions of reputation and trust of the callers or the callers' domains. If the trust level (which derives either by past communications or by information exchange between domains) is above a pre-defined threshold then the communication is permitted, otherwise it is rejected.

Users' addresses management: These frameworks include the techniques of address obfuscation and use of multiple addresses. The goal is to make address harvesting by spammers (spitters) as difficult as possible.

Charging-based: This approach charges users for each call or message. This charging can either be economic or computational resources. Since spammers (spitters) rely on sending bulk unsolicited calls or messages, the overall cost increases for each attack.

2.4 Feature of SPAM Caller

There have been several researches related to features of SPIT calls. The document [5] defines features to distinguish SPIT calls from normal calls. The confidence of incoming calls can be determined by whether a caller has identity with high degree of trust and whether an incoming call is free of charge or not. Usually normal callers make normal calls and most charged calls income from them. Therefore, *Identity strength* and *Cost of call* need to be considered as a static factor to evaluate suspicious level of incoming calls.

Spammers, in general, tend to make a phone call frequently per a predefined time period. Most callees, of course, do not want to receive SPIT calls; hence, they tend to

Table 1. Features to evaluate SPIT calls

	Features
To be considered statically	Identity strength
	Cost of call
To be considered dynamically	Call rate
	Call completion success rate
	Call duration consistency
	SPIT suspect

hang it up immediately. As a natural consequence it follows that spammers have poor *Call completion success rate* and *Call duration consistency;* nevertheless, they have a high *Call rate* compared with normal callers. To evaluate SPIT call, these features need to be considered comprehensively and calculated as a *SPIT suspect* score.

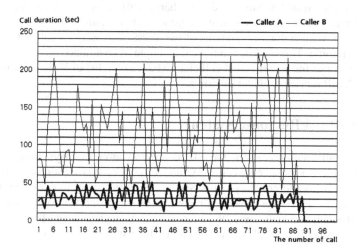

Fig. 3. The analysis of call duration. In general, since callees never want to speak with spammers for a long time, they tend to hang spam calls up immediately. As a result, spammers can not help having very short and even call duration patterns relatively. While on the other, normal callees usually make phone calls with a variety of intention such as greeting, friendship, or relationship with others; thus, the user B has uneven call duration patterns from about 25 to 225 seconds.

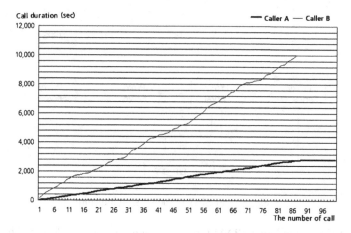

Fig. 4. The analysis of accumulated call charge. If the VoIP service provider charges 36.7 won[1] for a phone call per 180 seconds, user A is charged about 565.67 won and user B is charged about 2119.8 won. It is natural that the more the number of call increases, the more widen the gap of the accumulated charge between two users is.

---

[1] A currency unit of Korea, 13,000 won is about 1 dollar.

2.5 Cost of VoIP SPAM Call

VoIP Service provider emphasizes that the moderate call charge is the distinguished difference from non IP-based communication; however, the cost efficiency could be attractive to spammers rather than general users. The analysis of the correlation between call duration and accumulated call charge will show the reason why VoIP is more attractive to spammers as a means to generate bulk spam calls.

Figure 3 shows call duration patterns of two users. The user A's call duration is not exceeded 1 minute. This pattern is a typical example of spammers.

Figure 4 shows the accumulated call charge based on a list of VoIP call charges offered by a VoIP service provider in Korea.

3 VoIP SPAM Response System

Like the e-mail communication, the SIP communication has asynchronous feature during initiating a session between UAC and UAS. For this reason, a VoIP SPAM response system should able to process SIP signaling messages in real-time; thus, the system needs to have three phases for countering spam: prevention, detection, and handling of spam and spammers. We recommend managing these phases as policies which can be selectively deployed according to the necessity of each domain.

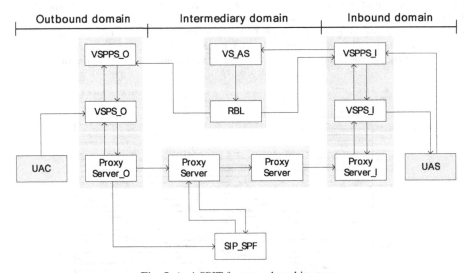

Fig. 5. Anti-SPIT framework architecture

Figure 5 shows the VoIP SPAM response system which was designed based on the SIP architecture in figure 1. The system consists of the policy manager and its enforcer.

- VoIP Spam Prevention Policy Server (VSPPS) is a server to control what and how the administrator deploys anti-spit solutions to this anti-spit system.

- VoIP Spam Prevention System (VSPS) enforces the policy behind the SIP Proxy.
- VoIP Spam Acceptance Server (VS_AS) is a server to check spam contents directly reported from UAS. If investigated contents are spam clearly, the administrator registers the spammer to the blacklist managed in RBL.
- RBL(Real-time Blockhole List) manages a blacklist to be shared with VSPPS_I and VSPPS_O.

Figure 6 describes how each server shares policy and applies it to SIP calls.

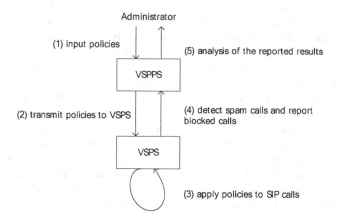

Fig. 6. Policy sharing and communication between VSPPS and VSPS

4 Implementation of a Phased ANTI-SPIT Framework

We implemented the multilayered ANTI-SPIT framework. Figure 7 shows the anti-spit solutions implemented in each domain. For the purpose of focusing on the prevention and detection of spam and spammers in the outbound domain, we implemented three filters and one challenge and response system.

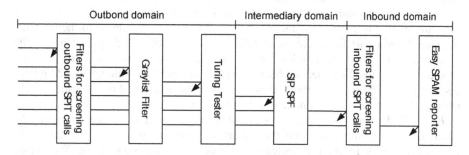

Fig. 7. The multilayered anti-spit framework

The *blacklist filter* is used for screening calls from the black-listed SIP URI (Uniform Resource Identifier).

The *keywords filter* is used for screening calls including spam keywords into the "*From*" or "*Subject*" filed of the INVITE message header field. If spammers want to deliver media spam only, they need not send abnormal INVITE messages because their goal is to establish the sessions between others; so, such spammers can detour these filters. To detect a spammer who disguises his identity as a normal user's identity, the administrator needs to monitor each user's call traffic pattern.

The *Graylist filter* is used for detecting users who have call traffic pattern similar with that of spammer. As the specific features, a spammer generally has a number of callee, short call duration, short inter-call time, and so on. The Graylist filter uses these factors to calculate each user's SPIT level. The Graylist filter is a middle layer between a blacklist and a whitelist. If a caller has higher SPIT level score than the threshold configured by the administrator, the caller can be suspicious as a potential spammer. Some normal callers, however, could have similar call traffic pattern with that of spammers. In this case, they can be suspicious as a potential spammer regardless of their intention. To prevent such misclassification, the callers should have the opportunity to prove they are not a spammer.

Turing Tester is used for screening real spammers from suspicious callers. In general, spammers tend to automatically send unsolicited bulk messages or media to others using software, but software is not able to response the answer from a callee. Therefore, if a suspicious caller provides the correct answer to turing tester, the caller is classified into the normal caller group; otherwise, the caller should be classified into the blacklist and his call is blocked continuously without further test. Although the turing test is easy enough to provide the correct answer, we should consider that some callers could be classified into blacklist due to their mistake. Thus, the administrator should able to recovery the caller's status when the caller requests it.

In the intermediary domain, spammers can attempt to directly send the forged INVITE messages to other domains. The reason why they forge the message is to disguise their identity as normal users' identity. *Sender Policy Framework (SPF)* identifies messages that are or are not authorized to use the domain name in the "*From*" field of the INVITE message header, based on information published in a sender policy of the domain owner [6]. SIP_SPF needs to be deployed in the inbound domain as well as the intermediary domain because the inbound domain asks whether the incoming INVITE messages are authorized by the previous domain.

The inbound domain has the blacklist and keywords filter too. Callees, however, may not be able to receive the incoming calls from callers registered to the blacklist because the blacklist filter screens all callers regardless of callee's preference to the specific callers. *Whitelist* enables a callee to selectively receive incoming calls regardless of whether the caller has been registered to blacklist. Whitelist should reflect just individual callee's preference; thus, it needs to be configured by the callee on his dedicated phone such as softphone or hardware terminal.

Easy SPAM reporter enables a victim to report received spam information to the administrator. Victims can report the spammer's number, types of spam, and a wav file which is a media spam recorded by their dedicated hardware phone. We implemented a hardware phone with a dedicated button to support the easy SPAM reporter function.

4.1 Graylist Module and SPIT Level Decision Model

As the criterion to evaluate how callers' call traffic is similar with that of spammers, we calculated SPIT level from six call traffic factors: *Call Rejection Rate (Call$_{RR}$)*, *Number of Call Recipient (Call$_{NC}$)*, *Call Duration (Call$_D$)*, *Call Traffic (Call$_T$)*, *Call Rate (Call$_R$)*, and *Inter-call time (Call$_{IC}$)*. The calculated caller's SPIT level is compared with the SPIT threshold configured by the administrator. The graylist has three states which are *Su* unknown, *Sg* gray, and *Sb* black respectively. The state of new users without any call traffic information is *Su*. If they generate call traffic, their state is transited to *Sg*. Among callers in gray state, if someone has higher SPIT level than the threshold, then his state is transited to *Sb*.

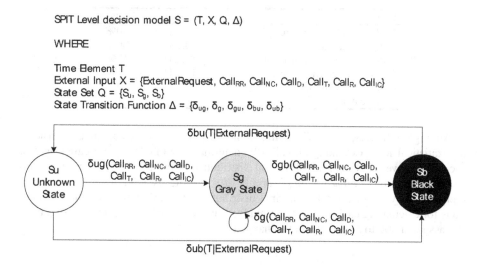

SPIT Level decision model S = (T, X, Q, Δ)

WHERE

Time Element T
External Input X = {ExternalRequest, Call$_{RR}$, Call$_{NC}$, Call$_D$, Call$_T$, Call$_R$, Call$_{IC}$}
State Set Q = {S$_u$, S$_g$, S$_b$}
State Transition Function Δ = {δ$_{ug}$, δ$_g$, δ$_{gu}$, δ$_{bu}$, δ$_{ub}$}

Fig. 8. State transition flow of SPIT level decision model

SPIT level decision model consists of *T*, *X*, *S*, and *Δ*. Time element *T* is used for defining state transition that can occur after a regular time.

Figure 8 depicts a caller's state transition among Su, Sg, and Sb respectively. By increasing SPIT level, a caller's state can be transited to the next state. As a general rule, the transition advances toward just one direction from Su to Sb and it does not allow a caller's current state to be get back to previous state; however, we have two exceptions that allow it. The one is when a caller's SPIT level comes down close to the threshold level for transition of previous state with the passage of time. The other is when an administrator or a caller request to correct a specific caller's distorted SPIT level reasonably.

4.2 SPIT Level Decision Algorithm

Call Detail Records (CDR) [7] include several factors such as caller identity, callee identity, call start time, call end time, call traffic, and call rejection. Using these factors, we propose a SPIT level decision algorithm. To define SPIT level, these factors need to be calculated as a quantitative value respectively. Above all, the calculated result should be regulated and reflected to a SPIT level. To evaluate the social network linkage and global reputation of a caller, research [8] deems the caller's call duration consistency important. Also we deem "$Call_{NC}$"and "$Call_D$" important; thus, two factors are given much weight in the six factors. Table 2 shows how each factor and its portion. The range of SPIT level against each factor is from 0 to 1. Note that, each portion can be changed according to administrators' experience or preference. Administrators, of course, should find the most reasonable portion of each factor thorough their empirical investigations.

Table 2. Factors to calculate SPIT level and portion of factors

Factor	Range	Portion
$Call_{NC}$: number of call recipient	[0…1]	50%
$Call_D$: call duration	[0…1]	30%
$Call_T$: average call traffic rate	[0…1]	10%
$Call_{RR}$: call rejection rate	[0…1]	5%
$Call_{IC}$: inter call time	[0…1]	3%
$Call_R$: call reate	[0…1]	2%

Among six factors, "$Call_{RR}$", "$Call_{IC}$", and "$Call_R$" should be calculated considering statistical features among all calls. To determine a SPIT level of a caller against each factor, we make individual normal distribution using the average and the standard deviation of "$Call_{RR}$" "$Call_{IC}$", and "$Call_R$" factors. A SPIT level of a caller is represented by his location in a normal distribution. The followings are the formulations for calculating each factor. Commonly, N is the number of recent calls of a user. We assigned 100 to N, but it can be changed.

$$Call_{NC} = \frac{Call\,Recipient_{Num}}{N} \tag{1}$$

From 100 calls of a caller, $CallRecipient_{Num}$ means the caller has how many callees who were not duplicated.

$$Call_D = \frac{CallDuration_{Num\_Short}}{N} \tag{2}$$

From 100 calls of a caller, individual call duration is calculated by (call end time-call start time). $CallDuration_{Num\_Short}$ means the number of call durations which is shorter than call duration threshold configured by the administrator.

$$Call_T = \frac{CallTraffic_{Num\_High}}{N} \tag{3}$$

From 100 calls of a caller, individual call traffic is extracted. $CallTraffic_{Num\_High}$ means the number of call traffic rate (byte/sec) which is larger than call traffic threshold configured by the administrator.

$$Call_{RR} = \frac{1}{\sqrt{2\pi Call\,Re\,j_{StdDev}}} \exp\left(-\frac{1}{2Call\,Re\,j_{StdDev}{}^2}(Call\,Re\,j_{Num} - Call\,Re\,j_{Mean})^2\right) \tag{4}$$

From 100 calls of a caller, $CallRej_{Num}$ is how many call tries of the caller are rejected by callees. To make a normal distribution, we got $CallRej_{Mean}$ which is the average of the number of rejected calls of all callers and the standard deviation. $Call_{RR}$ is a ratio of the caller's $CallRej_{Num}$ in the normal distribution.

$$Call_{IC} = \frac{1}{\sqrt{2\pi}ICT_{StdDev}}\exp\left(-\frac{1}{2ICT_{StdDev}^2}(ICT_{Num} - ICT_{Mean})^2\right) \tag{5}$$

From 100 calls of a caller, average of the caller's ICT_{avg} is calculated by (current call start time-previous call end time)/N. To make a normal distribution, we got ICT_{Mean} which is the average of ICT_{avg} of all callers and the standard deviation. $Call_{IC}$ is a ratio of the caller's ICT_{avg} in the normal distribution.

$$Call_{R} = \frac{1}{\sqrt{2\pi}CR_{StdDev}}\exp\left(-\frac{1}{2CR_{StdDev}^2}(CR_{Num} - CR_{Mean})^2\right) \tag{6}$$

From 100 calls of a caller, we calculated the time range of the caller's call try and got CR_{avg} which is the average of the time range. To make a normal distribution, we got CR_{Mean} which is the average of CR_{avg} of all callers and the standard deviation. $Call_{R}$ is a ratio of a caller's CR_{avg} in the normal distribution. These six factors can be synthesized considering its portion denoted in table 2. Note that, $\alpha + \beta + \gamma + \delta + \varepsilon + \zeta = 100\%$

$$SPIT\_LevelCaller = \alpha \times Call_{NC} + \beta \times Call_{D} + \gamma \times Call_{T} + \delta \times Call_{RR} + \varepsilon \times Call_{IC} + \zeta \times Call_{R}$$

4.3 SIP_SPF Module

The main idea of SIP_SPF is from RFC 4408 [9]. Figure 10 shows how SPF is deployed to VoIP service environment. (1) Each administrator publishes SPF records to DNS zone file. SPF records might be stated as Figure 9. The underlined sentence means SPF configuration. If a host wants to send emails using outbound.org domain name, the IP address of the host have to belong to C class subnet of an IP address registered on MX record managed by the outbound.org domain.

```
;  Name Server

;

   IN   NS      ns.outbound.org.

   IN   MX 10   sip.outbound.org.

   IN   TXT     "v=spf1 mx ip4:outbound.org/24 -all"

   IN   A       10.1.1.101

;
```

Fig. 9. An example of SPF record published to DNS

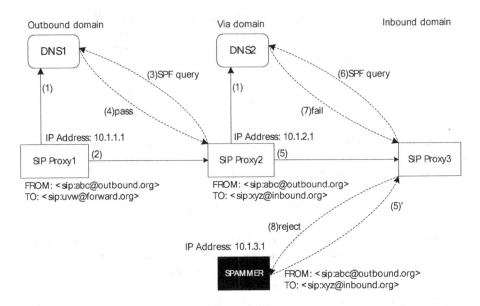

Fig. 10. A barebones SIP-based VoIP service network adopting SPF

(5)' a spammer forges his return-path and directly forwards it to SIP Proxy3. (6) SIP Proxy3 extracts an IP address from "*From*" field of the incoming INVITE message header. Then, SIP Proxy3 asks whether the IP address belongs to one of the IP addresses registered on SPF record managed by via domain. (7) If the answer includes "*fail*", SIP Proxy3 rejects the incoming message; otherwise, it accepts the message.

Since the INVITE messages are routed through several proxies, message forwarding problem can occur in inbound SIP proxy. This problem occurs due to the following reason. SPF depends on IP addresses; hence, SPF query could return "*fail*" message if the relationship between a domain name and its addresses changes by forwarding SIP messages to the next proxy. To fix it, researches [10] and [11] have proposed Sender Rewriting Scheme (SRS); however, the forwarding problem can be easily fixed using the "*Via*" field of the INVITE message. Figure 9 explains the reason why SIP proxy servers should extract "*Via*" header from the INVITE message in order to fix the message forwarding problem in detail. Since a value of "*From*" header is used at only the first outbound server, if the value normally relays the next hop, then it becomes useless because SIP Proxy2 queries to DNS1 using "<*sip:abc@outbound.org*>" of "*From*" header and "*10.1.1.1*" assigned to SIP Proxy1. Of course, the answer is "*pass*". Then SIP Proxy2 relays the INVITE message to SIP Proxy3. SIP Proxy3 queries to DNS2 using "<*sip:abc@outbound.org*>" and "*10.1.2.1*". In this case, the answer is "*fail*" because the IP address is not authorized to use the domain name "*outbound.org*". For this reason, SIP proxies should parse "*Via*" header instead of "*From*" header from the incoming INVITE message.

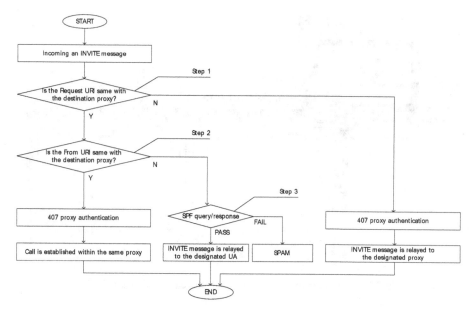

Fig. 11. Processing flows of proxy server with SPF module

Figure 11 describes the transactions of SIP_SPF query and response. When an IN-VITE message reaches the destination SIP proxy server, the proxy server checks whether the *"Request URI"* is same with its own URI. In step 1, if two URIs are not same, the INVITE message is relayed to the designated SIP proxy server in other domain; otherwise, the proxy server checks whether the *"From URI"* is same with its own URI. In step 2, if two URIs are same, it means the message sender and the receiver exist within the same domain. So the inbound proxy server needs not to perform SPF record query, otherwise the inbound proxy server queries SPF records to DNS. In step 3, if the answer is *"fail"*, the INVITE message is being sent by a spammer; otherwise it is relayed to the designated UAS. The overall processes for checking SIP message sender in VoIP service environment are done through three steps.

4.4 Easy SPAM Reporter Module

Although keywords filter and blacklist filter are effective to the inbound domains, these filters are based on a list containing reserved information such as spam keywords which have already been reported. So spammers can detour these filters if they do not use the registered information into such filters. To enhance static filters, victims of spam need to be able to report their received spam contents to administrators directly. We propose to deploy "easy spam reporter" system in the inbound domain.

Figure 12 is the hardware phone we produced. We deployed "easy spam reporter" module on the phone. The #1 box is an incoming call from a spammer. The callee chooses that number, and then its information is displayed on the right pane. By clicking the button "Spam Report" in #2 box, the spammer is reported to VS_AS.

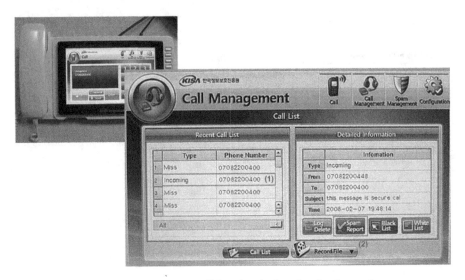

Fig. 12. "Easy spam reporter" function deployed on hardware phone

5 Experiments

5.1 Evaluation Factors for Spam Filters

In general, performance evaluation methods of spam filter are hm%, sm%, error rate, accuracy, and precision of a spam filter [12]. Table 3 shows six factors to calculate value of such methods.

Table 3. Evaluation Factors for A Spam Filter

Variable	Description
a	Ham: the number of clear normal calls
b	Spam: the number of clear spam calls
c	The number of classified calls as spam among normal calls
d	The number of classified calls as normal among spam calls
e	The number of classified calls as spam among spam calls
f	The number of classified calls as normal among normal calls

The followings are the formula to get each value.

$$hm\% = c/(c+f) \qquad (1)$$

hm% means a ratio that Ham is classed into Spam.

$$sm\% = d/(d+e) \qquad (2)$$

sm% means a ratio that Spam is classed into Ham.

$$\text{Error rate} = (c+d)/(a+b) \qquad (3)$$

Error rate means a ratio that spam filter misclassifies Ham and Spam.

$$Accuracy = (e+f)/(a+b) \qquad (4)$$

Accuracy means a ratio that spam filter correctly classifies Ham and Spam.

$$Precision = e/(c+e) \qquad (5)$$

Precision means a ratio that is real spam among things blocked by spam filter.

5.2 Experimental Results

To perform experiment, we prepared clear normal calls and spam calls. Against the proposed VoIP SPAM response system, 28 normal callers and 2 spammers performed 3,000 call tries respectively. Table 4 shows the experimental results. Among 2,800 normal calls, 2 calls were classified as spam calls.

Table 4. Experimental Results

Variable	Number of Calls	Characteristics	
a	2,800	False positive rate = c/(c+f) = 0/(0+200)	0%
b	200	False negative rate = d/(d+e) = 2/(2+198)	1%
c	0	Error rate = (c+d)/(a+b) = (0+2)/(2800+200)	0.06%
d	2	Accuracy = (e+f)/(a+b) = (198+2800)/(2800+200)	99.93%
e	198	Precision = e/(c+e) = 198/(0+198)	100%
f	2,800	-	-

Figure 14 illustrates the individual status of anti-spam solutions deployed in the proposed VoIP spam response system. The capital 'O' and 'I' mean the outbound domain and the inbound domain respectively. 'SPIM' is the filter for screening the SIP message with spam keywords.

6 Conclusion and Future Work

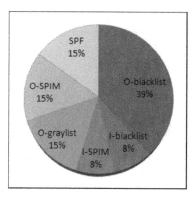

Fig. 14. Blocking status of each solution

In order to counter SPIT, we proposed various anti-spit solutions and implemented VoIP SPAM response system adopting them. Especially, the proposed system makes administrator take into account both objective and subjective basis of distinguishing spam calls. Considering SPIT level, administrator can distinguish suspicious callers. Easy spam reporter function enables administrator to get definite spam caller list.

In the future work, we plan to implement a RBL system based on user reputation. Generating user reputation means that an administrator can merge multi-leveled anti-spit policies into the integrated one policy.

References

1. Hype Cycle for Consumer Technologies in 2007 (2007), http://www.gartner.com
2. Rosenburg, J., et al.: SIP: Session Initiation Protocol. RFC 3261 (June 2002)
3. Korea Information Security Agency, VoIP Security Guide (December 2005)
4. VoIPSA (VoIP Security Alliance).:
   http://www.voipsa.org/Activities/taxonomy.php
5. Schwartz, D., Sterman, B., Katz, E., Tschofenig, H.: SPAM for Internet Telephony (SPIT) Prevention using the Security Assertion Markup Language (SAML) (December 2006), IETF-DRAFT http://draft-schwartz-sipping-spit-saml-01.txt
6. Allman, E., et al.: Domain Keys Identified Mail (DKIM) Signatures. RFC 4871 (May 2007)
7. CDR (Call Detail Records).:
   http://en.wikipedia.org/wiki/Call_detail_record
8. Balasubramaniyan, V., Ahamad, M., Park, H.: CallRank: Combating SPIT Using Call Duration. Social Networks and Global Reputation (2007)
9. Wong, M.: Sender Policy Framework (SPF) for Authorizing the Use of Domains in E-Mail, Version 1. RFC 4408 (April 2005)
10. Wong, M.: SPF, MTAs and SRS. Linux J (May 2004)
11. SRS (Sender Rewriting Scheme).: http://www.openspf.org/SRS
12. Gordon, V.C., Thomas, R.L.: Online supervised spam filter evaluation. ACM Trans. Inf. Syst. 25(3) (July 2007)

Feature Extraction for IRIS Recognition

Debnath Bhattacharyya[1], Poulami Das[1], Samir Kumar Bandyopadhyay[2],
and Tai-hoon Kim[3]

[1] Computer Science and Engineering Department, Heritage Institute of Technology,
Kolkata-700107, India
{debnathb,dasp88}@gmail.com
[2] Department of Computer Science and Engineering, University of Calcutta,
Kolkata-700009, India
skb1@vsnl.com
[3] Hannam University, Daejeon – 306791, Korea
taihoonn@empal.com

Abstract. In this paper we propose a new biometric-based Iris feature extraction system. The system automatically acquires the biometric data in numerical format (Iris Images) by using a set of properly located sensors. We are considering camera as a high quality sensor. Iris Images are typically color images that are processed to gray scale images. Then the Feature extraction algorithm is used to detect "IRIS Effective Region (IER)" and then extract features from "IRIS Effective Region (IER)" that are numerical characterization of the underlying biometrics. Later on this work will be helping to identify an individual by comparing the feature obtained from the feature extraction algorithm with the previously stored feature by producing a similarity score. This score will be indicating the degree of similarity between a pair of biometrics data under consideration. Depending on degree of similarity, individual can be identified.

Keywords: Biometric, eyeprint, IRIS, IER, Pattern Recognition and Degree of Freedom.

1 Introduction

The human iris recently has attracted the attention of biometrics-based identification and verification research and development community. The iris is so unique that no two irises are alike, even among identical twins, in the entire human population.

Automated biometrics-based personal identification systems can be classified into two main categories: identification and verification. In a process of verification (1-to-1 comparison), the biometrics information of an individual, who claims certain identity, is compared with the biometrics on the record that represent the identity that this individual claims. The comparison result determines whether the identity claims shall be accepted or rejected. On the other hand, it is often desirable to be able to discover the origin of certain biometrics information to prove or disprove the association of that information with a certain individual. This process is commonly known as identification (1-to-many comparison).

T.-k. Kim, T.-h. Kim, and A. Kiumi (Eds.): SecTech 2008, CCIS 29, pp. 31–39, 2009.

Actual iris identification can be broken down into four fundamental steps. First, a person stands in front of the iris identification system, generally between one and three feet away, while a wide angle camera calculates the position of their eye. A second camera zooms in on the eye and takes a black and white image. After the iris system has one's iris in focus, it overlays a circular grid (zone's of analysis) on the image of the iris and identifies where areas of light and dark fall. The purpose of overlaying the grid is so that the iris system can recognize a pattern within the iris and to generate 'points' within the pattern into an 'eyeprint'. Finally, the captured image or 'eyeprint' is checked against a previously stored 'reference template' in the database. The time it takes for a iris system to identify your iris is approximately two seconds.

In the iris alone, there are over 400 distinguishing characteristics, or Degrees of Freedom (DOF), that can be quantified and used to identify an individual (Daugman, J. & Williams, G. O. 1992). Although, approximately 260 of those are possible to captured for identification. These identifiable characteristics include: contraction furrows, striations, pits, collagenous fibers, filaments, crypts (darkened areas on the iris), serpentine vasculature, rings, and freckles. Due to these unique characteristics, the iris has six times more distinct identifiable features than a fingerprint.

Iris recognition has many advantages over the other forms of biometric identification like –

Accuracy – Simply put, iris recognition is the most accurate form of identification known to man. Genetically identical individuals have completely independent iris textures, whereas DNA (genetic "fingerprinting") is not unique for the about 1.5% of the human population who have a genetically identical monozygotic twin. So it is more accurate than even DNA matching.

Speed - our iris recognition system is capable of making a match from a database of over 1 million records in less than a second. Conversely, fingerprint, hand and voice systems are challenged by large databases. Not only does the time taken to register a match increase, but also the accuracy of the system falls unlike iris recognition.

Stability - The iris image remains stable from the age of about 10 months up until death. This means that an iris image need only be captured once and does not need to be updated. Other biometric measures change over time. Hands and fingers grow, our voices change, our skin degrades and other biometric measures are subject to labor, health, genetics, climate and age.

Non-invasive - Users wearing gloves, protective wear, glasses, safety goggles and even contact lenses can operate iris recognition systems. No contact is required with a touch pad or screen meaning that iris recognition is ideal in environments where hygiene is at a premium. It is also important to note that iris recognition is a completely separate technology to retinal scanning. No bright lights or lasers are beamed into the eye, only a digital photograph is taken. This means that not only is iris recognition the most accurate biometric technology, it is also the safest.

HUMANS have used body characteristics such as face, voice, and gait for thousands of years to recognize each other. Alphonse Bertillon, chief of the criminal identification division of the police department in Paris, developed and then practiced the idea of using a number of body measurements to identify criminals in the mid-19th century. Just as his idea was gaining popularity, it was obscured by a far more significant and practical discovery of the distinctiveness of the human fingerprints in the late

19th century. Soon after this discovery, many major law enforcement departments embraced the idea of first "booking" the fingerprints of criminals and storing it in a database (actually, a card file). Later, the leftover (typically, fragmentary) fingerprints (commonly referred to as latents) at the scene of crime could be "lifted" and matched with fingerprints in the database to determine the identity of the criminals. Although biometrics emerged from its extensive use in law enforcement to identify criminals (e.g., illegal aliens, security clearance for employees for sensitive jobs, fatherhood determination, forensics, and positive identification of convicts and prisoners), it is being increasingly used today to establish person recognition in a large number of civilian applications.

What biological measurements qualify to be a biometric? Any human physiological and/or behavioral characteristic can be used as a biometric characteristic as long as it satisfies the following requirements:

- Universality: each person should have the characteristic.
- Distinctiveness: any two persons should be sufficiently different in terms of the characteristic.
- Permanence: the characteristic should be sufficiently invariant (with respect to the matching criterion) over a period of time.
- Collectability: the characteristic can be measured quantitatively.

However, in a practical biometric system (i.e., a system that employs biometrics for personal recognition), there are a number of other issues that should be considered, including:

- performance, which refers to the achievable recognition accuracy and speed, the resources required to achieve the desired recognition accuracy and speed, as well as the operational and environmental factors that affect the accuracy and speed;
- acceptability, which indicates the extent to which people are willing to accept the use of a particular biometric identifier (characteristic) in their daily lives;
- circumvention, which reflects how easily the system can be fooled using fraudulent methods.

A practical biometric system should meet the specified recognition accuracy, speed, and resource requirements, be harmless to the users, be accepted by the intended population, and be sufficiently robust to various fraudulent methods and attacks to the system.

2 Previous Works

Plenty of works are done on Iris Recognition System, since last 3-4 years. Most of the cases, authors claimed the better performance of speed in capturing images and recognition over the existing systems available at that time. To gather the knowledge, we have considered the following selective works.

Lye Wi Liam, Ali Chekima, Liau Chung Fan and Jamal Ahmad Dargham, in 2002, proposed [1] a system consisting of two parts: Localizing Iris and Iris Pattern Recognition. They used digital camera for capturing image; from the captured images Iris is extracted. Only the portion of selected Iris then reconstructed into rectangle format, from which Iris pattern is recognized.

Eric Sung, Xilin Chen, Jie Zhu and Jie Yang, December 2002, proposed a modified Kolmogora, complexity measure based on maximum Shannon entropy of wavelet packet reconstruction to quantify the iris information [2]. Real-time eye-corner tracking, iris segmentation and feature extraction algorithms are implemented. An ordinary camera with a zoom lens captures video images of the iris. Experiments are performed and the performances and analysis of iris code method and correlation method are described. Several useful findings were reached albeit from a small database. The iris codes are found to contain almost all the discriminating information. Correlation approach coupled with nearest neighbors classification outperforms the conventional thresholding method for iris recognition with degraded images.

Jiali Cui, Yunhong Wang, JunZhou Huang, Tieniu Tan and Zhenan Sun have proposed [3] the iris recognition algorithm based on PCA (Principal Component Analysis) is first introduced and then, iris image synthesis method is presented. The synthesis method first constructs coarse iris images with the given coefficients. Then, synthesized iris images are enhanced using super resolution. Through controlling the coefficients, they create many iris images with specified classes. Extensive experiments show that the synthesized iris images have satisfactory cluster and the synthesized iris databases can be very large.

Hyung Gu Lee, Seungin Noh, Kwanghyuk Bae, Kang-Ryoung Park and Jaihie Kim have introduced [4] the invariant binary feature which is defined as iris key. Iris image variation is not important in their work. Iris key is generated by the reference pattern, which is designed as lattice structured image to represent a bit pattern of an individual. Reference pattern and Iris image are linked into filter. In the filter Iris texture is reflected according to the magnitude of iris power spectrum in frequency domain.

Zhenan Sun, Yunhong Wang, Tieniu Tan, and Jiali Cui, in 2005, proposed [5] to overcome the limitations of local feature based classifiers (LFC). In addition, in order to recognize various iris images efficiently a novel cascading scheme is proposed to combine the LFC and an iris blob matcher. When the LFC is uncertain of its decision, poor quality iris images are usually involved in intra-class comparison. Then the iris blob matcher is resorted to determine the input iris identity because it is capable of recognizing noisy images. Extensive experimental results demonstrate that the cascaded classifiers significantly improve the system's accuracy with negligible extra computational cost.

Kazuyuki Miyazawa, Koichi Ito, Takafumi Aoki, Koji Kobayashi, Hiroshi Nakajima developed [6] phase-based image matching algorithm. The use of phase components in 2D (two-dimensional) discrete Fourier transforms of iris images makes possible to achieve highly robust iris recognition in a unified fashion with a simple matching algorithm.

Pan Lili and Xie Mei, proposed [7] a new iris localization algorithm, in which they adopted edge points detecting and curve fitting. After this, they set an integral iris image quality evaluation system that is necessary in the automatic iris recognition system.

Iris image denoising algorithm is proposed by Wang Jian-ming and Ding Run-tao [8], in which phase preserving principle is held to avoid corruption of iris texture features. Importance of phase information for iris image is shown by an experiment and the method to implement phase preserving by complex Gabor wavelets is explained. To verify the algorithm, white noise is added to iris images and Hamming distances between the iris images are calculated before and after the denoising algorithm is applied.

Weiki Yuan, Zhonghua Lin and Lu Xu have analyzed eye images [9] that they have based on structure characteristics of eyes, they put forward a rapid iris location arithmetic. Firstly, they have got an approximative center by gray projection, have got two points that located at left and right boundary by threshold value respectively, and have got a point that located at the lower boundary by direction edge detection operators, then they ensured the boundary of pupil and probable center. Secondly, they have got exact pupil boundary and center by Hough transform that is processed at a small scope surrounding the probable center. Thirdly, they have searched two points that located at left and right boundaries between iris and sclera along horizontal direction by using the exact center and direction edge detection operators. Then they ensured the horizontal coordinate of the center of iris based on the above two point accurately. Finally, they have searched two points that located at upper and lower boundaries between iris and sclera beginning at the horizontal coordinate of the center of iris along the directions that making plus and minus thirty angles between horizontal direction respectively by using direction edge detection operators, so they ensured the coordinate of the center of iris and the boundary between iris and sclera. The experiments indicated that this method reached about zero point two second at speed and percentage of ninety nine point forty five at precision. This method is faster than existing methods at speed, they claimed.

3   Our Work

We have divided our work into three main phases related with three different algorithms, which are given and discussed hereunder:

3.1   24-bit Bitmap Color Image to 8-bit Gray Scale Conversion

a)   At first a picture of an individual's Eye with a Powerful Digital Camera, such that the picture must be a size of 100*100 in 24-Bit BMP format.

b)   Take this 24-Bit BMP file as Input file and open the file in Binary Mode.

c)   Copy the ImageInfo (First 54 byte) of the Header from Input 24-Bit Bmp file to a newly created BMP file and edit this Header by changing filesize, Bit Depth, Colors to confirm to 8-Bit BMP.

d)   Copy the ColorTable from a sample gray scale Image to this newly created BMP at 54th Byte place on words.

e)   Convert the RGB value to Gray Value using the following formula-
blueValue = (0.299*redValue + 0.587*greenValue + 0.114*blueValue);
greenValue = (0.299*redValue + 0.587*greenValue + 0.114*blueValue);

redValue = (0.299*redValue + 0.587*greenValue + 0.114*blueValue);
grayValue = blueValue = greenValue = redValue;

f)   Write to new BMP file.

Take 24-bit BMP color image as input. Then convert it to 8-bit Gray Scale image by following this algorithm. This 8-bit Gray Scale image is the output of the algorithm. In this algorithm, first read the red, blue and green value of each pixel and then after formulation, three different values are converted into gray value.

3.2 IRIS Edge Detection

a)   Load resultant 8-bit Grayscale Image from Algorithm1 into memory
b)   Convert the Loaded Image into PlanarImage
c)   Set the Horizontal and Vertical kernels (3 x 3; float type), respectively as follow:

$$\begin{bmatrix} 1.0 & 0.0 & -1.0 \\ 1.0 & 0.0 & -1.0 \\ 1.0 & 0.0 & -1.0 \end{bmatrix} 3 \times 3 \qquad \begin{bmatrix} -1.0 & -1.0 & -1.0 \\ 0.0 & 0.0 & 0.0 \\ 1.0 & 1.0 & 1.0 \end{bmatrix} 3 \times 3$$

d)   Generated PlanarImage in Step-b, is passed through kernels created in Step-c.
e)   Modified fine-grained PlanarImage is stored into Image File.
f)   Close all Image file(s).

Here we are considering 8-bit Image, two-pass masking is used, namely, Horizontal and Vertical kernels. The PlanarImage now passed through these masks or kernels. Resultant transformed Image generates the distinct marks for IRIS area; the process is edge detection [10].

3.3 IRIS Effective Region Extraction and Pattern Generation

(Extracting a 8*12 Iris Pattern from Edge Detected IRIS Image)

a)   Take the 8-Bit BMP Image produced from previous Algorithm as Input and open this BMP file in binary Read Mode.
b)   Read the raster Data and Store the raster Data into a Matrix of vectorsize. Where vectorSize = filesize - (54+(4*256)).
c)   Then a 8*12 Iris Pattern is extracted from Edge Detected BMP using following logic-

```
for (x=0;x<=originalImage.rows-1;x++) {
  for (y=0;y<=originalImage.cols-1;y++) {
  if ( y<30 && x=((originalImage.rows/2)+4) && GrayValue == 255) {
      for (i=0;i<8;i++) {
      for (j=0;j<12;j++) {
        *(edgeImage.data + (i * edgeImage.cols) + j) = *(originalImage.data
        + (x * originalImage.cols) - (i * originalImage.cols) + (y + j));
```

```
Write to new BMP Image file
      }
   }
}
}
}
```

Take 8-bit BMP image produced from previous step as an input. Then convert it to 12X8 8-bit BMP image by following this algorithm. This 12x8 8-bit BMP image is the output of the algorithm. In this algorithm, first go to the middle row and first column of the input image, then go to the 4 pixels upward and check the gray value of each pixel until gray value becomes 255 (white). After this start reading the pixels and store the corresponding gray value into a 8x12 matrix.

4 Result

Our testing results shown in Fig. 1 through Fig. 4. 24-bit Color eye picture is taken by using a powerful digital camera, located in a suitable position. Numerous pictures are

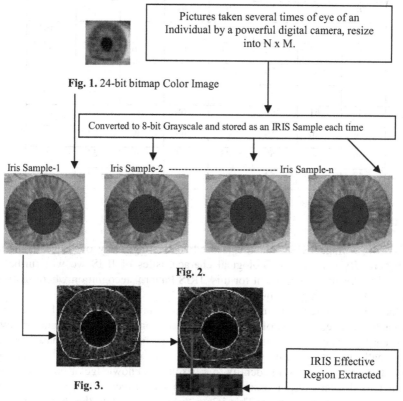

Pictures taken several times of eye of an Individual by a powerful digital camera, resize into N x M.

Fig. 1. 24-bit bitmap Color Image

Converted to 8-bit Grayscale and stored as an IRIS Sample each time

Iris Sample-1   Iris Sample-2 ---------------------------------- Iris Sample-n

Fig. 2.

IRIS Effective Region Extracted

Fig. 3.

Fig. 4. Highlighted [n x m] Red Rectangle from Fig. 3 Sample-1.

taken and these are resized and converted to 8-bit Images, here, these are considered as Iris Samle-1 through Iris Sample-n, which are displayed in Fig. 2. For every sample Edge detection is done, here shown for Iris Sample-1 in Fig. 3.

Now using algorithm "IRIS Effective Region Extraction and Pattern Generation" Iris Effective Region is extracted, which is clearly shown in Fig. 4 surrounded by rectangle. From this rectangle the following 2D-Array is generated, shown in Table-1.

In this process n number of 2D-Arrays will be generated for n number of IRIS Images.

We are considering the Table-1 is the IRIS Pattern of Iris Sample-1, so, we will get n number of IRIS Patterns of an individual. From this n number of IRIS Patterns one single 'IRIS Pattern' of an individual can be generated by Statistical Analysis, which can be strongly used for Pattern Recognition or over all Human Recognition.

Table 1. 8*12 Matrix IRIS Pattern

61	56	66	67	67	82	57	72
61	56	66	67	67	82	57	72
56	50	56	63	63	84	79	90
63	57	54	67	67	73	93	104
63	57	49	67	67	73	93	104
48	65	56	61	61	76	91	94
48	65	56	61	61	76	91	94
39	61	69	68	68	73	77	80
39	61	69	68	68	73	77	80
36	40	50	43	43	56	67	80
36	40	50	43	43	56	67	80
42	49	53	56	56	67	67	65

5 Conclusion

In this work a huge IRIS Database is used for testing. Only one such example is shown here. By considering Biological characteristics of IRIS we will further use Statistical Correlation Coefficient for this 'IRIS Pattern' recognition where Statistical Estimation Theory can play a big role.

Reliable personal recognition is critical to many business processes. Biometrics refers to automatic recognition of an individual based on her behavioral and/or physiological characteristics. The conventional knowledge-based and token-based methods do not really provide positive personal recognition because they rely on surrogate representations of the person's identity (e.g., exclusive knowledge or possession). It is thus obvious that any system assuring reliable personal recognition must necessarily involve a biometric component. This is not, however, to state that biometrics alone can deliver reliable personal recognition component. In fact, a sound system design will often entail incorporation of many biometric and nonbiometric components (building blocks) to provide reliable personal recognition.

References

1. Liam, L.W., Chekima, A., Fan, L.C., Dargham, J.A.: Iris Recognition using Self-Organizing Neural Network. In: IEEE 2002 Student Conference on Research and Development Proceedings, Shah Alam, Malaysia, pp. 169–172 (2002)
2. Sung, E., Chen, X., Zhu, J., Yang, J.: Towards non-cooperative iris recognition systems. In: Seventh international Conference on Control, Automation, Robotics And Vision (ICARCV 2002), Singapore, December 2002, pp. 990–995 (2002)
3. Cui, J., Wang, Y., Huang, J., Tan, T., Sun, Z.: An Iris Image Synthesis Method Based on PCA and Super-resolution. In: 17th International Conference on Pattern Recognition (ICPR 2004), Cambridge, UK, August 23-26, vol. 4, pp. 471–474 (2004)
4. Lee, H.G., Noh, S., Bae, K., Park, K.-R., Kim, J.: Invariant biometric code extraction. In: IEEE Intelligent Signal Processing and Communication Systems (ISPACS 2004), Seoul, Korea, November 18-19, pp. 181–184 (2004)
5. Sun, Z., Wang, Y., Tan, T., Cui, J.: Improving iris recognition accuracy via cascaded classifiers. IEEE Transactions on Systems, MAN, and CYBERNETICS - Part C: Applications and Reviews 35(3), 435–441 (2005)
6. Miyazawa, K., Ito, K., Aoki, T., Kobayashi, K., Nakajima, H.: An Efficient Iris Recognition Algorithm Using Phase-Based Image Matching. In: IEEE Image Processing Conference, 2005 (ICIP 2005), Genoa, Italy, September 11-14, vol. 2, pp. II-49–52 (2005)
7. Lili, P., Mei, X.: The Algorithm of Iris Image Preprocessing. In: Fourth IEEE Workshop on Automatic Identification Advanced Technologies (AutoID 2005), October 17-18, pp. 134–138 (2005)
8. Jian-ming, W., Run-tao, D.: Iris Image Denoising Algorithm Based on Phase Preserving. In: Sixth IEEE International Conference on Parallel and Distributed Computing, Applications and Technologies, PDCAT 2005, Dalian, China, December 05-08, pp. 832–835 (2005)
9. Yuan, W., Lin, Z., Xu, L.: A Rapid Iris Location Method Based on the Structure of Human Eyes. In: Proceedings of the 2005 IEEE Engineering in Medicine and Biology 27th Annual Conference, Shanghai, China, September 1-4, pp. 3020–3023 (2005)
10. Bhattacharyya, D., Bandyopadhyay, S.K., Das, P.: Handwritten Signature Verification System using Morphological Image Analysis. In: CATA-2007 International Conference, A publication of International Society for Computers and their Applications, Honolulu, Hawaii, USA, March 28-30, pp. 112–117 (2007)

Bidirectional Quantum Secure Direct Communication Based on Entanglement

Dazu Huang[1,2], Zhigang Chen[1], Jianquan Xie[1,2], and Ying Guo[1]

[1] School of Information Science and Engineering, Central South University,
Changsha, 410083 China
[2] Department of Information Management,
Hunan College of Finance and Economics,
Changsha, 410205, China

Abstract. Based on entanglement,a bidirectional quantum secure direct communication scheme is proposed to exchange directly the communicators' secret messages . In this scheme the messages are encoded in the entanglement state. our scheme has great capacity to distribute the secret messages since these messages have been imposed on high-dimensional Bell states via the local unitary operations with superdense coding. Security analysis indicates that this scheme is secure against the present Trojan horse attack and the current attack strategyand it can also ensure the security of the messages in a low noisy channel.

Keywords: Bidirectional Quantum secure direct communication, entanglement state, quantum cryptography.

1 Introduction

With the rapid development of information technology, dramatic progress in quantum information has been made. Quantum key distribution (QKD) is one of the most important applications of quantum mechanics. It can establish a common private key between two legitimated users to ensure secret messages protected from being altered or stolen. Many QKD protocols [1,2,3] have been put forward constantly since Bennett and Brassard proposed BB84 protocol [4] in 1984. However, their basic theorem is identical for communication, i.e., the two legitimated parties first create a shared private key, and then use it to encrypt the transmitted messages. On the other hand, the nondeterministic property in the standard QKD scheme leads loss of lots of qubits since many qubits have to be discarded. As far as communication is concerned, this beforehand step and loss of many qubits undoubtedly reduce the efficiency of communication. So how to improve both efficiency and security of quantum communication is a hot issue at all times. In recent years, there has been much attention focused on both deterministic secure quantum communication (DSQC) [5,6,7,8,9,10,11, 12,13,14,15] and quantum secure direct communication (QSDC) [16,17,18,19, 20,21,22,23,24,25,26,27].

Recently, a novel deterministic QKD, which is also called as the deterministic secure quantum communication (DSQC) [5], was proposed.However, its

T.-k. Kim, T.-h. Kim, and A. Kiumi (Eds.): SecTech 2008, CCIS 29, pp. 40–49, 2009.

deterministic measurement can not be performed, so there are not any practical values. In DSQC, the receiver can read out the secret message by exchanging additional classical bits for qubits. It is just a slight modification of the usual QKD with classical communications. To some extent, DSQC process is similar to the QKD protocol [1]. but it can obtain deterministic messages rather than a random binary string, that is, QKD protocols can not predict whether an instance is useful or not. In 2004, Gao et al [6] proposed a DSQC scheme based on EPR pairs and entanglement swapping, in which the users can complete the eavesdropping check before they take a swapping. It is the first valuable DSQC protocol. Later, Yan et al [7] proposed several DSQC protocols based on quantum teleportation and entanglement swapping. Song [8] and Wang et al [9] presented DSQC protocols based on secret transmission order of particle or blind polarization bases, but they are vulnerable to eavesdroppers. Li et al [10] proposed a DSQC protocol without maximally entanglement states. Man et al. [11] exploited entanglement swapping to design a DSQC protocol by using Einstein-Podolsky-Rosen (EPR) pairs as the quantum carriers. Wang *et al.* [12] put forward a protocol for DSQC based on the secret transmitting order of the travel particles. Zhu *et al.* [13] proposed another protocol for DSQC based on the rearrangement of orders of particles, which follows some ideas in the QKD protocol [14], Li et al [15] presented a Trojan horse attack strategy and a possible improvement to Zhu's protocol.

Different from DSQC, whose object is to establish a deterministic key between the communicators, the receiver can read out the secret message without exchanging additional classical bits for qubits.the goal of quantum secure direct communication (QSDC) is also to transmit directly the secret messages without first establishing a key to encrypt them. DSQC and QSDC are both the deterministic quantum communications. However, DQSC does require additional classical messages to read out the secret messages while QSDC does not require any additional classical information in communications. In 2002, Bostrom et al [16] proposed a QSDC protocol by using EPR pairs as quantum information carriers. It was proven to be insecure in a noise channel . In 2003, Deng et al [17] proposed a two-step QSDC protocol using an EPR pair block. It was the first completely secure QSDC protocol, and the phrase set "quantum secure direct communication (QSDC)"was used for the first time in Ref. [17].

Since Deng *et al.* proposed a QSDC scheme using EPR pairs [17], many QSDC schemes have been actively suggested and pursued (More QSDC and DSQC protocols have been mentioned in Ref. [18] and Refs. [19,20,21]). Boström and Felbinger presented a "ping-pong" protocol (PP protocol) [22], which is intended to be a QSDC protocol, to distribute a bit message based on an EPR pair. However, an eavesdropper, Eve, may eavesdrop on information if quantum channel is imperfect (noisy or lossy), and it can also be attacked without eavesdropping [23]. It is a quasi-deterministic quantum communication protocol. The capacity is restricted since an entangled state carries only one bit message in each a protocol run. Afterward, Cai and Li gave an improved PP protocol [24], which allows one entangled state to carry two bit messages. The PP protocol and its revised versions [24] are all insecure if there is loss or noises in the quantum channel. These schemes only satisfy the first requirement of the Deng-Long security criteria for QSDC [18]. In addition, Wang *et al.* presented another novel QSDC protocol [25] to distribute the high-dimensional messages via quantum superdense coding in high-dimension Hilbert space. This superdense-coding-based QSDC scheme improves the two-step QSDC scheme [17] as it does not require the sender to determine whether some of the quantum signals sent by the receiver are lost or not [18].

Currently, quantum entanglement swapping has offered an elegant method that enables one to entangle two quantum systems to achieve the secret message without having direct interaction with each other [26]. Based on entanglement swapping, there have been many applications in quantum information [27], such as constructing quantum teleportation, speeding up the distribution of entanglement, correcting errors or loss in Bell states, preparing entangled states of particles, and sharing the secret message. In this paper, we consider the other application of entanglement swapping, i.e., establishing a bidirectional quantum secure direct communication (QSDC) based on the identification of the high-dimensional Bell states. It combines the ideas of PP protocol with block transmission, quantum superdense coding and entanglement swapping. So the present scheme has the feature of exchanging the communicators' messages with enhenced security by distributing the high-dimensional messages with quantum superdense coding and entanglement exchanging.

2   QSDC Protocol

Before presenting the QSDC, let us introduce the local unitary operations which can impose the secret messages on Bell states. Four two-dimensional Bell states can be defined as

$$|\Psi^{\pm}\rangle = \frac{1}{\sqrt{2}}(|01\rangle \pm |10\rangle),$$

$$|\Phi^{\pm}\rangle = \frac{1}{\sqrt{2}}(|00\rangle \pm |11\rangle). \tag{1}$$

Let $U_{00} = |0\rangle\langle0| + |1\rangle\langle1|$, $U_{01} = |0\rangle\langle0| - |1\rangle\langle1|$, $U_{10} = |0\rangle\langle1| + |1\rangle\langle0|$ and $U_{11} = |0\rangle\langle1| - |1\rangle\langle0|$ be four local unitary operators acting on one qubit of a Bell state in Eq.(1). The encodings of the secret messages $\{ij : i, j \in \{0, 1\}\}$ can hence be imposed on Bell states by using the local unitary operations $\{U_{ij} : i, j \in \{0, 1\}\}$, respectively. For two unitary operations U_{ij}^{A} and U_{mn}^{B}, we can calculate the following equation

$$|\Theta_1\rangle = (U_{ij}^{A}|\Psi_{AB_a}^{-}\rangle) \otimes (U_{mn}^{B}|\Psi_{A_bB}^{-}\rangle)$$

$$= \frac{1}{2}(U_{ij}^{A} \otimes U_{mn}^{B})(|\Psi_{AA_b}^{-}\rangle|\Psi_{B_aB}^{-}\rangle - |\Psi_{AA_b}^{+}\rangle|\Psi_{B_aB}^{+}\rangle$$

$$+ |\Phi_{AA_b}^{+}\rangle|\Phi_{B_aB}^{+}\rangle - |\Phi_{AA_b}^{-}\rangle|\Phi_{B_aB}^{-}\rangle), \tag{2}$$

where $U_{ij}^A, U_{mn}^B \in \{U_{ij} : i,j \in \{0,1\}\}$ are two unitary operations performed on the first qubit of $|\Psi_{AB_a}^-\rangle$ and the second qubit of $|\Psi_{A_bB}^-\rangle$, respectively. Similarly, we can also obtain

$$
\begin{aligned}
|\Theta_2\rangle &= (U_{ij}^A|\Psi_{AB_a}^-\rangle) \otimes (U_{mn}^B K_B|\Psi_{A_bB}^-\rangle) \\
&= \frac{1}{2\sqrt{2}}(U_{ij}^A \otimes U_{mn}^B)[|\Psi_{AA_b}^-\rangle(|\Psi_{B_aB}^-\rangle - |\Phi_{B_aB}^+\rangle) \\
&\quad - |\Psi_{AA_b}^+\rangle(|\Psi_{B_aB}^+\rangle + |\Phi_{B_aB}^-\rangle) + |\Phi_{AA_b}^+\rangle(|\Phi_{B_aB}^+\rangle \\
&\quad + |\Psi_{B_aB}^-\rangle) - |\Phi_{AA_b}^-\rangle(|\Phi_{B_aB}^-\rangle - |\Psi_{B_aB}^+\rangle)],
\end{aligned} \tag{3}
$$

$$
\begin{aligned}
|\Theta_3\rangle &= (U_{ij}^A K_A|\Psi_{AB_a}^-\rangle) \otimes (U_{mn}^B|\Psi_{A_bB}^-\rangle) \\
&= \frac{1}{2\sqrt{2}}(U_{ij}^A \otimes U_{mn}^B)[(|\Psi_{AA_b}^-\rangle - |\Phi_{AA_b}^+\rangle)|\Psi_{B_aB}^-\rangle \\
&\quad - (|\Psi_{AA_b}^+\rangle + |\Phi_{AA_b}^-\rangle)|\Psi_{B_aB}^+\rangle + (|\Phi_{AA_b}^+\rangle + |\Psi_{AA_b}^-\rangle)|\Phi_{B_aB}^+\rangle \\
&\quad - (|\Phi_{AA_b}^-\rangle - |\Psi_{AA_b}^+\rangle)|\Phi_{B_aB}^-\rangle],
\end{aligned} \tag{4}
$$

$$
\begin{aligned}
|\Theta_4\rangle &= (U_{ij}^A K_A|\Psi_{AB_a}^-\rangle) \otimes (U_{mn}^B K_B|\Psi_{A_bB}^-\rangle) \\
&= \frac{1}{4}(U_{ij}^A \otimes U_{mn}^B)[(|\Psi_{AA_b}^-\rangle - |\Phi_{AA_b}^+\rangle)(|\Psi_{B_aB}^-\rangle - |\Phi_{B_aB}^+\rangle) \\
&\quad - (|\Psi_{AA_b}^+\rangle + |\Phi_{AA_b}^-\rangle)(|\Psi_{B_aB}^+\rangle + |\Phi_{B_aB}^-\rangle) + (|\Phi_{AA_b}^+\rangle \\
&\quad + |\Psi_{AA_b}^-\rangle)(|\Phi_{B_aB}^+\rangle + |\Psi_{B_aB}^-\rangle) - (|\Phi_{AA_b}^-\rangle \\
&\quad - |\Psi_{AA_b}^+\rangle)(|\Phi_{B_aB}^-\rangle - |\Psi_{B_aB}^+\rangle)],
\end{aligned} \tag{5}
$$

where $K = \frac{1}{\sqrt{2}}(|0\rangle\langle 0| - |1\rangle\langle 0| + |0\rangle\langle 1| + |1\rangle\langle 1|)$. It is easy to prove that $\langle\Theta_u|\Theta_v\rangle \neq 0$ for $u \neq v$.

From Eqs.(2-5), one can see that there is an explicit correspondence between two initial Bell states and the outcomes of Bell-state measurement (BM) after quantum entanglement swapping. To exchange the different secret messages with each other, two communicators, Alice and Bob, should agree on that each an operation, say U_{ij}, can carry two bit messages "ij". Then, they act as follows:

(1) Alice and Bob prepare their ordered N Bell states in the same Bell state, say $|\Psi_{AB_a}^-\rangle$ and $|\Psi_{A_bB}^-\rangle$, where the subscripts AB_a and A_bB indicate Alice's and Bob's pair particles, respectively. Denote all particles of these entangled states with $\{[p_A(k), p_{B_a}(k)] : 1 \leq k \leq N\}$ and $\{[p_{A_b}(k), p_B(k)] : 1 \leq k \leq N\}$, where k represents the state order in two respective Bell state sequences. Alice takes one particle from each Bell state to form an ordered Bell partner particle sequence, say $\{[p_A(k)] : 1 \leq k \leq N\}$, which is called as the home sequence or HA-sequence for short. The remaining particles constitute another partner particle sequence $\{[p_{B_a}(k)] : 1 \leq k \leq N\}$ called as the travel sequence or TA-sequence. Similarly, Bob regards $\{[p_B(k)] : 1 \leq k \leq N\}$ and $\{[p_{A_b}(k)] : 1 \leq k \leq N\}$ of his ordered Bell state sequence as the home sequence (HB-sequence) and the travel sequence (TB-sequence), respectively.

(2) Alice (Bob) performs a random operation $\tau_A(\tau_B) \in \{I, K\}$ on each particle of HA(HB)-sequence. Then, she (he) selects several particles in TA(TB)-sequence

as the checking particles denoted by CA(CB)-sequence with the partner particles in HA(HB)-sequence of the same Bell states denoted by WA(WB)-sequence. The remaining particles of TA(TB)-sequence are denoted by EA(EB)-sequence with the partner particles in HA(HB)-sequence denoted by DA(DB)-sequence.

(3) Alice (Bob) applies the unitary operations U_{ij} (U_{mn}) on DA(DB)-sequence to encode the secret messages "ij" ("mn"). Then, she (he) disturbs the initial order of all particles in TA(TB)-sequence and distributes the resulting sequence to Bob (Alice).

(4) When Alice and Bob receive the respectively disturbed TB-sequence and TA-sequence, they announce the initial order of their travel sequences. Then, they rearrange the particles of two received travel sequences and switch to *the detecting mode* in step (5) to check whether two-way quantum channel is secure. Otherwise, they proceed to *the message mode* in step (6) to decode the distributed messages, i.e., Alice and Bob exchange their own secret messages.

(5) After performing τ_A onto WA-sequence, Alice selects randomly one of two sets of measurement basis, say, $\mathcal{X}_z = \{+, -\}$ and $\mathcal{X}_x = \{|0\rangle, |1\rangle\}$, to measure the particles of CB-sequence and WA-sequence with the outcomes denoted by $|M_{CB}\rangle$ and $|M_{WA}\rangle$, respectively. She tells Bob which basis has been used for the measurement. Then, Bob applies τ_B onto WB-sequence and makes use of Alice's basis to measure WB-sequence and CA-sequence with the outcomes denoted by $|M_{WB}\rangle$ and $|M_{CA}\rangle$, respectively. Finally, Alice and Bob compare all of the measurement outcomes. If no eavesdropping exists, their outcomes should be completely opposite, i.e., $\langle M_{CB}|M_{WB}\rangle = 0$ and $\langle M_{CA}|M_{WA}\rangle = 0$. When Alice and Bob ascertain that there is no eavesdropper, they proceed to step (6). Otherwise, the communication is aborted.

(6) Alice (Bob) performs the proper BM to measure the pair particles in DA-sequence and EB-sequence (DB-sequence and EA-sequence) according to Eq.(2-5). Without loss of the generality, assume that $\tau_A = \tau_B = I$. In this case, Alice first applies a BM with Bell measurement basis $\mathcal{B} = \{|\Psi^{\pm}\rangle, |\Phi^{\pm}\rangle\}$ on a two-particle pair and announces her measurement outcomes. After that, Bob also performs a BM on its partner two-particle pair in DB-sequence and EA-sequence, and records his measurement outcomes. In fact, after Alice's BM on a selected two-particle pair, Bob's partner two-particle pair should project to one of four Bell states. According to Alice's outcomes, Bob can deduce the exact unitary operations that Alice has performed locally on DA-sequence. As an example, assume that Alice and Bob's outcomes are $|\Phi^-_{AA_b}\rangle$ and $|\Psi^+_{B_aB}\rangle$, respectively. Since Alice's N initially ordered Bell states are all $|\Psi^-_{AB_a}\rangle$, Bob can judge that $|\Psi^-_{AB_a}\rangle$ has been projected to $|\Phi^+_{AB_a}\rangle$ by Alice applying the local unitary operation U_{10}. It can be illustrated by the following equation

$$(U_{10}^A|\Psi^-_{AB_a}\rangle) \otimes |\Psi^-_{A_bB}\rangle = |\Phi^+_{AB_a}\rangle \otimes |\Psi^-_{A_bB}\rangle$$

$$= \frac{1}{2}(|\Phi^-_{AA_b}\rangle|\Psi^+_{B_aB}\rangle - |\Psi^+_{AA_b}\rangle|\Phi^-_{B_aB}\rangle$$

$$-|\Psi^-_{AA_b}\rangle|\Phi^+_{B_aB}\rangle + |\Phi^+_{AA_b}\rangle|\Psi^-_{B_aB}\rangle). \tag{6}$$

Thus, Bob can deduce that Alice's secret message is "10". Similarly, after Bob performs his BM on the selected two-particle pair and announces the measurement outcomes, Alice can also deduce Bob's secret message after applying her BM on the partner two-particle pair. In this way, Alice and Bob can exchange the secret messages with each other. (We note that in the second case of $\tau_A = I$ and $\tau_B = K$, Alice and Bob should apply the Bell measurement basis $\mathcal{B}$ and the state measurement basis $\mathcal{S} = \{|\Psi^+\rangle \pm |\Phi^-\rangle, |\Psi^-\rangle \pm |\Phi^+\rangle\}$ respectively to deduce the secret messages in terms of Eq.(3). Similarly, in the third case of $\tau_A = K$ and $\tau_B = I$, Alice and Bob should apply $\mathcal{S}$ and $\mathcal{B}$ in terms of Eq.(4). In the fourth case of $\tau_A = \tau_B = K$, both Alice and Bob should apply $\mathcal{S}$ in terms of Eq.(5).)

As discussed above, Alice and Bob can ensure the security of two travel sequences by using *the detecting mode*. Eve can not read out the exchanged messages in Bell states without two home sequences. Even if Eve captures all particles of two travel sequences, she can not gain any information about the encoded messages by measuring one particle of an Bell state alone [22]. In this way, no secret message will be leaked to Eve. Moreover, since Alice and Bob have applied the random operations τ_A and τ_B on two respective home sequences before distributing two travel sequences, it makes more difficult for Eve to distinguish $|\Theta_u\rangle$ from $|\Theta_v\rangle$. Thus, it enhances the security of the exchanged secret messages.

3 Security Analysis

So far, we have proposed a Bidirectional QSDC scheme based on quantum entanglement swapping and the identification of Bell states. Now, we are faced with the security of this scheme. To get the secretly exchanged messages, Eve would intercept some particles in travel sequences and replace them with her own particles prepared in advance. However, this eavesdropping may be detected in *the detecting mode*. This scheme is based on the entanglement of Bell states and the secure transmissions of travel sequences, so the proof of the security is similar in essence to those presented in Refs. [16], [2]. If Eve could not be detected in *the detecting mode*, she would capture easily some travel particles and take BM on them. However, Eve could not read out the secret messages without the partner particles preserved in the communicators' home sequences. Thus, this scheme is secure against eavesdropping.

It seems that this scheme should be designed only for ideal quantum channels, in which the reliable sharing of an entangled state between Alice and Bob is important and necessary. It is known that when a qubit of an entangled pair travels in imperfect quantum channel, the initial entanglement might be lost. Hence, a security problem for this scheme implementing in imperfect quantum channel seems arise. Fortunately, it has been proven that Alice and Bob can reliably share an entangled pair over any long distance by using quantum repeater techniques [28], containing the entanglement purification and teleportation. Once Alice and Bob have shared a two-qubit entangled state, Eve can be detected by the communicators using the techniques of BM. Thus, this scheme may also be acted securely even in imperfect quantum channel.

We have presented a QSDC scheme for two communicators to exchange two bit messages via quantum superdense coding implemented in two-dimensional Hilbert space. In fact, this scheme can be easily generalized to exchange two d-dimensional $(d \geq 3)$ messages via quantum superdense coding with the d-dimensional Bell states [29]

$$|\bar{\Psi}^{mn}\rangle = \frac{1}{\sqrt{d}} \sum_j e^{2\pi ijm/d}|j\rangle \otimes |j+n \mod d\rangle, \tag{7}$$

where $m, n \in \{0, 1, \cdots, d-1\}$. The unitary operations that are used for the encoding of the secret messages can be described as

$$\bar{U}_{mn} = \sum_j e^{2\pi ijm/d}|j+m \mod d\rangle\langle j|, \tag{8}$$

which can transform $|\bar{\Psi}^{00}\rangle$ into $|\bar{\Psi}^{mn}\rangle$, i.e., $\bar{U}_{mn}|\bar{\Psi}^{00}\rangle = |\bar{\Psi}^{mn}\rangle$. It implies that one particle can carry $2\log_2 d$ bits of classical information.

To illustrate the QSDC scheme via quantum superdense coding with d-dimensional Bell states, we make use of a d-dimensional quantum system in the present scheme. Before exchanging the secret messages, Alice and Bob should agree on that each unitary operation $\bar{U}_{ij}$ can carry the d-dimensional messages "ij", and prepare two sequences of N ordered d-dimensional Bell states, say $|\bar{\Psi}^{00}_{AB_a}\rangle$ and $|\bar{\Psi}^{00}_{A_bB}\rangle$, respectively. After Alice (Bob) applies her (his) unitary operations $\bar{U}_{ij}$ ($\bar{U}_{mn}$) on DA(DB)-sequence to encode the d-dimensional messages "ij" ("mn"), she (he) disturbs the initial order of the particles of TA(TB)-sequence and distributes the resulting TA(TB)-sequence to Bob (Alice). While receiving the disturbed TB(TA)-sequence, the communicators announce the initial order of TA(TB)-sequence. Then, they rearrange the particles of two travel sequences and switch to two communication modes, i.e., *the detecting mode* and *the message mode*. In *the detecting mode* Alice selects randomly one of several sets of measurement basis (as an example, for a qutrit system there are four sets of measurement basis chosen as $\mathcal{X}_1 = \{|n\rangle : n \in \{0, 1, 2\}\}$, $\mathcal{X}_2 = \{\frac{1}{\sqrt{3}}\sum_{k=0}^2 e^{2nk\pi i/3}|k\rangle : n \in \{0, 1, 2\}\}$, $\mathcal{X}_3 = \{C_n^+ \sum_{k=0}^2 |k\rangle : n \in \{0, 1, 2\}\}$ and $\mathcal{X}_4 = \{C_n^- \sum_{k=0}^2 |k\rangle : n \in \{0, 1, 2\}\}$, where $C_n^{\pm} = \frac{1}{\sqrt{3}}e^{\pm 2\pi i/3}\sum_{k=0}^2 |n+k\rangle\langle n+k|$) to measure the particles of CB-sequence and WA-sequence with the outcomes $|\bar{M}_{CB}\rangle$ and $|\bar{M}_{WA}\rangle$. She tells Bob which basis has been used for the measurement. Then, Bob makes use of Alice's basis to measure WB-sequence and CA-sequence and gets the outcomes $|\bar{M}_{WB}\rangle$ and $|\bar{M}_{CA}\rangle$. Finally, Alice and Bob gather together to compare their measurement outcomes. If no eavesdropping exists, their measurement outcomes should satisfy the following conditions

$$|\bar{M}_{CB}\rangle = |\bar{M}_{WB}\rangle, |\bar{M}_{CA}\rangle = |\bar{M}_{WA}\rangle. \tag{9}$$

In *the message mode*, Alice and Bob perform the proper d-dimensional BM to measure the particle pairs (DA-EB)-sequence (composed of DA-sequence and EB-sequence) and (DB-EA)-sequence (composed of DB-sequence and EA-sequence) to exchange their secret messages as the proposed processes in *the message mode* of the two-dimension system. In the similar way, Alice and Bob can exchange their *d*-dimensional messages with the security.

Our proposed protocol is secure to Trojan horse attack. As described in Ref. [15], There are two kinds of Trojan horse attack strategies, i.e. the invisible photon eavesdropping (IPE) scheme proposed by Cai et al [30]and the delay-photon Trojan horse attack [31, 32]. To defeat impersonation attack is based on the secret order of the particles according to the above analysis. However, the secret order will be published by Alice after the security checking. Provided that the legitimate users only check the security once in the third line from Alice to Bob, Eve can choose either a special wavelength l' which is close to the legitimate one (l' l) to produce a invisible photon or the same wavelength l'(l'= l) as the legitimate one with a delay time to produce a delay photon. Thus Eve inserts a spy photon in each legitimate photon of EPR pairs. When Alice and Bob perform their operations on the legitimate photons they also execute the same operation on the corresponding spy photon. When photons are transmitted over the quantum channel, Eve captures his spy photons and stores them. Eve's operations have no effect on the secret order and the secret states of the T sequence under the precondition we assume that Eve is so powerful that his technological capabilities is confined only by the laws of quantum physics mechanics. After Alice and Bob finish the security checking, Eve can rearrange the spy photon sequence order according to the information announced by Alice and measures them to obtain Alice's secret messages without being detected in principle. [15]

Our proposed protocol is also secure against the intercept-and-resend attack. The decoy photons are produced by choosing randomly one of the two bases Z and X, and are inserted into the traveling sequence randomly. Suppose Eve can take the intercept-and-resend attack. To acquire the secret message, in step 3 when the DA-sequence (DB-sequence) is sent to Bob (Alice), Eve would capture the DA-sequence (DB-sequence) and replace them with her own particles prepared in advance. Eve does not know the states of the traveling sequences sent and cannot resend a perfect copy of the original signals she intercepts according to the properties of quantum physics such as Heisenberg uncertainty principle and quantum no-cloning principle. We let the number of eavesdropping photons in each traveling sequence $TA(TB)$ be b, in which the number of the eavesdropping photons with the basis X is $b/2$, the length of the photon sequence $HA(HB)$ is a, and hence the total length of the sequence TA (TB)is $a + b$. Thus, the probability with which Eve's presence is not detected is

$$P_e = \frac{\left(\frac{1}{4}b\right)^4}{P_{a+b}^b}$$

$$= \frac{1}{(a+b)(a+b-1)\dots(a-b+1)}\left(\frac{1}{4}b\right)^4. \tag{10}$$

and hence the probability of detecting Eve is

$$1 - P_e = 1 - \frac{1}{(a+b)(a+b-1)\dots(a-b+1)}\left(\frac{1}{4}b\right)^4. \tag{11}$$

Thus, for example, let $b = 10$, $a = 40$, the probability with which Eve's presence is detected is

$$1 - \frac{1}{(50)(49)\ldots(31)}(2.5^4) \approx 1. \tag{12}$$

Consequently, Eve's eavesdropping will inevitably disturb the states of the decoy photons and be detected from the higher error rate. As soon as they find that Eve is online they terminate the communicating process.

4   Conclusions

In summary, a bidirectional quantum secure direct communication is presented based on entanglement state. In this scheme the messages are encoded in the entanglement state. our scheme has great capacity to distribute the secret messages since these messages have been imposed on high-dimensional Bell states via the local unitary operations with superdense coding. Security analysis indicates that this scheme is secure against the present Trojan horse attack and the current attack strategyand it can also ensure the security of the messages in a low noisy channel with the assistances of quantum privacy application with quantum purification and quantum error-correction.

Acknowledgements

This work was supported in part by National Natural Science Foundation of China (No.60873082), Scientific Research Fund of Hunan Provincial Education Department (No.08B011), and the Young Core Instructor and Domestic Vistor Foundation from the Education Department of Hunan Province,and Natural Science Foundation of Hunan Province (No.07JJ3128), and Postdoctoral Science Foundation of China (No.20070420184).

References

1. Deng, F.G., Long, G.L.: Phys. Rev. A 69, 052319 (2004)
2. Long, G.L., Liu, X.S.: Phys. Rev. A 65, 032302 (2002)
3. Guo, Y., ZengCommu, G.H.: Theor. Phys. 47(3), 459-463 (2007)
4. Bennett, C.H., Brassard, G.: Advances in Cryptology:Proceedings of Crypto 1984, p. 175. Springer, Heidelberg (1984)
5. Shimizu, K., Imoto, N.: Phys. Rev. A 60, 157, (1999); Beige, A., Englert, B.G., Kurtsiefer, C., Weinfurter, H.: Acta. Phys. Pol. A 101, 357 (2002)
6. Gao, T., Yan, F.L., Wang, Z.X.: Nuovo Cimento Della Societa talianaDi Fisica B-general Physics Relativity Astronomy and Mathematical Physics and Methods. 119, 313-318 (2004)
7. Yan, F.L., Zhang, X.Q.: European Physical Journal B 41, 75-78 (2004)
8. Song, J., Zhu, A.D., Zhang, S.: Chin. Phys. 16, 621-623 (2007)
9. Wang, J., Zhang, Q., Tang, C.J.: Phys. Lett. A 358, 256-258 (2006)

10. Li, X.H., Deng, F.G., Li, C.Y., et al.: Journal of the Korean Physical Society 49, 1354–1359 (2006)
11. Man, Z.X., Zhang, Z.J., Li, Y.: Chin. Phys. Lett. 22, 18 (2005)
12. Wang, J., Zhang, Q., Tang, C.J.: Phys. Lett. A 358, 256 (2006)
13. Zhu, A.D., Xia, Y., Fan, Q.B., Zhang, S.: Phys. Rev. A 73, 022338 (2006)
14. Deng, F.G., Long, G.L.: Phys. Rev. A 68, 042315 (2003)
15. Li, X.H., Deng, F.G., Zhou, H.Y.: Phys. Rev. A 74, 054302-1-054302-5 (2006)
16. Bostrom, K., Felbinger, T.: Phys. Rev. Lett. 89, 187902-1-187902-4 (2002)
17. Deng, F.G., Long, G.L., Liu, X.S.: Phys. Rev. A 68, 042317 (2003)
18. Long, G.L., Deng, F.G., Wang, C., Li, X.H., Wen, K., Wang, W.Y.: Front. Phys. China 2(3), 251–272 (2007)
19. Wang, C., Li, Y.S., Long, G.L.: Commun. Theor. Phys. 46(3), 440–442 (2006); Chen, P., Li, Y.S., Deng, F.G., Long, G.L.: Commun. Theor. Phys. 47, 49–52 (2007)
20. Xia, Y., Song, J., Song, H.S.: Commun. Theor. Phys. 49, 919–924 (2008); Liu, J., liu, Y.M., Xia, Y., Zhang, Z.J.: Commun. Theor. Phys. 49, 887–890 (2008)
21. Guo, Y., Zeng, G.H.: Commun. Theor. Phys. 47, 459–463 (2007)
22. Boström, K., Felbinger, T.: Phys. Rev. Lett. 89, 187902 (2002)
23. Wójcik, A.: Phys. Rev. Lett. 90, 157901(2003); Cai, Q.Y.: Phys. Rev. Lett. 91, 109801(2003)
24. Cai, Q.Y., Li, B.W.: Phys. Rev. A 69, 054301 (2004)
25. Wang, C., Deng, F.G., Li, Y.S., Liu, X.S., Long, G.L.: Phys. Rev. A 71, 044305 (2005)
26. Pan, J.W., et al.: Phys. Rev. Lett. 80, 3891 (1998); Lee, J., et al.: Phys. Rev. A 70, 032305 (2004)
27. Bose, S., Vedral, V., Knight, P.L.: Phys. Rev. A 57, 822 (1998)
28. Waks, E., Zeevi, A., Yamamoto, Y.: Phys. Rev. A 65, 052310 (2002)
29. Liu, X.S., et al.: Phys. Rev. A 65, 022304 (2002)
30. Cai, Q.Y.: Phys. Lett. A 351, 23–25 (2006)
31. Gisin, N., Ribordy, G., Tittel, W., et al.: Q Rev. Mod. Phys. 74, 145–195 (2002)
32. Deng, F.G., Li, X.H., Li, C.Y., et al.: e-print quant-ph/0508168

Study and Implementation of SELinux-Like Access Control Mechanism Based on Linux[*]

Gaoshou Zhai and Yaodong Li

School of Computer and Information Technology, Beijing Jiaotong University,
Shang Yuan Cun 3#, Hai Dian District, Beijing 100044, China
gszhai@bjtu.edu.cn

Abstract. It's very important to study security mechanisms inside an operating system, among which access control mechanisms are indispensable for system security. Nowadays, Linux is becoming more and more popular for its excellent performance and open source philosophy. Meanwhile, access control mechanisms of Linux have been improved ceaselessly to satisfy arisen security requirements. For instance, SELinux is integrated into Linux kernel 2.6 and it can enforce a policy based on mandatory access control (MAC). However, there are still some defects in these mechanisms. In this paper, available Linux access control mechanisms are analyzed at first, while permission division principle is summarized. Then a SELinux-like MAC mechanism characteristic of cross-layered permission assignment is devised based on some popular information security models such as RBAC, DTE and etc. And a corresponding prototype system is implemented based on Linux. Finally, some preliminary test results are analyzed and further research directions are pointed out.

Keywords: Operating system security, access control mechanisms, mandatory access control, SELinux, cross-layered permission assignment, RBAC, DTE.

1 Introduction

Human society is going through a digitized era because of the explosion of information technology. A great lot of information has been digitized and maintained centrally by information systems. More and more valuable and critical information are being managed by information systems. Hence, the security capability of an information system is now becoming bottleneck of an information system. On the other hand, security of an operating system is the precondition to guarantee security of an information system because operating system is the base and the kernel of an information system. Therefore, it is very important and necessary to study security mechanisms provided by an operating system [1]. The foremost target of information security is to assure data security which can be protected by enforcing access control. Currently, Linux is becoming one of the most popular operating systems because of its excellent performance and open source philosophy. Since lots of individuals and

---

[*] The research presented in this paper was performed with the support of Beijing Jiaotong University Grants for 2005SM016.

T.-k. Kim, T.-h. Kim, and A. Kiumi (Eds.): SecTech 2008, CCIS 29, pp. 50–66, 2009.

enterprises are switching to Linux, access control mechanism of Linux has been improved from time to time for new security requirements (Fig. 1 shows a whole framework for security mechanisms of Linux).

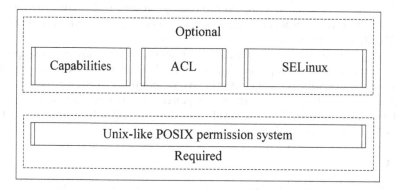

Fig. 1. Security Mechanisms of Linux

For instance, SELinux sub-system can enforce a policy based Mandatory Access Control (MAC) and provide flexible security policy configuration. However, there are still some defects in current Linux access control mechanism. The main target of this paper is to analyze and improve access control mechanism of current Linux operating system. To achieve this goal, available Linux security mechanisms ought to be analyzed at first.

2   Discretionary Access Control Mechanism of Linux

The foremost security mechanism inside Linux kernel is Unix-like POSIX permission system, and then capabilities and access control lists (ACL) permission are later introduced as optional components.

2.1   Unix-Like POSIX Permissions System

Unlike a Microsoft ACE/DACL control system, Linux implements a Unix POSIX permissions system [2]. In this system, every file and directory can have a combination of read, write and execute privileges and these permissions are represented numerically with different binary bits. At the same time, these permissions are organized and be set according to ownership, group membership and others.

Although it is simple and convenient to configure the system permissions and the corresponding cost is saving. But its granule for permission control is too big to satisfy permission configuration requirement with fine granules. For example, it can't be used to define per-user or per-group permissions. Meanwhile, controlled objects are limited to files and the other potential objects such as processes are ignored. Furthermore, security identification information of a file can be modified dynamically during the system running period. In addition, the existence of super-user or administrator is the hidden trouble of system security.

2.2 Capabilities

Capabilities [3] and [4] are introduced in order to solve super-user problems. The essential principle of capabilities is to add a 32-bit permission map into process control block so as to control the corresponding process under given permissions. Because each bit is corresponding to a kind of permission, capabilities can describe at most 32 different permissions.

Capabilities have refined system permissions and can effectively control super-user under the precondition of proper configuration. And they can implement process-level permission control with compact but effective descriptions. However, they focus on subjects and objects are ignored and impaired. Moreover, they can't improve confidentiality of system data effectively and there is still a long way to reach the target of flexible security policy configuration.

2.3 ACL

To configure the system permissions with well-fined granules, ACL [5] can be employed. Furthermore, each file is equipped with an access control list as an extended attribute to describe all permissions for different subjects as to it. Thus any given permissions can be assigned for any special user as to any file.

ACL improves flexibility of permission configuration with refined granules (subjects). But operation granules for permission are still rough and it requires excessive storage space to save ACL. Nevertheless, it can't control process-level permissions effectively.

3 Mandatory Access Control Mechanism of Linux (SELinux)

The up-to-date Linux kernel has been integrated with SELinux [6] which enforces a MAC policy and its security performance is improved to a great extent.

3.1 Architecture and Principle of SELinux

SELinux employs role-based access control (RBAC), type enforcement (TE) and an optional multi-level security (MLS) synthetically (Fig. 2 shows access control model of SELinux).

According to RBAC models, permissions are assigned to different roles, and any system user can then be appointed of one or more roles so as to be granted to special permissions. But in SELinux, permissions are not directly assigned to roles. Instead, types are introduced to be assigned some permission to, and one or more types can be appointed to any role so that the role can own corresponding permissions. At the same time, user defined in SELinux is different from conception of system user, and one or more roles can be mapped onto a user in session. Moreover, subjects and objects in system are identified by security context like ternaries of <User, Role, Type> while each security context can be mapped onto a unique security identifier (SID) in kernel space. In addition, objects are divided into some classes and corresponding operations are defined as to the objects of special class.

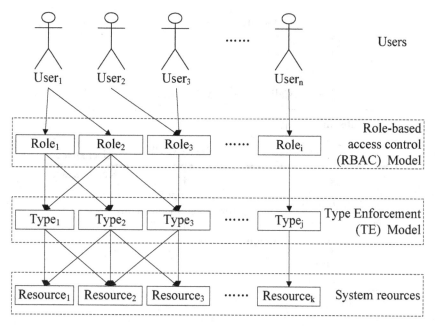

Fig. 2. Access control model of SELinux

In Linux kernel 2.6, SELinux is build on the framework of Linux security modules (LSM) and the architecture of SELinux can be referred to Fig. 3. SELinux are made up of security server, security policy base, security policy enforcement mechanism, access vector caches (AVC) and SELinux pseudo-file-system (SELinuxFS) in kernel space and object manager and libselinux in user space. SELinux is to be activated whenever some controlled subject requests to access a controlled object. First, parameters with LSM hook functions are verified and security contexts for corresponding subject and object are extracted from their security fields. Second, the access vector is searched for in AVC according to SIDs for subject and object and operation type. If it's found, then it can be judged directly as YES or NO for the access request at once. Otherwise, related information are transferred to security server and corresponding access vector is calculated based on security policies and decision result is returned finally. Furthermore, SELinuxFS provides interfaces for applications to access SELinux components in kernel space and these interfaces are encapsulated into libselinux for use in user space. Object manager can process requests for security policy query from applications and it receives messages from kernel by netlink mechanism.

3.2 Policy Configuration of SELinux

Security policy configuration for SELinux is made up of definitions for TE access vector rules, RBAC rules and constraints rules. All of these are described in special security policy description language provided by SELinux.

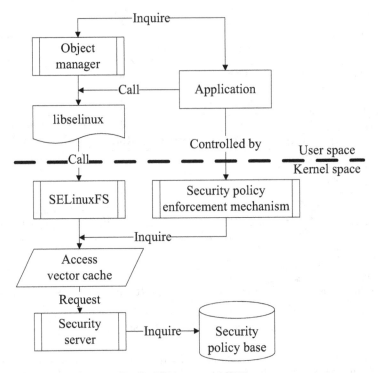

Fig. 3. Architecture of SELinux

3.3   Evaluation of SELinux

SELinux supports multiple security models and MAC policy. It is extensible and flexible with refined permission configuration. But it is the bottleneck of SELinux to configure the security policy of the system correctly. Moreover, flexibility of policy configuration is always weakened because there are close relationships among multiple models of SELinux. In addition, policy description and policy configuration of SELinux is too complicated to be mastered.

4   A New Mandatory Access Control Mechanism

It can be concluded that permission (or privilege) division is the essential way to solve systematic security problem. In another word, security performance of a system is dependent on the way of permission (or privilege) division.

Firstly, conception of permission (or privilege) must be clarified. In general, it can be defines as a binary group like < *mList, xID*> where *xID* represents identifier of an object or a type of objects and *mList* represents a list of those access modes permitted. Secondly, conception of user group or role is always introduced to represent a set of some identified permissions so that system permissions can be separated from fixed users and that can make permission management more flexible. Similarly, a role can be defined as a binary group like *<RID, PList>* where *RID* represents identifier of a role and *PList* represents a permission list. Thirdly, conception of domain (that is similar to domain or privilege level in computer architecture) should be introduced in order to describe permission division at process or thread levels because a process or thread (that performs tasks on behalf of user) usually needs only a small part of permission set corresponding to its user role. Finally, problems ought to be solved in order to design a access control model which include how to assign system permissions to subjects, how to control subjects move among permission sets, how to optimize control granule of information flow among objects and etc.

4.1 LYSLinux Access Control Model

Therefore, a hybrid access control model named LYSLinux is devised by integrating RBAC and Domain Type Enhancement (DTE) together (refer to Fig. 4).

System space are partitioned into subject set *S*, object set *O*, Operation Set *Op* and Permission Set *Perm*. Moreover, *S* is divided into user set *U* and process set *Ps* and a user in *U* can create one or more processes in *Ps*. Similarly, *O* is divided into resource set *R* and process set *Po*, where *R* consists of all available files, system devices, net sockets and etc that can carry information while *Po* involves those processes existing in passive status of operation. In addition, *Op* includes all possible operation modes for any subject performs on any object while *Perm* is in essence a set of binary group like *<op, o>* where *o* and *op* is element belongs to *O* and *Op* respectively.

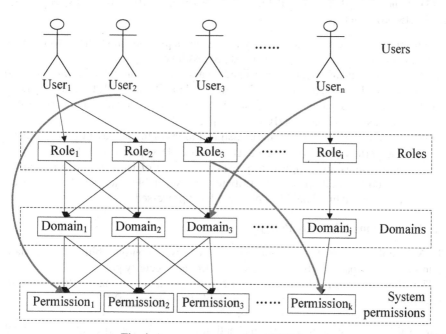

Fig. 4. Access control model of LYSLinux

Conception of type is introduced to identify object instead of using *SID* (in SELinux) in order to improve efficiency of permission control for it can provide more flexible granule for object control. Conception of domain is introduced to describe set of permission required for performing special task and to support permission control at process levels. Permission set can be divided at user level, role level and domain levels. Thus any subject can be mapped into a permission set and any object can be mapped into a domain identifier so that subjects and objects are separated completely and it makes permission assignment more clearly.

In addition, it's supported that roles and users can be granted permission directly so that RBAC and DTE models can be integrated more flexibly. In another word, although the model is a layered permission assignment model, permissions can be assigned crossing layers, as is more consistent with that in real world. Naturally, it can simplify the security policy configuration.

To demonstrate authorization based on LYSLinux, an example is given as follows. Suppose that:

(1) $S = Ps \cup U$ where $Ps = \{p1, p2, p3, p4, p5, p6, p7, p8\}$ and $U = \{U1, U2\}$;

(2) Four roles responsible for performing four types of tasks are defined according to security requirements, so role set *RS* can be described as {Role1, Role2, Role3, Role4};

(3) $O = R \cup Po$ where $R = \{f1, f2, f3, f4, f5, f6, f7, f8, f9, f10\}$ and $Po = Ps$;

(4) $Op = \{op1, op2, op3\}$;

(5) *Perm* = {<op1, f1>, <op1, f2>, <op1, f3>, <op1, f10>, <op2, f4>, <op2, p1>, <op3, p1>, <op3, p8>};

Thus, permission can be assigned by following steps (corresponding to four levels, i.e. domain level, role level, user level and process level):

(1)   A few domains can be created and be assigned permissions. For instance, D1 = {<op1, f1>, <op1, f3>}, D2 = {<op2, f4>}, D3 = {<op1, f1>, <op3, p1>}.

(2)   Permissions can be assigned to roles in the way of domains and permissions. For instance, Role1 = D1∪D2∪{<op3, p8>}.

(3)   Similarly, Permissions can be assigned to users in the way of roles, domains and permissions. For instance, U1 = Role1∪D3∪{<op1, f10>}.

(4)   Permissions are assigned to processes in term of least privilege principles. To do so well, privilege attribute for executable files and even process privilege status should be considered and processed.

4.2 Description of Security Policy

FLASK architecture ought to be adopted so as to ensure configurability of systematic permission and separation between access control and security policy.

The whole security model can be described by type table, permission table, domain table, role table, user table and relationship table (refer to Fig. 5).

Type Table. It consists of related information about different types of objects. Each type is described by type identifier, type name, file path, resource classification (e.g. FILE, DEVICE, TASK and etc), domain identifier, role identifier and user identifier. The latter three items are only required for objects of TASK type.

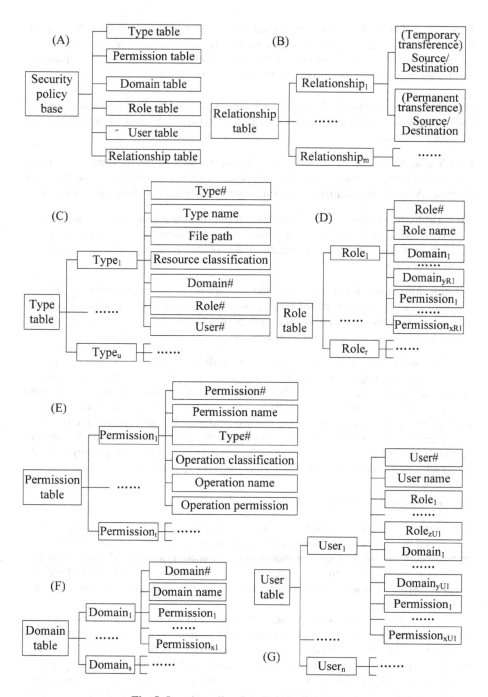

Fig. 5. Security policy description of LYSLinux

Permission Table. It consists of related information about available permissions. Permission is described by permission identifier, permission name, type identifier, operation classification, operation name and operation permission. If operation permission is not set, it means that operation is not permitted.

Domain Table. It consists of related permission information about different domains. Each domain is described by domain identifier, domain name and identifiers for one or more permissions.

Role Table. It consists of related permission information about different roles. Each role is described by role identifier, role name and identifiers for permissions or domains. At least one identifier for permissions or domains is required for each role.

User Table. It consists of related permission information about different users. Each user is described by user identifier, user name and identifiers for permissions or domains or roles. At least one identifier for permissions or domains or roles is required for each user.

Relationship Table. It consists of related transference information between different domain or between different roles or between different users. Transference can be divided into temporary transference and permanent transference. Transference is described by pair of transference source and transference destination.

It is obvious that the relationships among different tables are more like tree structure. For example, one domain entry can be mapped into more permission entries, and one role entry can be mapped into more domain entries or more permission entries, and one user entry can be mapped onto more domain entries or more permission entries or more role entries. And it is well known that tree structure can be easily described in extensible mark language (XML) that is simple, legible and verifiable. So XML file is used to describe security policies in our prototype while XML schema is used to describe file format for security policies.

4.3 Storage and Management of Security Policy

It is quite frequent to enforce security decision according to security policy configured in the system during the system running period. So it's necessary to circumspectly design storage and management of security policy. All factors such as interaction modes between user space and kernel space, communication efficiency between MAC enforcement module and security policy server, and etc. are considered.

Undoubtedly, users can describe security policies in XML, but a more concentrated and efficient way (for space saving) ought to be selected for systematic management of security policy. Because large numbers of processes can be executed concurrently, and they can frequently activate access control management and security policy search and computation (who are running in kernel space for security and communication efficiency reasons) so that security policies should be stored or cached in memory when system runs. As a matter of fact, security policies should be stored in an equally concentrated and efficient way or a same way both in memory and hard disk. Thus time can be saved when security policies are loaded from security policy base (stored in hard disk) to memory for security server and other kernel modules to enforce security decision.

Therefore, a special data structure is build up between security server and security policy base (in XML files) to store and describe security policy. When security module is start-up, security policy is read from file system and the data structure is initialized. And in order to be convenient for security server to build up security policy data structure, corresponding binary security policy description file format ought to be designed and the transformation from XML descriptive file to the binary file can be executed in user space.

The binary file for security policies stores security policy information, type table, permission table, domain table, role table, user table, domain relationship table, role relationship table and user relationship table orderly from beginning (i.e. 0 offset) of the file (refer to Fig. 6).

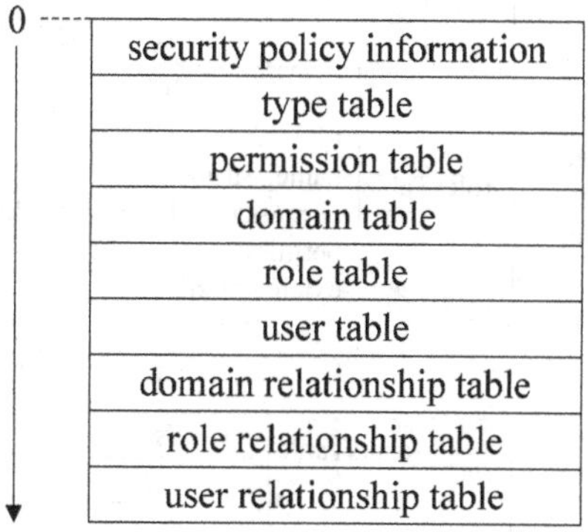

0
| security policy information |
| type table |
| permission table |
| domain table |
| role table |
| user table |
| domain relationship table |
| role relationship table |
| user relationship table |

Fig. 6. Storage Layout of Security Policy Binary File Image

Fig. 7 shows data structure for LYLinux security policies (PolicyDB) which is created and maintained by security policy server. Note that U32 represents unsigned integer of 32 bits and String represents string type coded in ASCII.

5 Prototype Design and Implementation

A prototype is designed and implemented based on Linux to verify feasibility and validity of the above SELinux-like access control mechanism.

5.1 Security Facilities Inside Linux Kernel

Security facilities provided by Linux Kernel involve LSM, extended attributes with inodes in file system and loadable kernel module (LKM).

LSM. It makes that feasible to intercept and capture the operation for subjects accessing objects by placing hook function calling inside kernel source codes. It provides security fields for most kernel objects such as process control blocks (i.e. task_struct), inode and files that have already been opened and system can obtain

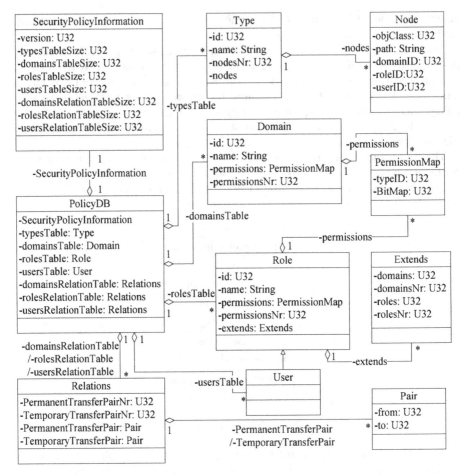

Fig. 7. Data Structure for LYSLinux Security Policies

security identifiers for subjects and objects by extracting from information for security fields of kernel objects. Whenever an application invokes a system call, original logic of Linux kernel is executed to perform resource allocation, error checking and classical UNIX discretionary access control firstly. Before Linux try to access kernel objects, a hook will transfer control to the corresponding helper function and the latter will be obligated to decide whether the current process can access the kernel object in the specified operation mode.

File System Extended Attributes. Extended attributes are a series of entries stored with inodes and each entry is a binary group like <name, value> where name and value represents attribute name and attribute value respectively. Extended attributes of a file can be obtained or set by invoking system call of *getxattr()* and *setxattr()* in user space or by invoking function of *getxattr()* and *setxattr()* at VFS level in kernel space.

LKM. It is introduced to enlarge functions of Linux kernel more flexibly. LKM modules can be dynamically loaded upon running and can be executed in kernel space without compile the whole kernel. Main framework of applying LKM involves module initialization, module clearance, module registration, module cancellation and module installation.

5.2 Structural Design of LYSLinux Access Control Module

Fig. 8 shows the structure of LYSLinux access control module. It can be seen that LYSLinux access control module is build up on Flask architecture and has two parts. One part is security policy enforcement mechanism which is made up of security enforcer, object manager and AVC, and the other part is security policy management mechanism which consists of security server and security policy base.

Security enforcer performs access control by LSM as to security check points where LSM has already involved. But as to those none-involved such as security audit for TCP data packet, other ways ought to be taken.

Object manager is responsible for management of permissions as subjects and security identified information as to objects. It takes uniform format, i.e. ternaries like <domain, role, user> to describe permission set for a subject and intersection of these three permission set forms actual permission set for that subject. Meanwhile, identifier is introduced to map special permission set for subjects so as to reduce redundant data. On the other side, type is used to identify objects, and security information for objects (both files and processes) is stored in security fields provided by LSM and extended attributes of file system.

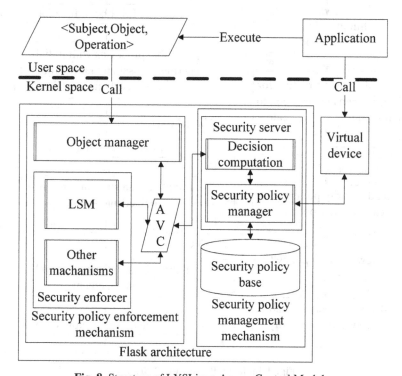

Fig. 8. Structure of LYSLinux Access Control Module

AVC is introduced to reduce time for decision computation and to improve system performance. Obviously, access vectors in AVC ought to be maintained according to some replacement policy or algorithm.

Security server is obligated to load and maintain security policies and to perform decision computation according to security identifiers for subject and object and permission of request.

In addition, a kernel virtual char device is introduced to satisfy extensible requirement. Moreover, it provides a safe way for applications in TCB to read or write kernel data for LYSLinux.

All components of access control modules are running in kernel space and can be implemented in a loadable kernel module.

5.3   Process Design of Mandatory Access Control Based on LYSLinux

Because LYSLinux is implemented in LKM, initialization functions for LYSLinux kernel modules will perform a series of initialization operations whenever they are loaded into the system.

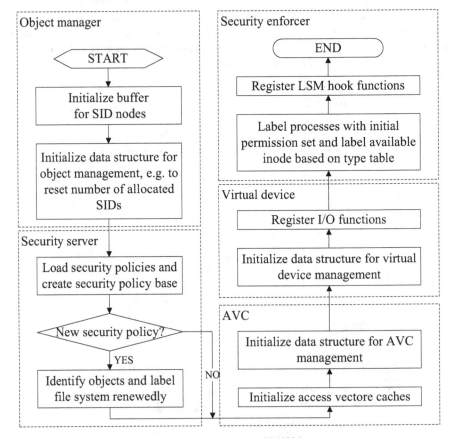

Fig. 9. Initiation Process of LYSLinux

The initialization procedure can be divided into five steps, i.e. initialization of object manager, initialization of security sever, initialization of AVC, initialization of virtual devices and initialization of security enforcer (refer to Fig. 9).

And when the whole initialization procedure for LYSLinux kernel modules is finished, security policy enforcement mechanism begins to intercept and capture access request and carry mandatory access control into execution.

Furthermore, when some subject request to access an object, LSM hook functions in kernel transfer program workflow to corresponding helper functions for security policy enforcement mechanism with pointer parameters pointing to the subject and the kernel object. Then the helper functions will startup following operations:

(1) Related security information such as current effective SID for subject and type identifier for object is extracted from kernel objects.

(2) Query parameter is formed as ternary group like <SID, objType, operationClassification> and then is transferred to AVC for searching.

(3) If corresponding access vector is found in AVC, then decision result is generated and jump to step (6); else go to step (4).

(4) AVC mechanism invokes object manager for subject permission information and then transferred it (with object type and operation classification) to security sever for decision computation.

(5) According to decision result and access vector returned from security server, AVC mechanism updates AVC and return decision result to security enforcer.

(6) Security enforcer returns decision result to Linux kernel.

5.4 Prototype Implementation

The prototype is made up of two parts, .i.e. mandatory access control modules and compiler for security policies. While the former part is programmed in C language, the latter is programmed in Java.

Mandatory access control modules in the prototype can be divided into security server, AVC mechanism, object manager, security enforcer, and etc.

Security server consists of security policy loader and security policy querier. The former is responsible for creating and maintaining security policy base, and the latter is responsible for decision computation.

AVC mechanism is responsible for management of AVC, and AVC is organized as hash table in order to improve search efficiency.

Object manager is responsible for security labeling of subjects and objects.

Security enforcer is responsible for perform mandatory access control, and there are four types of hook functions provided in our prototype, i.e. process related hook functions, file related hook functions, inode related hook functions and hook functions for loading and executing binary programs. They are responsible for initialization and clearance of security information, security control as to processes, files, inodes and binary programs respectively.

6 Prototype Test and Results

Prototype test is to verify the validity of the prototype and the feasibility of LYSLinux access control mechanism.

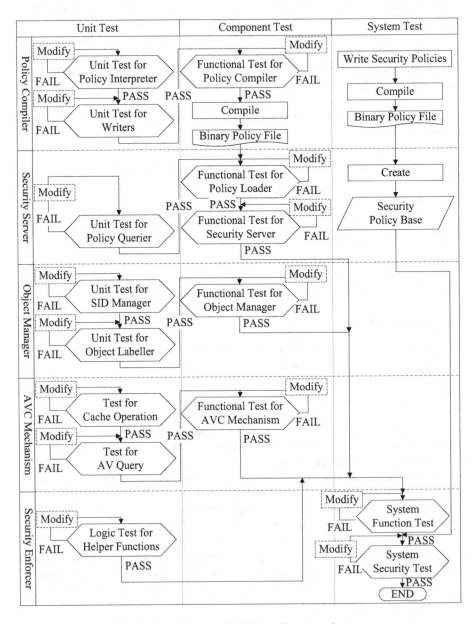

Fig. 10. Test Scheme of LYSLinux Prototype System

Prototype test involves unit test, component test, system function test and system security test. The former three types of tests focus on function implementation, while the last test focus on security enforcement based on special security policies. Fig.10 shows the whole test scheme for the prototype.

Junit framework is utilized to perform systematically unit test for policy compiler. All other modules of the prototype are running in kernel space and no unit test framework is provided by Linux kernel, so that they have to be tested by LKM way and manual analysis ought to be carried out according to test results output.

At stage of unit test, unit test for modules belong to different component can be performed synchronously, because components are independently at that time. However, at stage of component test, policy compiler must be tested before security server, because the latter depends on the former.

The prototype is tested comprehensively, and test results show that:

(1)   Policy compiler can offer proper interpretation of all security policy configuration tables and it can perform writing operation of binary policy data correctly.

(2)   Security server can create security policy base successfully and perform all kinds of permission query and computation correctly upon request of allowable operation, not allowable operation, unavailable object type in security policy for the subject, permission defined in the *extends* (only for roles or users), transference between domains, roles and users, and etc.

(3)   AVC mechanism can insert or delete access vector correctly.

(4)   Object manager can label objects correctly and perform SID allocation and reclaim successfully.

(5)   The prototype can enforce access control rules and security functions based on special security policy written for simple application environment.

7 Summary

Preliminary test results of the prototype show that the SELinux-like MAC mechanism in this paper is functional and feasible. Nevertheless, some aspects ought to be improved in future. For example, security model can be improved to support role ranking, access control for resources other than files (such as special files, network operation) and even other file systems (not ext3) can be supported and security policy configuration tools can be develop to simplify the configuration work.

References

1. Zhai, G., Zeng, J., Ma, M., Zhang, L.: Implementation and Automatic Testing for Security Enhancement of Linux Based on Least Privilege. In: Proceedings of the 2nd International Conference on Information Security and Assurance (ISA 2008), pp. 181–186. IEEE Computer Society, Los Alamitos (2008)
2. Linux Introduction and POSIX Permissions and Commands, http://www.networkingprogramming.com/1024x768/linux1.html

3. Tu, W., Guan, H., Bai, Y.: Enhancing Access Control Function in Linux File System. Computer Applications and Software 23(2), 117–118, 119 (2006) (in Chinese)
4. Bacarella, M.: Taking Advantage of Linux Capabilities. Linux Journal 2002(97) (2002)
5. Access Control Lists in Linux,
   `http://www.suse.de/~agruen/acl/chapter/fs_acl-en.pdf`
6. Smalley, S., Vance, C., Salamon, W.: Implementing SELinux as a Linux Security Module, NAI Labs Report #01-043 (February 2006)
7. Zanin, G.: Towards a formal model for security policies specification and validation in the SELinux system. In: Proceedings on the Ninth ACM Symposium on Access Control Models and Technologies (SACMAT 2004), pp. 136–145. ACM Press, New York (2004)

Research on Streaming Data Integration System about Security Threat Monitor

Aiping Li, Jiajia Miao, and Yan Jia

Computer Institute, National University of Defence Technology,
410073, ChangSha, China
apli1974@gmail.com

Abstract. Computer networks have become ubiquitous and integral part of the nation's critical infrastructure. How to grasp the real-time overall situation of the network security is very noteworthy to study. An increasing number of network security systems have been deployed in the backbone and the gateways of enterprises, including various Netflow systems, IDS, VDS, VS and firewalls. These products make great contributions in enhancing the network security. However, current network security systems are independent and autonomous. Consequently, such solutions cannot figure out an overview of the network security situation. In another perspective, building a new global monitoring system will suffer from redundant construction and longer deploying time. We propose a novel and high assurance solution called GS-TMS which reuses the log data generated by the existing systems. Based on the data stream and data integration technologies, GS-TMS provides a desirable capability in quickly building a large-scale distributed network monitoring system. Furthermore, GS-TMS has additional notable advantages over current monitoring systems in scalability and flexibility.

Keywords: Data Stream, Threat Monitor System, Security Log.

1 Introduction

The Internet is now regarded as an economic platform and a vehicle for information dissemination at an unprecedented scale to the world's population. But this success has also enabled hostile agents to use the Internet in many malicious ways [1], and terms like spam, phishing, viruses, self propagating worms, DDoS attacks, etc. Hence, mitigating threats to networks have become one of the most important tasks of several governmental and private entities.

1.1 Limitations of the Current System

Mitigating threats to networks have become one of the most important tasks of several governmental and private entities. Intrusion detection systems (IDSes), such as Snort[2], monitor all incoming traffic at an edge network's DMZ, perform TCP flow reassembly, and search for known worm signatures. Cisco's NBAR[3] system for routers searches for signatures in flow payloads, and blocks flows on the fly whose

T.-k. Kim, T.-h. Kim, and A. Kiumi (Eds.): SecTech 2008, CCIS 29, pp. 67–78, 2009.

payloads are found to contain known worm signatures. There are two notable limitations in the above systems:

- **The Autonomy System Is Closed.** IDSes and other security products are autonomy systems, which cannot share the monitor results with each other . For example, even though the IDS of enterprise A detects a paragraph DDoS attack, the IDS of enterprises B might fail to get this situation in time. Therefore, enterprise B will trend to be compromised by the same attack.
- **The detection is on the lower level.** Most IDS are on the enterprise level[4] but not the ISP level. When the IDS of enterprise A finding a bots net and informing the ISP, we can thoroughly block the source IPs of the bots net within the backbone.

In the database research field, the independent data, which cannot be shared, is termed as "island". Data integration is a widely adopted solution to solve this problem. This guides us to build an integrated network security platform to share the security information.

1.2 Requirements in Reality

The continuous growth of the network, coupled with the increasing number of the connected computers, poses more challenges to the network monitoring systems:

- **Data arriving at a high rate.** Such security systems monitor variety of continuous data that may be characterized as unpredictable and arriving at a high rate, including both packet traces and network performance measurements. For example, the ISP with high-speed switches, the data flow comes up to 40 Gbit/s.
- **Data generating and monitoring tasks are continuous.** In the network monitoring system of a large network, e.g., the backbone network of an ISP, the query result with the latest monitoring data changes constantly. So the query is not an one-shot query, but a continuous query.
- **Real-time response is pivotal.** With the development of computer technologies, hackers and virus technologies also improve rapidly. The attacks will do great harm due to the delayed protecting responses. Therefore, the monitoring system requires real-time data processing.

1.3 Our Solution

Examining the data stream applications in network security, we come up with a new idea: the security log data can serve as the input of *Data Stream Manager System (DSMS)* to analyze the network security events in real time.

As a summary, we propose a novel technology to materialize a global view of the network security status based on existing applications, as illustrated in Figure. 1. Our system, called *Global Stream-based Threat Monitor System (GS-TMS)*, utilizes existing enterprise gateway security systems, such as IDS, firewall, DDoS protection systems and so on. We retrieve the logs from these systems as the input stream of DSMS. Based on the technologies of data stream and data integration, GS-TMS can provide the users with a unified interface to perform real-time monitoring and analyzing.

From the perspectives of the implementation, constructing such a system faces the following challenges:

- How to automatically convert the existing security system logs to the input data stream?
- How to build the mapping between the heterogeneous data streams?
- How to design a suitable data stream query language for the network monitoring?
- How to solve the heterogeneity in query language level and data schema level?
- How to share and merge the results from the distributed heterogeneous systems?
- How to guarantee the validity of the input data streams from the distributed nodes?

In one word, the research on GS-TMS aims to help government make use of the existing security logs to monitor the network status efficiently. But due to the autonomic, heterogeneous, distributed and dynamic features of the Internet, there are many challenging research issues in this area. In this paper, a comprehensive solution is presented and my current and future research works in this area is discussed.

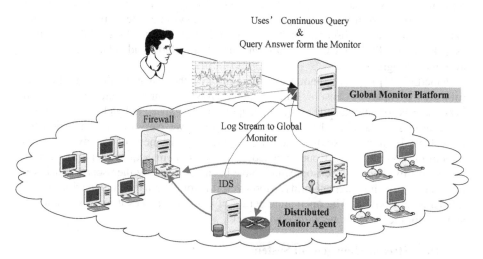

Fig. 1. The deployment of GS-TMS

1.4 Paper Organization

The research on GS-TMS aims to help government make use of the existing security logs to monitor the network status efficiently. In the remainder of this paper, we proceed as follows: the related work is described in section 2. In Section 3, we catalog the goals of GS-TMS. we describe the architecture of GS-TMS in Section 4. Next, in Section 5, we present the methods to verify our system in the artificial environment and the real-world environment. The conclusion about our work is given in the last section.

2 Related Work

2.1 Existing Network Monitor System

As the variety and the sophistication of attacks grow, early detection of potential attacks will become crucial in mitigation the subsequent impact of these attacks.

More recently, distributed network monitoring has received much attention from the research community. Projects such as Neti@Home[18], ForNet[19], DIMES [20] and Domino[21] all use agents on end systems to monitor network traffic, whether for intrusion detection and response or for straightforward network mapping and performance.

There are also many similar monitors deployed around the World. For example, the NCS plans to build GEWIS[22] (Global Early Warning Information System) around existing Internet performance tools integrated into a cohesive suite that can provide a top-level view of system performance. GEWIS monitor the performance of the Internet and provide warnings to government and industry users of threats that could degrade service, such as denial-of-service attacks against the DNS that control Internet traffic.

JPCERT/CC has started deploying the ISDAS[23] (Internet Scan Data Acquisition System). ISDAS has a wide distributed arrangement of sensors, and observes various scan activities; worm infections, probing vulnerable systems, etc. It provide the summarized scan treands observed on the web page. Moreover, the observed data are used as a basis of JPCERT/CC activities on publishing alerts and advisories, security awareness programs, etc.

PlanetLab[24] has also announced a plan to build their own monitor based on distributed wide aperture sensors. Building and deploying a threat monitor is not a cumbersome task for anyone with some unoccupied address space in hand.

According to the related work mentioned above, we can draw a conclusion that there have been many studies focusing on the establishment of the overall threat monitoring system, but to our knowledge, most of them acquire network security events just by their own sensors which have been deployed by themselves. Such system cannot have high expansibility. Moreover, it is totally a national behavior, but not a federative behavior. The open architecture of GS-TMS makes it more scalable and suitable for the dynamic network environment.

2.2 Data Stream Management System

DSMS has been proposed to integrate data collection and processing of network streams in order to support on-line processing for various network management applications. The STREAM[25] and Gigascope[26] projects have made performance evaluations on their DSMSs for network monitoring. In both projects, several useful tasks have been suggested for network monitoring. Plagemann et al. have evaluated an early version of the TelegraphCQ[11] DSMS as a network monitoring tool by modeling and running queries and making a simple performance analysis.

Examining existing work, the data stream management technologies are become increasingly perfect, more and more network monitoring applications have adopted the data stream technologies.. Therefore, there are two key challenging issues: how to integrate these distributed data management systems and how to provide a top-level security view? How to share the early warning information deployed in the different internal monitoring systems? The key to figure out these two questions is no other than the data stream integration technology.

3 Desiderata for GS-TMS System

3.1 Continuous

From the user point of view, the query answers returned from GS-TMS is continuous instead of one-shot query. The feedbacks which users desire to retrieve from our system are continuously changing over time.

3.2 Automatic and Robust

To be adapted to the Internet characteristics of distribution and dynamic, our system should deal with the joining and leaving requests of the distributed monitoring nodes automatically. The automation characteristic of our system consists of two sub-requirements: Automatically converting the log database into the data stream input and detecting the failure nodes.

3.3 Transparent

To eliminate the heterogeneity of the distributed nodes, all the heterogeneous systems which need to provide unified the upper interface for users should construct a map between the top-level view and the local view of the distributed nodes.

3.4 Efficient

Our system is set up in the distributed network. Consequently Global Monitor Platform should communicate with all the distributed monitor agent frequently. It is necessary to reduce the communication costs. Usually, monitoring node is high-load, so it's also important to minimize the computing overhead.

3.5 Simple

We must simplify the user interface, including the query language and the results presentation styles, to make the system as simple as possible.

4 The System Architecture

4.1 The Components of the System

In this section, we will detailed introduce the architecture of GS-TMS. As illustrated in Fig. 2, GS-TMS comprises two primary components: Global Monitor Platform (GMP) and Distributed Monitor Agent (DMA). GMP is mainly responsible for interacting with users, as well as merging the query rewriting, results and other tasks;

DMA is in charge of the log conversion, i.e., executing the specific query tasks from the GMP. We describe the GS-TMS architecture with two stages: initializing phase and processing phase.

As shown in Fig. 2, in the initializing stage, the main task is: 1) After the agents have been installed in the distributed nodes, DMA will convert local log database to the stream input of Light DSMS. Firstly, the log to stream module automatically extracts an entity relationship schema from the local log database through reverse engineering. Secondly, it analyses the main log table, and convert it to stream data as the input of Light DSMS. 2) Schema mapping module takes the global schema and local schema as input, then outputs the mapping results. Then, this mapping result will be submitted to Global Monitor Platform.

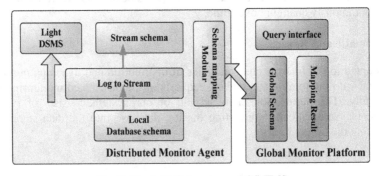

Fig. 2. The initializing stage of GS-TMS

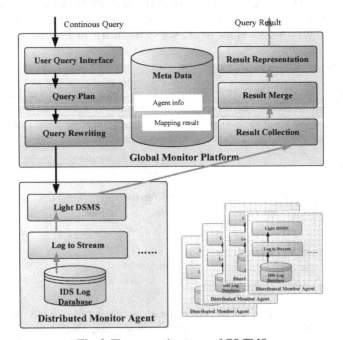

Fig. 3. The processing stage of GS-TMS

As shown in Fig. 3, in the processing stage, the main task is: 1) Accepting the user's submission of query, executing the query plan (for minimizing communication costs), query rewriting according to the results of schema mapping and decomposing query into the specific monitoring agents; 2) When DMA gets the specific query sentence, it will analyze the log stream, and then returns the query answer to GMP; 3) Result Merge Module merges the query answers from different nodes according to the schema mapping results and specific policies, and then presents the final query answers to users; 4) The attack events, which were detected by DMA will be shared among all the other distributed nodes.

4.2 Log to Stream

One advantage of our system is that GS-TMS can coexist with legacy security systems, reusing the existing security log database. Existing security systems, such as IDS, firewall and DDoS detecting systems have a large number of attack-warning logs[5][6], but these logs are only available to local users, as a time log is also the basis of the analysis. GS-TMS also gives support to convert the logs of these legacy systems to the local stream input of DMA. This advantage enables the log information sharing and data stream processing.

We use a case to present our idea, such as Snort's log conversion process. As shown below, that is the database schemas of Snort V1.06[2].As shown in Fig. 4, we can observe that: 1) Table event with timestamp is the core of these tables. 2) Table iphdr includes source IP address and destination IP address. So, we can draw the following laws:

1. The core table must include timestamp field.
2. The core table will continuously increase larger with the time going on.

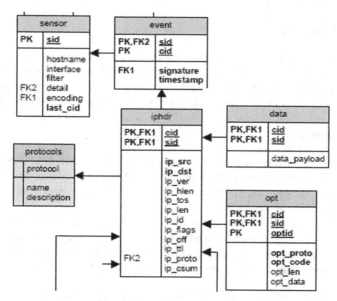

Fig. 4. The snort schema v1.06

3. The main table, which contains the basic information (for example, IP info, and etc.) should has a high degree and has the same keys as the core table.

Based on the above analysis, we must firstly extract an E-R graph from a relational database through reverse engineering [7], and then utilize the matrix compute to find the highest degree of the tables. Finally, we will work out the optional core tables and main tables.

4.3 Stream Schema Matching

A fundamental operation in the manipulation of schema information is matching, namely, taking two schemas as the inputs and producing a mapping between the elements of the two schemas that correspond semantically to each other[8].

We will take the global schema and local schema as the inputs. DMA then gives the mapping between two schemas as the outputs. This results are stored in GMP for future query writing and result merging.

Following the case we motioned above, we have the some observations:

– The scale of the input schema should be as less as possible to make the match in our system simple.
– The data instances of that case should be organized in fixed format. As an illustration, the source address and destination address are formatted in form of 'XXX.XXX.XXX.XXX'.

In GS-TMS matching is relatively simple in schema scale. We consider of the specific application, using a hybrid algorithm to improve the performance, with high recall rate and high precise rate.

4.4 Query Language

These data management systems adopt a variety of query language, such as CQL[9], TQL[10], TelegraphCQ[11] language and so on. The CQL is an expressive SQL-based declarative language for registering continuous queries against streams and stored relations. Taking into account we build our query language prototype based on CQL.

4.5 Query Rewriting

In this system, we address the problem of query rewriting in global-as-view data integration systems. User queries are formulated over the global schema, and the system suitably queries the sources, providing an answer to the user, who is not obliged to have any information about the sources.

Many techniques haven been provided to solve the heterogeneous schema issues[12]. In other word, system interpreted the user-input query, which according to the global schema, to some specific query, which according to the local schema. In GS-TMS, we need to query rewriting module work in two-level heterogeneous:

– Heterogeneity between the global schema and the local source schema.
– Heterogeneity between the different DSMS.

4.6 Broken Mapping Detection

In a dynamic environment, sources frequently change their query interfaces, data formats[13]. Such changes often invalidate semantic mappings and cause system failure. Hence, once the system is deployed, the administrator has to monitor it over time to detect and repair the broken mappings. Today, such continuous monitoring is well-known to be extremely labor intensive. Hence, developing techniques to reduce the maintenance cost is critical for the widespread deployment of data integration systems in practice. We proposed the Detecting Broken Mappings Based on Fuzzy Reasoning module, which improve the correct ratio of checking invalidation mapping[14].

4.7 Summarization

We recall the architecture and design goals that we set out in Table 1 with their relationship. Table 1 reports that the goal 'Continuous' is support by 'Light DSMS module', and so on.

Table 1. Relationship between goals and modules

Goal	Module
Continuous	Light DSMS
Automatic & Robust	Log to stream
Transparent	Schema matching
Efficient	Qeury plan & Query executing
Simple	Query interface & Result representation

5 Evaluation Design

Our evaluation for GS-TMS is performed in the simulation experiment.

The purpose of simulation experiment is to verify the functionality of the system, and evaluate the system performance both in the initializing phase and the processing phase. In the initializing phase, we select the most popular IDS system in China, like TopSec[15], ICEYE[16], Snort[2] to construct the testbed. These produces occupy over 80% of the market quotient. We focus the performance of converting log database to data stream and the precise of schema mapping algorithm here. We use *Precision* to describe the performance of converting log data to stream, *Recall* to express the precise of schema map algorithm, which is as :

$$Precision = \frac{total\ convert\ data}{total\ data} \quad Recall = \frac{correct\ convert\ data}{total\ convert\ data}.$$

We simulated the log data produced speed from 2M/s to 12MB/s, then get the experiment data in Figure5. As shown in Figure 5, all the *Precision* of legacy system log data is above 95%, we think the result is good for the legacy systems. What's more, the *Recall* of each system is fairly good, almost above 90%, the reason we think maybe the meta map data has some problem, we will try again to improve the recall ratio of each system.

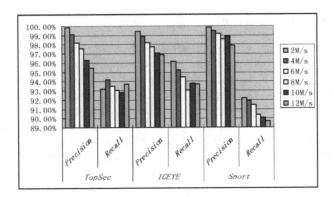

Fig. 5. The initializing phase experiment result

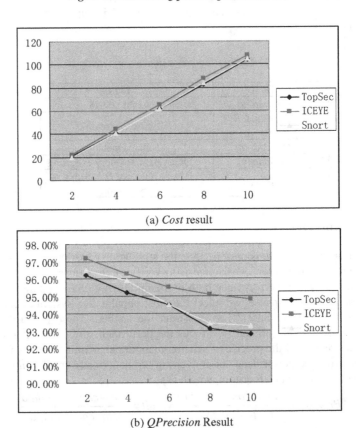

(a) *Cost* result

(b) *QPrecision* Result

Fig. 6. The processing phase experiment result

In the processing phase, we use the log data from Dshield, due to its data is more comprehensive than the log that we can provide. Here we focus how to reduce the communicate costs between GMP and DMAs and how to improve the precise of query rewriting algorithm. Follow the above description, we use *Cost* express the communicate costs and *QPrecision* to express the query precision. We get the experiment result in Figure 6. The Cost is described in milliseconds, where the experiment environment is 100M/s. The *QPrecision* is described as:

$$QPrecision = \frac{correct\ query\ result}{total\ data}$$

As shown in Fig. 6, the communication cost is almost line increase along the data stream increase, this is fairly good. What's more, the extra commutation cost is very small as shown in Fig 6(a). The *QPrecision* of each system is also above 92%, and the decrease of *QPrecision* is not very fast, and when the data scale is increase, the *QPrecision* tends to the constant. The result has shown the architecture are good.

The purpose of the experiments is only to show the algorithms and architecture we given is logical. The optimization of the algorithms will be done in the future work. The experiments we made are not very perfect, the purpose of the experiments is only to show the algorithms and architecture we given is logical. The optimization of the algorithms will be done in the future work.

6 Conclusion

With the rapid increasing of the internet attack events, it is impending to have a Global Early Threat Monitor System. In this paper, we propose a comprehensive solution for Global Threat Monitor System. There are a number of components in the solution, and each of them is also a research issue in this area. Our main contribution in this paper is to present a set of new methods for integration distributed security system and provide a global view of the security status. Moreover, we adapt the legacy systems to our stream-based agents, so we can deal with the attack events more promptly.

There are still many problems need to be solved, including reducing communication costs, providing more supports for different operators in language, etc. Finally, real-world environment experiment to test the system is needed.

Acknowledgements. This work is supported by the National High-Tech Research and Development Plan of China ("863" plan) under Grant No. 2006AA01Z451, No. 2007AA01Z474 and No. 2007AA010502.

References

1. Technical Cyber Security Alerts, http://www.us-cert.gov/cas/techalerts
2. The de facto standard for intrusion detection/prevention, http://www.snort.org/
3. NBAR System, http://www.cisco.com/en/US/products/ps6616/

4. Siegel, C.A., Sagalow, T.R.: Cyber-Risk Management: Technical and Insurance Controls for Enterprise Security. Information Systems Security 11 (2002)
5. Kandula, S.: Botz-4-sale: Surviving organized DDoS attacks that mimic flash crowds. In: 2nd Symposium on Networked Systems Design and Implementation (2005)
6. Kim, H.A., Karp, B.: Autograph: Toward Automated, Distributed Worm Signature Detection. USENIX (2005)
7. Anderson, M.: Extracting an Entity Relationship Schema from a Relational Database through Reverse Engineering, pp. 13–16. IEEE Press, Manchester (1994)
8. Bernstein, P.A., Melnik, S., Mork, P.: Interactive schema translation with instance-level mappings. In: Proceedings of the 31st VLDB, pp. 12–83 (2005)
9. Arasu, A., Babu, S., Widom, J.: The CQL continuous query language: semantic foundations and query execution. The VLDB Journal 15, 121–142 (2006)
10. Barbara, D.: The Characterization of Continuous Queries. International Journal of Cooperative Information Systems 8, 295–323 (1999)
11. Chandrasekaran, S.: TelegraphCQ: continuous dataflow processing. In: Proceedings of the 2003 ACM SIGMOD, pp. 668–668. ACM, California (2003)
12. Cali, A., Lembo, D., Rosati, R.: Query rewriting and answering under constraints in data integration systems. In: Proc. of the 18th IJCAI, pp. 16–21 (2003)
13. McCann, R.: Mapping maintenance for data integration systems. In: Proceedings of the 31st VLDB, pp. 1018–1029 (2005)
14. Miao, J., et al.: Detecting Broken Mappings for Deep Web Integration, Semantics, Knowledge and Grid. In: Third International Conference, pp. 56–61 (2007)
15. TopSentry product introduction,
    http://www.topsec.com.cn/products/ids.asp
16. ICEYE product introduction,
    http://www.nsfocus.com/1_solution/1_2_2.html
17. The annual report 2007, http://www.cert.org.cn/
18. Simpson Jr C.R., NETI@ home (2003), http://neti.gatech.edu
19. Shanmugasundaram, K., et al.: ForNet: A Distributed Forensics Network, Computer Network Security. In: Gorodetsky, V., Popyack, L.J., Skormin, V.A. (eds.) MMM-ACNS 2003. LNCS, vol. 2776, pp. 1–16. Springer, Heidelberg (2003)
20. The DIMES project, http://www.netdimes.org/new/
21. Yegneswaran, V., Barford, P., Jha, S.: Global Intrusion Detection in the DOMINO Overlay System. In: Proceedings of NDSS (2004)
22. Brewin, B.: Feds planning early-warning system for Internet,
    http://www.computerworld.com/securitytopics/security/
    hacking/story/0,10801,75248,00.html
23. Internet Scan Data Acquisition System (ISDAS);
    http://www.jpcert.or.jp/isdas/index-en.html
24. Feds planning early-warning system for Internet,
    http://www.computerworld.com/
25. PlanetLab, An open platform for developing, deploying, and accessing planetary-scale services, http://www.planet-lab.org/
26. Arasu, A., et al.: STREAM: The Stanford Data Stream Management System, a book on data stream management edited by Garofalakis, Gehrke, and Rastogi (2004)
27. Cranor, C., et al.: Gigascope: a stream database for network applications. In: Proceedings of the ACM SIGMOD, pp. 647–651 (2003)

Using Honeypots to Secure E-Government Networks

Bahman Nikkhahan, Sahar Sohrabi, and Shahriar Mohammadi

Information Technology Engineering Group, Department of Industrial Engineering,
K.N. Toosi University of Technology, Tehran, Iran
Bahman616@gmail.com, shr.sohrabi@gmail.com,
smohammadi40@yahoo.com

Abstract. Nowadays governments are moving to provide their services online for all of their citizens. In the online world, security is one of the most important issues. As a result, citizens want to trust on a secured E-government network. Generally, E-government security and E-commerce security are the same, but E-government has some extra features. Usually government agencies can cooperate better than businesses, because, most of them are connected to form a big governmental network, but businesses are competitors and they don't want to lose their market share. In this paper, "connectedness" of E-government networks is used to design a honeynet for tracing hackers. Because of possible damages to this network, it must be fault tolerance. This framework provides interesting resources for hackers and at the same time it prevents them from misusing those resources for future attacks.

Keywords: E-government, Honeypot, Security.

1 Introduction

Information and Communication Technologies (ICT) is transforming the governmental processes in serving citizens (G2C), businesses (G2B) and governments (G2G).

While E-government is subject to the same threats as e-business, E-government operates within different constraints. Most businesses deal only with a subset of the population, and they can choose the how and the when they do it. But the government must deal with everyone [10]. Therefore, in order to the huge number of users and transactions, and sensitivity of this field, like citizen's private information or government's secret information, and other issues, securing governmental networks is more important than businesses [2]. One of the main issues of trust in E-government implementation is security [11]. Citizens prefer to use traditional ways rather than using an unsecured web site. On 14 June 2002 the UK's Inland Revenue withdrew its online tax filing service amid complaints that users could see other people's tax returns. This public humiliation, however temporary, reveals part of the price paid when E-government initiatives are not secure [10].

Henriksson et al. (2006) divided the factors that influence the quality of government websites to 6 major categories: (1) Security and Privacy; (2) Usability; (3) Content; (4) Services; (5) Citizen Participation; and (6) Features [4].

T.-k. Kim, T.-h. Kim, and A. Kiumi (Eds.): SecTech 2008, CCIS 29, pp. 79–88, 2009.

Wimmer and Bredow (2001) proposed a holistic concept that integrates security aspects from the strategic level down to the data and information level in order to address different security aspects of E-government in a comprehensive way. Their holistic approach consists of 4 layers: strategic, process level, interaction and information [12].

Hof and Reichstädter surveyed security, peculiarities and implementations of security requirements within governmental structures, based on three interaction points (citizen to government C2G, government to government G2G and government to citizen G2C) [5].

This paper introduces a fault tolerance honeynet to strengthen the security of governmental network. At first, we will describe E-government, honeypots and honeynet in detail, and then we will show the proposed framework.

2 E-Government

The initiatives of government agencies and departments to use ICT tools and applications, Internet and mobile devices to support good governance, strengthen existing relationships and build new partnerships within civil society, are known as eGovernment initiatives (see table 1). As with e-commerce, eGovernment represents the introduction of a great wave of technological innovation as well as government reinvention. It represents a tremendous impetus to move forward in the 21st century with higher quality, cost effective government services and a better relationship between citizens and government [6].

Table 1. Reinventing Local Governments and the E-government Initiative [6]

Paradigm shifts in public service delivery		
	Bureaucratic paradigm	EGovernment paradigm
Orientation	Production cost-efficiency	User satisfaction and control, flexibility
Process organization	Functional rationality, departmentalization, vertical hierarchy of control.	Horizontal hierarchy, network organization, information sharing.
Management principle	Management by rule and mandate	Flexible management, interdepartmental team work with central coordination
Leadership style	Command and control	Facilitation and coordination, innovative entrepreneurship.
Internal communication	Top down, Hierarchical	Multidirectional network with central coordination, direct communication.
External communication	Centralized, formal, limited channels	Formal and informal direct and fast feedback, multiple channels
Mode of service delivery	Documentary mode and interpersonal interaction	Electronic exchange, non face to face interaction
Principles of service delivery	Standardization, impartiality, equity.	User customization, personalization

E-government means different things for different people. Some simply define it as digital governmental information or a way of engaging in digital transactions with customers. For others E-government simply consists of the creation of a web site where information about political and governmental issues is presented. These narrow ways of defining and conceptualizing E-government restrict the range of opportunities it offers [6].

Different authors have different definition of E-government:

Richard Heeks propose that the term "E-governance" should be seen to encompass all ICTs, but the key innovation is that of computer networks, from intranet to the Internet, which have created a wealth of new digital connections:

- Connections within government, permitting "joined-up thinking."
- Connections between government and NGO/citizens, strengthening accountability.
- Connections within and between NGOs, supporting learning and concerted action.
- Connections within and between communities, building social and economic development.

As a result, Heeks suggest, the focus of e-governance shifts from just parts of e-administration, in the case e-government, to also encompass e-citizens, e-services and e-society [3].

- Whitson and Davis (2001): "Implementing cost-effective models for citizens, industry, federal employees, and other stakeholders to conduct business transactions online".
- Tapscott (1996): "An inter-networked government".
- Luling (2001): "online government services, that is, any interaction one might have with any government body or agency, using the Internet or the World Wide Web" [8].

Inter-networked government is the best definition for the purpose of this paper.

3 Honeypots

Honeypots are a security resource whose value lies in being probed, attacked or compromised. This means that whatever we designate as a honeypot, our expectations and goals are to have the system probed, attacked, and potentially exploited. It does not matter what the resource is (a router, scripts running emulated services, a jail, an actual production system). What does matter is that the resource's value lies in its being attacked. If the system is never probed or attacked, then it has little or no value. This is the exact opposite of most production systems, which you do *not* want to be probed or attacked [9].
The primary purpose of a honeypot is to proactively gather information about security threats by providing a real system with real applications and services for the attacker to interact with, but with no production value: we can safely watch and learn from an intruder without fear of compromising our systems [1]. The value of a honeypot is weighed by the information that can be obtained from it [7].

Traditionally, the attacker has always had the initiative. They control whom they attack, when, and how. All we can do in the security community is defend: build security measures, prevent the bad guy from getting in, and then detect whenever those preventive measures fail. As any good military strategist will tell you, the secret to a good defense is a good offense. But how do the good guys take the initiative in cyberspace? Security administrators can't go randomly attacking every system that probes them. We would end up taking down the Internet, not to mention the liability issues involved. Organizations have always been limited on how they can take the battle to the attacker. Honeypots give us the advantage by giving us control: we allow the bad guys to attack them [9].

Honeypots can run any operating system and any number of services. The configured services determine the vectors available to an adversary for compromising or probing the system [7].

Honeypots are categorized by the level of interaction into high-interaction and low-interaction.

Level of interaction gives us a scale with which to measure and compare honeypots. The more a honeypot can do and the more an attacker can do to a honeypot, the greater the information that can be derived from it. However, by the same token, the more an attacker can do to the honeypot, the more potential damage an attacker can do [9].

A high-interaction honeypot provides a real system the attacker can interact with. It can be compromised completely, allowing an adversary to gain full access to the system and use it to launch further network attacks.

In contrast, a low-interaction honeypots simulates only some parts — for example, the network stack. These honeypots simulate only services that cannot be exploited to get complete access to the honeypot. A low-interaction honeypot often implements just enough of the Internet protocols, usually TCP and IP, to allow interaction with the adversary and make her believe she is connecting to a real system [7].

Whether you use a low-interaction or high-interaction honeypot depends on what you want to achieve. Table 2 summarizes the tradeoffs between different levels of interaction in four categories [9].

Table 2. Tradeoffs of honeypot levels of interaction [9]

Level of Interaction	Work to Install and Configure	Work to Deploy and Maintain	Information Gathering	Level of Risk
Low	Easy	Easy	Limited	Low
Medium	Involved	Involved	Variable	Medium
High	Difficult	Difficult	Extensive	High

The first category is installation and configuration, which defines the time and effort in installing and configuring your honeypot. In general, the greater the level of interaction a honeypot supports, the more work required to install and configure it. This is simply common sense. The more functionality you provide an attacker, the more options and services must be installed and configured.

The second category is deployment and maintainance. This category defines the time and effort involved in deploying and maintaining your honeypot after you have built and configured the system. Once again, the more functionality your honeypot provides, the more work required to deploy and maintain it.

The third category is information gathering—how much data can the honeypot gain on attackers and their activities? High-interaction honeypots can gather vast amounts of information, whereas low-interaction honeypots are highly limited.

Finally, level of interaction impacts the amount of risk introduced. We are concerned about the risk of a honeypot being used to attack, harm, or infiltrate other systems or organizations. The greater the level of interaction, the more functionality provided to the attacker, and the greater the complexity. Combined, these elements can introduce a great deal of risk. On the other hand, low-interaction honeypots are very simple and offer little interaction to attackers, creating a far lower risk solution[9].

We also differentiate between physical and virtual honeypots.

3.1 Physical Honeypot

Physical honeypot means that the honeypot is running on a physical machine. Physical often implies high-interaction, thus allowing the system to be compromised completely. They are typically expensive to install and maintain. For large address spaces, it is impractical or impossible to deploy a physical honeypot for each IP address. In that case, we need to deploy virtual honeypots [7].

3.2 Virtual Honeypot

Compared to physical honeypots, this approach is more lightweight. Instead of deploying a physical computer system that acts as a honeypot, we can also deploy one physical computer that hosts several virtual machines that act as honeypots. This leads to easier maintenance and lower physical requirements. Usually VMware or User-Mode Linux (UML) are used to set up such virtual honeypots. These two tools allow us to run multiple operating systems and their applications concurrently on a single physical machine, making it much easier to collect data [7].

3.3 Advantages and Disadvantages of Various Kinds of Honeypots

With the help of a high-interaction honeypot, we can collect in-depth information about the procedures of an attacker [7]. We can watch how she attacks and what kinds of tools and approaches she uses.

High-interaction honeypots — both virtual and physical — also bear some risks. In contrast to a low-interaction honeypot, the attacker can get full access to a conventional computer system and begin malicious actions. For example, she could try to attack other hosts on the Internet starting from your honeypot, or she could send spam from one of the compromised machines [7].

Low-interaction honeypots can be used to detect known exploits and measure how often your network gets attacked. The advantages of low-interaction honeypots are manifold. They are easy to set up and maintain. They do not require significant computing resources, and they cannot be compromised by adversaries. The risk of running low-interaction honeypots is much smaller than running honeypots that adversaries can break into and control. On the other hand, that is also one of the main disadvantages of the low-interaction honeypots. They only present the illusion of a machine, which may be pretty sophisticated, but it still does not provide an attacker with a real root shell [7].

One disadvantage of virtual honeypot is the attacker can differentiate between a virtual machine and a real one. It might happen that an advanced attacker compromises a virtual honeypot, detects the suspicious environment, and then leaves the honeypot again. Moreover, she could change his tactics in other ways to try to fool the investigator. So virtual honeypots could lead to less information about attackers [7].

3.4 Honeynet and Honeywall

Honeynet is a group of linked honeypots behind a special firewall called a honeywall [1]. Usually, a honeynet consists of several honeypots of different type (different platforms and/or operating systems). This allows us to simultaneously collect data about different types of attacks. Usually we can learn in-depth information about attacks and therefore get qualitative results of attacker behavior [7].

Also, the Honeywall is normally set up as a transparent bridge that limits the amount of malicious traffic that can leave the honeynet, keeping an attacker from attacking other machines on the Internet [1]

4   The Proposed Model of a Fault Tolerance Honeynet for Securing E-Government

Securing E-government networks is similar to other networks. Many approaches like cryptography, PKI, firewalls, digital signatures are employed in these networks. However, as mentioned above, E-government is an inter-networked government. In most of the cases, government agencies in a country are connected to each other for communicating the information about citizens. This is one of the main differences between government networks and business networks. Because, the businesses are competitor and do not disclose their network to each other, but in most of the governments, co-operation is more critical than competition. So we can use this connectedness to set up a honeynet.

The main goal of honeypots is to trace the hackers and obtain information about their approaches and tools. One of the most important challenges of honeypots is the degree of their interaction. If we use low-interaction honeypots, a hacker cannot utilize all of the resources of the system, so she probably won't be able to use all of her approaches and tools. Therefore we will lose a suitable opportunity for obtaining information. In the other side if she can completely utilize all of the resources, maybe she can use the information that she obtained from the honeypot for attacking other hosts or send spam from one of the compromised machine [7]. As a result, this trade off must be managed effectively.

Security in the governmental networks is more critical than business networks. So if we want to use honeypots in these networks, we must consider the trade off related to interaction, precisely. We need at least a high-interaction honeypot for each agency's network. So we have a network of honeypots through the government, called honeynet. With this network we can increase the possibility of attacks; because our honeypots are dispersed all over the government and all of them are high-interaction. Furthermore we have a Honeycentre server. This server is the manager of the honeynet. It aggregates all of the honeypots logs and then summarizes the results. Honeycentre then informs the web servers about the results, so the administrators of those web servers make an appropriate defensive decision to cover the security holes.

Now we have a network that traces the attacks, all over the government, with a high degree of interaction to hackers. On the other hand, we can cover our security holes as soon as possible.

Honeypots are subject to damage. So, various attacks may disable the honeypots. So we must have a fault tolerance network to predict these problems and react as soon as possible. For this purpose, Honeycentre can help. Honeycentre is gathering information and logs from honeypots all of the times. When a honeypot is down, Honeycentre cannot receive the logs from that honeypot, so it informs the web server of that network and simultaneously assigns a virtual honeypot instead of the damaged honeypot. Honeycentre allots IP address of the damaged honeypot to the virtual honeypot. We may have an additional server for assigning these virtual honeypots (figure1).

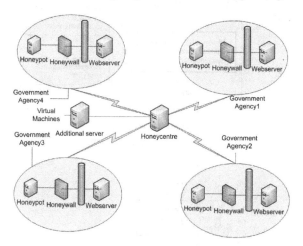

Fig. 1. Fault tolerance honeynet for securing e-government

In figure 1, other network components like user stations, gateways, routers, and connections between agencies are not shown for avoiding complexities.

As mentioned in section 2.2, virtual honeypots are more lightweight than a high-interaction or low interaction honeypot. At a given time, we may have some damaged honeypots in the network, and we cannot fix all of them very soon. In the other hand we cannot assign some high or low interaction honeypot instead of all damaged honeypots to the network, because maybe they are too many and we don't have required resources. So if we use virtual honeypots temporarily, we can solve this problem with just one additional server.

These virtual honeypots must act like the original honeypot. So each government agency replicates its minimum data into Honeycentre or additional server in every specified period of time. These data are minimum, because they should only help the system work, until the problem is solved and the real honeypot returns back to its logical position.

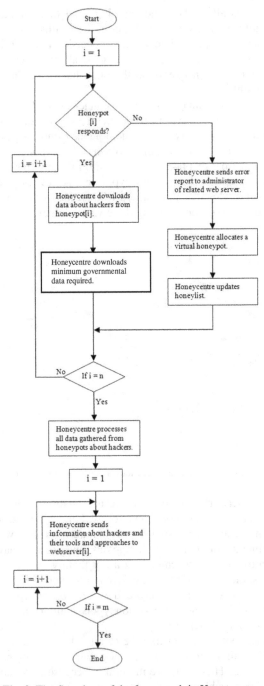

Fig. 2. The flowchart of the framework in Honeycentre

Such a situation enables the Honeycentre to create a real fault tolerant system which would be strong enough to deal with attacks without any interruption.

Figure 2 shows this process in the Honeycentre. Honeycentre wants to gather data from all of the honeypots; for this purpose, Honeycentre checks responses from all of the honeypots. If a honeypot did not respond in a specific period of time, Honeycentre finds out a problem with that honeypot. So, it sends an error report to the administrator of the network, then allocates a virtual honeypot for that network and finally updates honeylist. Honeylist consists of addresses of all honeypots and their related web servers and administrators of their networks. If the honeypot responds, Honeycentre downloads data about hackers from the honeypot. Then it downloads required governmental data into additional server for running virtual honeypot, if needed.

When Honeycentre collected the data from all honeypots, processes them and converts these data to useful information. Then, it sends information to all of the web servers. This information consists of approaches and tools that hackers employ and their anti hack solutions.

With this framework, we can consider the interaction trade off, that mentioned above, effectively. From one point of view, we utilize high interaction honeypots and from other point of view, we create boundaries to prevent hackers from doing more than their permission.

5 Conclusion

Designing and implementing more effective approaches for securing E-government is an important issue, because, the governmental information is usually so sensitive. Furthermore, security has an important role in trust formation of citizens and their adoption of e-government. In this paper, one of the main differences of government and business networks is exploited: connectedness. This useful property used to form a network of honeypots. Furthermore, this honeynet is fault tolerance; so if some honeypots are damaged, the Honeycentre allots some virtual honeypots with minimum resources needed, and evicts the damaged honeypot from the network. So the proposed framework causes interaction with the hackers completely and simultaneously prevents them from damaging the network.

References

1. Barfar, A., Mohammadi, S.: Honeypots: Intrusion deception. ISSA Journal, 28–31 (2007)
2. Conklin, A., White, G.B.: E-government and Cyber Security: The Role of Cyber Security exercises. In: Proceedings of the 39th Annual Hawaii International Conference on System Sciences (2006)
3. Fallahi, M.: The obstacles and guidelines of establishing E-government in Iran, MSc. Thesis, Luleå University of Technology, Sweden (2007),
   http://epubl.ltu.se/1653-0187/2007/052/
   LTU-PB-EX-07052-SE.pdf

4. Henriksson, A., Yi, Y., Frost, B., Middleton, M.: Evaluation instrument for e-government websites. In: Proceedings Internet Research 7.0: Internet Convergences, Brisbane, Queensland, Australia (2006)
5. Hof, S., Reichstädter, P.: Securing e-Government. In: EGOV 2004, pp. 336–341. Springer, Heidelberg (2004)
6. Ndou, V.: E-government for developing countries: opportunities and challenges. The Electronic Journal on Information Systems in Developing Countries 18(1), 1–24 (2004)
7. Provos, N., Holz, T.: Virtual Honeypots: From Botnet Tracking to Intrusion Detection. Addison Wesley Professional, Reading (2008)
8. Sharifi, H., Zarei, B.: An adaptive approach for implementing E-government. In: Iran, I.R. (ed.) Journal of Government Information, vol. 30(5-6), pp. 600–619 (2004)
9. Spitzner, L.: Tracking Hackers. Addison Wesley Professional, Reading (2002)
10. Stibbe, M.: E-government security. Infosecurity Today 2(3), 8–10 (2005)
11. The E-government handbook for developing countries Infodev. (2002)
12. Wimmer, M., von Bredow, B.: E-Government: Aspects of Security on Different Layers. In: Proceedings of the 12th International Workshop on Database and Expert Systems Applications, DEXA 2001 (2001)

Trust-Risk-Game Based Access Control
in Cross Domain Application

Yan Li[1], Jinqiang Ren[2], Huiping Sun[1], Haining Luo[2], and Zhong Chen[1]

[1] School of Software and Microelectronics, Peking University,
Beijing, China
hopelee47@gmail.com, sunhp@ss.pku.edu.cn, chen@ss.pku.edu.cn
[2] Information Security Research and Services Center, State Information Center,
Beijing, China
{renjq,lhn}@mx.cei.gov.cn

Abstract. With development of grid technology, sensitive data protection becomes a difficult task for accesses from heterogeneous domains. Moreover, anonymity and unknown peers worsen security problems. Traditional access control mechanisms are not suitable to distributed environment. Several models and mechanisms make use of trust evaluation to assist access control decision. But few explicitly consider trust and risk as two separate factors which affect interactions between peers. In this paper, we present an access control mechanism which considers both trust and risk as two vital parameters. We also introduce static game model with incomplete information to analyze the optimal decision. In addition, a new model of trust evaluation is proposed to represent the confidence in the peer. To appease people's anxiety about loss, a model of risk assessment is also presented to indicate impacts on resources. At the end of this paper, to describe how our mechanism works, a scenario is provided.

Keywords: Trust evaluation, risk assessment, game model, access control mechanism, cross domain, grid computing.

1 Introduction

Recently, with the development of distributed technology, interactions among multi-domains have been increasingly frequent and common. Grid computing technology, which is a typical cross domain application, has boomed as innovative distributed computing infrastructure for advanced science and engineering. However, sharing resources introduces resource security as a prime concern. Furthermore, if the goal is to allow arbitrary users to submit applications to the grid, new dimensions to security issues are introduced [1]. And since resources owners may come from various administrative domains or virtual organizations, the issues of authorization is addressed in great length in Globus [3]. Thus, these problems, if not addressed, will become significant obstacles.

Sharing resources is a fundamental concept for grid. To contribute to cooperative activities, grid entities have to expose their files and database to public. The exposure will probably invite the threats from thieves and hackers which are always

T.-k. Kim, T.-h. Kim, and A. Kiumi (Eds.): SecTech 2008, CCIS 29, pp. 89–102, 2009.

anonymous in cyberspace. If grid entities impose strict constraints on access to their resource in their own local systems, positive cooperation will be hindered by these constraints which are intended for malicious access. Cooperation cross organizations and domains turns to the virtual organization (VO) [4], which is a collection of distributed users and resources providers spread across multiple administrative domain with multiple policies. However, based on different policies defined by distinct domains, access control mechanisms have trouble in precise negotiations of these policies.

Trust, considered as a key factor in grid security [6], satisfies the requirement of access control mechanism in grid environment. Trust can meet needs of dynamic and multi-domains conditions. A certain amount of trust models have been proposed to satisfy the distributed environment. In [7, 9, 12, 13, 15], trust models are proposed to take anonymity, unpredictability and uncertain under control and assist decision arising from access from distinct domains. To reduce risk and inform mechanism of potential risks, risk assessment and management are important to control risks quantitatively. Risk is an evaluation that significantly indicates the extent to which their assets and resources will be influenced. [16, 17, 18, 19, 20] present various approaches and models for risk assessment and management to control and assess risk in network. [21, 22, 23] use trust to derive the risk of an action, while [25] use risk analysis to access user trust.

To control accesses from heterogeneous domains and to secure local system, trust is used to indicate the extent to which subjects of accesses can be trusted. Meanwhile, risk is utilized to present risks local systems may take if permit access to them. Trust and risk represent separate aspects of a transaction. Without the analysis of risk, trust value is often confusing and ambiguous to understand. Mechanisms don't know what proper action to take just with various trust value. Merely with risk assessment, mechanisms are likely to loose trust on transactions and may refuse to participate in grid computing and cooperation. Trust and risk indicate separate aspects of transactions. Attempting to combine trust and risk will ignore or misunderstand the relationship between trust and risk. Risk is prerequisite to trust. If there is no risk involved, there is no need to trust. The amount of trust required seems to depend on the risk involved. For analysis of requests and optimal solution, the static game model with incomplete information is introduced into the decision-making process.

In this paper, we propose a new access control mechanism in distributed environment based on trust evaluation and risk assessment for cooperation. We use trust evaluation and risk assessment as two key factors to assist to determine whether accesses to local systems are validated and inoffensive. To find the optimal solution with factors, a static game model can be the best tool for us to achieve the optimization of decision. The introduction of trust, risk and game model into access control mechanism makes systems more robust, flexible, and dynamic.

The rest of the paper is organized as follows: In section 2, we briefly introduce the related works. In section 3, we set forth our new access control mechanism in detail. In section 4, the static game model with incomplete information is depicted thoroughly. Section 5 describes the concept and evaluation of trust. And section 6 presents the definition and assessment of risk in detail separately. Scenario description example is discussed in section 7. Section 8 consists of conclusion and future work.

2 Related Work

Access control mechanism is vital to secure computer system. It allows owners of resources to define management and enforce access conditions applicable to each resource.

Discretionary Access Control (DAC) was designed for multi-user databases and systems with a few previously known users. Mandatory Access Control (MAC) is applied in military environments where the number of users can be enormous. Role-base Access Control (RBAC) is well-known because the introduction of user, role and group fits naturally in the organizational structures of the companies. However, these three access control methods are intended for special environment. None of them is suitable for distributed environment, not to mention grid and p2p technology.

In [26], a new technique is proposed to employ runtime monitoring and a restricted shell. This technique can be used for setting-up an execution environment that supports the full legitimate use allowed by security policy of a shared resource. This technique can't solve the problems caused by anonymity and unpredictability because it doesn't adjust the access control methods to the distributed environment.

Virtual Organization Management System (VOMS) [10] specifies the role and VO membership attribute to users. However, access control policies in CAS and VOMS are not appropriate for decentralized and autonomous requirements in dynamic virtual organization because they are controlled by centralized servers. Akenti [24] and PERMIS [14] are integrated into grid system by some efforts. But they don't provide actual policy management mechanism.

Trust evaluation is introduced to establish trustworthiness. Furthermore, numerous models for trust evaluation established and maintained in grid environment have been proposed. Alfarez Abdul-Rahman et al. [11] proposed a trust-reputation model which deals exclusively with beliefs about the trustworthiness of some agents based on experience and reputational information. To fill the gap caused by lack of the process of trust evolution, Mui et al. [7] proposed a Bayesian formalization for a distributed rating process. In [9, 12, 13, 15], trust models and reputation systems in distributed environment are proposed.

Now that plagued by various kinds of risk, risk assessment and management is also necessary to reduce and avoid these problems. To support risk assessment, a large amount of risk assessment models or frameworks are proposed. Bjorn Axel Gran [17] introduced an approach for model-based risk assessment that utilizes success-oriented models describing all intended system aspects. F. Baiardi and S. Suin [18] proposed a risk assessment framework that generalizes the notion of dependency with respect to security attributes such as the confidentiality, integrity or availability. Dariusz Wawrzyniak [19] presented a model for the information security risk assessment that consists of security threats, business impact, security measures and costs.

There are only a few models that take both trust and risk into account. But they just try to combine trust and risk. JoSang [8] analyzed the relationship between trust and risk and refined Manchala's model in order to derive a computational model integrating the two notions. In [21, 22, 23], trust value is used to determine cost-PDF(probability density function) access the risk of an action. In [25], G. Brandeland et al. advocated asset-oriented risk analysis as a means to help assess user trust.

However, most existing researches and mechanism, which are based on trust models, seldom explain the meaning of a particular trust value belonging to a user clearly and indicate the quantified risk. Risk assessment cannot help people establish trust in grid environment because it just informs mechanisms of the risk they may take. Moreover, the existing risk definition and evaluation cannot take profit and desire into account while the traditional risk definition is not directly related to the policy and profit. Solely based on trust or risk, it is a tough task to make policies for acceptance of a transaction. However, the attempt to combine trust and risk will surely complicate the trust evaluation and risk assessment.

3 Access Control Mechanism Based on Trust and Risk

Trust and risk are two significant factors for access control decision. Game theory provides analytical tools to predict the outcome of complex interactions among rational entities. Considering trust and risk as parameters, we utilize the static game model with incomplete information to analyze the possible outcomes and choose the optimal strategy. In our proposed access control mechanism, subject, type, object, operation, trust, risk and payoff function define the whole mechanism. Considering trust and risk as indicators, our mechanism dynamically analyzes requests and predicts outcomes with game model in order to restrict access and operation on the local resources.

Definition 1(Subject). *The entities that can perform actions in the system are called subjects. The set of potential subjects in system can be denoted as a finite set Sub =* $\{s_1, s_2, ..., s_n\}$.

Definition 2(Type). *The type fully describes the particular private information or attributes belonging to a subject. It cannot be common knowledge. A subject may have several types–even an infinity of types, one for each possible state of its private information. Supposing there are n subjects in the set Sub, the type space in system can be denoted as the type-profile space Type =* $\{\Theta_1, \Theta_2, ..., \Theta_n\}$.

Each subject knows its own type with complete certainty. The access control mechanism's beliefs about each subjects' types are captured by a common-knowledge joint probability distribution over their types. We refer to a type of subject i by θ_i, where this type is a member of subject i's type space i's type space Θ_i. Type may include abnormal user, normal user, malicious user, etc. It can be defined and classified by system's administrators.

Definition 3(Object). *The entities representing resources to which access may need to be controlled are called objects. Objects can include any data and files in the system. The set of objects in system can be denoted as a finite set Obj =* $\{obj_1, obj_2, ..., obj_n\}$.

Definition 4(Operation). *The actions that performed on objects by subjects in the computer system are called operations. Operations may include read, write, execute, etc. The set of potential operations in system can be denoted as a finite set Op =* $\{op_1, op_2, ..., op_n\}$.

Trust can be considered as a mapping from arbitrary point in space (Sub, Op) to trust value set T. Set T represents the set of all possible values of trust. We can predefine the minimum value 0 and maximum value m_t. The mapping function can be denoted as $F: Sub \times Op \rightarrow T$. Thus, the mapping represents the trust evaluation of the potential operation performed by the subject. Trust evaluation set ET can be denoted as

$$ET = \{(Sub, Op, T) \mid \exists t (s \in Subject \land op \in Op \land t \in T \land F(s, op) = t)\}$$

Risk can be viewed as the mapping from arbitrary point in space (Type, Op, Obj) to risk value set R. Set R includes all possible risk values based on a particular risk assessment model or methodology. The mapping indicates the risk assessment of the object on which an operation by the subject with a particular type may be performed. The mapping relationship can be described by the payoff function. The payoff function is a mathematical function describing the award given to a single subject at the outcome of an interaction. Given a subject i, i's operation set Op = \{op_1, op_2, ..., op_n\}, subject i's type space Θ_i = \{θ_1, θ_2,..., θ_k\}, required object obj. Then subject i's payoff function is $\pi_i(\theta_1, \theta_2,..., \theta_k, op_1, op_2, ..., op_n, obj)$. The risk assessment set can be denoted as

$$RA = \{(Type, Op, Object, R) \mid \exists r (\theta \in \Theta_i \land op \in Op \land$$
$$obj \in Object \land r \in R \land \pi(\theta, op, obj) = r)\}$$

Arbitrary points (s, θ, op, obj, t, r) in the space (Sub, Type, Op, Obj, T, R) present that if subject s tries to perform the operation op on object obj, mechanism makes a computation according to information about type, trust, payoff function and risk and concludes an optimal strategy for the system. Optimal strategy may indicate either accepting or denying. So let mapping from arbitrary points in the space (Sub, Type, Op, Obj, T, R) to set \{Accept, Deny\}

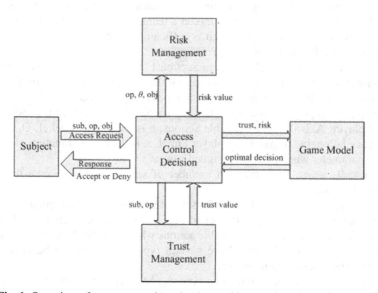

Fig. 1. Overview of access control mechanism architecture based on trust and risk

$$G: Sub \times Type \times Op \times Object \times T \times R \rightarrow \{Accept, Deny\}$$

If the point $(s, \theta, op, obj, t, r)$ is mapped to *Accept*, the access permission will be granted. And the subject can perform the operation on the objects. However, if point $(s, \theta, op, obj, t, r)$ is mapped to *Deny*, the access request will be denied. So the subject cannot perform operation on the objects.

Thus, according to policies, this novel access control mechanism can dynamically make decisions based on trust and risk, which can be applied appropriately to distributed environment and grid applications. Fig. 1 presents the access control mechanism architecture based on trust and risk.

4 Formal Game Model

Game theory has been used in many other problems involving attackers and defenders. The problem and decision process of access control mechanism are similar because a malicious user or attacker may wish to attack the system and the access control mechanism has to prohibit malicious and harmful actions activated by various users. Interaction can cause the system to change in security state, perhaps probabilistically. The malicious user or attacker can gain rewards such as thrills for self-satisfaction, steals secret data. The access control mechanism, however, may not have enough knowledge about the actual purposes of users which may probably be malicious. Access control mechanism tries to expect the possible outcomes and take optimal action to protect the system. So a static game model with incomplete information is ideal for capturing the properties of these interactions.

In real life, there can be more than one user interacting with the system resources. These users may include normal users and abnormal users. The system may have one access control mechanism at the same time. In essence, the game makes no distinction as to which user takes action. We can model a team of users at different locations as the same as an omnipresent user. Thus it is sufficient to use a two-player game model for the analysis of this access control problem.

With some concepts and definitions in Section 1, we introduce the formal model of static game model with incomplete information. Besides, we will also explain how to define or derive the belief function, payoff function, player set, action set.

Formally, a two-player static game is a tuple $<N, (A_i), (p), (\Theta_i), (\pi_i)>$, where N is the set of player, A_i is the set of feasible actions, p is the player's belief, Θ_i is the set of type space belonging to particular player i in N, π_i is the payoff function of player i. And i is a parameter which may be assigned s or ad.

$N = \{s, ad\}$, where s represents a member of set Sub, ad represents the access control mechanism.

$A_s = Op = \{op_1, op_2, ..., op_n\}$. A_s is the set of feasible actions belonging to s.

$A_{ad} = \{Accept, Deny\}$. A_{ad} is the set of feasible actions belonging to ad. Access control mechanism may have two feasible actions which may be *Accept* or *Deny*.

$\Theta_s = \{\theta_1, \theta_2, ..., \theta_n\}$. Θ_s may have several types which should be defined and classified by the system administrator.

$\Theta_{ad} = \{\theta_{ad}\}$. Θ_{ad} can have only one type θ_{ad} because access control mechanism makes any decision and takes all actions with the purpose of protecting the system.

$\pi_s = \pi_s(\theta_s, A_s, A_{ad}, obj)$. θ_s is the type of the subject s. A_s is the possible operation set when the subject s chooses θ_s as its type. A_{ad} includes feasible actions of ad. obj is the member of set Obj which belongs to the system.

$\pi_{ad} = \pi_{ad}(\theta_{ad}, A_{ad}, A_s, obj)$. θ_{ad} is the type of the access control mechanism ad. A_{ad} is feasible action set by the access control mechanism ad with the type θ_{ad}. A_s is the possible operation set chosen by the subject s. obj is the member of set Obj and may be accessed by the subject. Actually access control mechanism always makes a decision according to a subject and an operation. Thus there mostly exists one operation opi as a parameter in the payoff function π_{ad}.

Our research focuses on decision-making process by the access control mechanism. So we will ignore how attackers or users utilize the game model. To aid readability and describe our game model clearly, we provide the graphical representation of the game from the access control mechanism's view. In Fig. 2, a subject has n types. Supposing a subject can request only one operation on object each time, a trust value will be assigned to the subject with its operation op. Access control mechanism has two feasible actions–Accept, Deny. In the part under the dotted line in Fig. 2, our game model will analyze the reward or cost for each strategy.

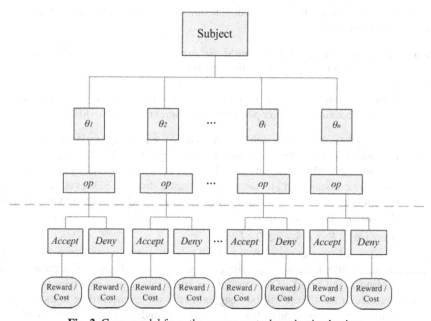

Fig. 2. Game model from the access control mechanism's view

According to Harsanyi transformation [27], we can think of the game as beginning with a move by player Nature, who to subject assigns a type. Nature's move is imperfectly observed. Each player observes the type which Nature has bestowed upon her, but no player directly observes the type bestowed upon any other player. Although the access control mechanism doesn't have any knowledge of subject's type, it knows its belief distribution in subject's type, denoted as p. We will introduce the belief function which considers subject's trust as the parameter, denoted as $B(t) =$

$\{p_1, p_2, ..., p_n\}$, where t is the trust value of the subject, and $p_1, p_2, ..., p_n$ are mechanism's belief in subject's types. Actually the belief in subject's type is a probability value. Given a game $< N, (A_i), (p), (\Theta_i), (\pi_i)>$, if strategy profile $a^* = (a^*_{ad}, a^*_s(\theta))$, for access control mechanism, is the optimal solution to the problem max $\sum p_i \pi_{ad}(\theta, a_{ad}, a_s(\theta), obj)$, a^* is the game's Bayes-Nash equilibrium.

5   Trust Conception and Evaluation

The trust is a complex notion that has been study long in the academic field. In this section, we use the following definition by Gambetta [5] and improve it to meet the need of distributed environment:

Definition 5(Trust). *Trust is a particular level of the subjective probability with which an agent will perform a particular action, both before we can monitor such action and in a context in which it affects our own action.*

In essence, trust involves the confidence in a consequence resulted from an action by the agent. So trust is subjective and probabilistic. It has direct influence on the expectation of the emergence of a particular outcome. Several attributes of definition should be laid emphasis on.

Definition 6(Context). *Trust is multi-dimension quantity. The different trust dimensions are contexts. Context is always related to operation. It can denoted as a set $C = \{c_1, c_2, ..., c_n\}$.*

For example, we may trust a doctor to operate on a patient, but we may not trust him to cook well because the two operations and contexts are quite different.

Definition 7(Agent). *Agents are subjects that can exchange reputational information through recommendations. We can denote the set of agents as $A = \{a_1, a_2, ..., a_n\}$.*

Then, assume that the level of trust LT={vt, t, u, vu}. And here we should introduce semantic distance [11]. Assuming semantic distance SD={svt, st, su, svu}. To determine a context, we should utilize the mapping function O: Sub×Op→C. And let set Q present the direct trust. $Q \subseteq C \times S \times LT$. And Let set R present the recommender trust. $R \subseteq C \times A \times SD \times LT$.

In the process of trust evaluation, we should determine the direct trust first. If the system has never interacted with the subject, the subject will assigned a default trust value according to the belief. If the system has some interaction experiences with the subject, a particular trust level will be assigned to the subject according to its records.

To calculate a recommender trust, the recommended trust degree should be adjusted by

$$rt = lt * sd \qquad (1)$$

The operator * denotes the operation that adjusts the recommender trust.

To combine recommendations, we must assign weights to recommenders. Agents, in the same administrative domain with resources owner, may be assigned greater weights, while those from heterogeneous domains may probably be assigned lower weights.

$$recommend = \sum_{i=1}^{|A|} w_i rt_i / |A| \tag{2}$$

Finally, we combine the direct trust and recommended trust.

$$Trust = direct \cdot \alpha + recommend \cdot \beta \tag{3}$$

where α and β are parameters separately indicating the weights of direct trust and recommended trust.

6 Risk Definition and Assessment

Risk is one of key tools for making decisions in a potential uncertain environment. Risk always emerges with both cost and reward when the outcome of a transaction is likely to be the one that may be quite different from user's expectation. There are many definitions of risk that vary by specific application and situational context.

Definition 8(Risk). *Risk is the mathematical expectation of the potential impact caused by the particular event. Risk = (probability of event occurring)×(impact of event occurring).*

Our risk definition includes the impact of event occurring which may be either positive or negative. So the assessment of risk will also include both reward and cost. For the metric of risk, we should introduce a basic concept – utility, which comes from economics.

Definition 9(Utility). *Utility is a scientific construct to that economists use to understand how rational consumers divide their limited resources among the commodities that provide them with satisfaction.* [2]

Definition 10(Utility function). *The function $u(x)$ calculates the utility derived from an outcome x according to x's impact on assets. Inputs and outputs are two key factors that influence the impact.*

Definition 11(Outcomes). *If transaction T is accept by resource owner, $o_1, o_2, ..., o_n$ are possible outcomes of T. There exists set O including all possible outcomes as its elements. It can be denoted as $O = \{o_1, o_2, ..., o_n\}$. Meanwhile, probability of o_i's occurrence is p_i. We also distinguish outcomes with regard to the type of the subject. So the set O will be separate into several subsets according to subject's types.*

The risk of a transaction can be evaluated and calculated by the following equation:

$$Risk(O, \theta) = p_1 o_1 + p_2 o_2 + ... + p_k o_k \tag{4}$$

where elements of subset $\{o_1, o_2, ..., o_k\}$ are the possible outcomes caused by a subject's operation on the object with a particular type θ. To calculate the value of risk, each outcome in set O will be transformed to a utility value by utility function $u(x)$.

The final utility value of x can be calculated by the operator ⌂ and the following equation:

$$u(x) = \text{INPUT} \vartriangle \text{OUTPUT} \tag{5}$$

INPUT is total amount of resources and assets which contribute to the output. OUTPUT is total amount of resources and assets which are produced through the transaction. $\vartriangle$ is an abstract operator used to combine the input and output. It can be specified by users.

7 Scenario Description Example

In this section, we describe a request and response scenario to present how our access control mechanism works. A user or subject, which may usually be a process, initializes a request for the service from a local system. All requests for resource of local systems should be checked and mediated by the access control mechanism in the system and theoretically cannot be bypassed in any way. Given a subject named s, it is the member of a heterogeneous domain D_h. It intends to download service list in the local system which belongs to domain D_l. In addition, s should also submit its evidences of the trust for its downloading operation. These evidences include recommended trust from four agents as recommender and direct trust according to the system. With all parameter, the access control mechanism begins to do calculation and analysis.

7.1 Trust Evaluation

Supposing that the subject s has never interacted with the system before, the direct trust for downloading by s can be assigned 40 according to system default policy, ie $direct = 40$. There are four agents provide recommended trust for s. Agent$_1$ is an agent from another heterogeneous domain G. The recommended trust value by Agent$_1$ is 80. Its semantic distance is 0.2. Agent$_2$ is an agent from another heterogeneous domain H. The recommended trust value by Agent$_2$ is 50. Its semantic distance is 0.3. Agent$_3$ is an agent from the domain D_1 which is the same as the local system. The recommended trust value by Agent$_3$ is 75. Its semantic distance is 0.8. It is reasonable that semantic distance is much higher when an agent belongs to the same domain. Agent$_4$ is an agent from domain D_h. The recommended trust value by Agent$_4$ is 85. Its semantic distance is 0.4.

Access control mechanism firstly calls trust management module to calculate the trust value for s. According to (1) and (2), the combined recommended trust $recommend = (80*0.2 + 50*0.3 + 75*0.8 + 85*0.4)/4 = 31.25$. Let $\alpha = 0.6$ and $\beta = 0.4$. According to (3), the combined trust value $Trust = 50 \cdot 0.6 + 31.25 \cdot 0.4 = 42.5$.

7.2 Risk Assessment

The object obj is obviously the service list in the system. The service list may include some basic and private information about the system. So if service list is downloaded, there will be four outcomes. The outcome o_1 can improve the collaboration between peers since the service list shows what services the system can provide. The outcome o_2 can increase the reputation of the system so that it may have more opportunities to get services from other peers when it needs. The outcome o_3 will leak the private information of the system and lead to violating the privacy. The outcome o_4 will lose control of the unauthorized copy of its important information such as the service list. p_1, p_2, p_3 and p_4 are the probabilities of o_1's, o_2's, o_3's and o_4's occurrence. Let $p_1 = 0.14$, $p_2 = 0.23$, $p_3 = 0.34$, $p_4 = 0.29$.

According to (5), to calculate and combine input and output, let $u(o_1) = 45$, $u(o_2) = 60$, $u(o_3) = -70$, $u(o_4) = -43$. Supposing the subject s has two types – normal and malicious, the outcome set can be separated into two subsets. They are $\{o_1, o_2\}$ and $\{o_3, o_4\}$. By (4), Risk(obj, normal) = $0.14 \cdot 45 + 0.23 \cdot 60 = 20.1$, Risk(obj, malicious) = $0.34 \cdot (-70) + 0.29 \cdot (-43) = -36.27$.

7.3 Analysis with Game Model

In the given game $<N, (A_i), (p), (\Theta_i), (\pi_i)>$, $N = \{s, ad\}$, $A_s = Op = \{download\}$, $A_{ad} = \{Accept, Deny\}$, $\Theta_s = \{normal, malicious\}$, $\Theta_{ad} = \{\theta_{ad}\}$, $\pi_{ad} = \pi_{ad}(normal, malicious, download, obj)$.

If ad chooses strategy Accept and the type of s is normal, the reward of ad will be 20.1. If ad chooses strategy Accept and the type of s is malicious, the reward of ad will be -36.27. If ad chooses strategy Deny, the reward of ad will be 0 whatever the type of s is. Table 1 depicts the strategy and payoff of access control mechanism.

Table 1. Strategy and payoff

		s	
		normal	*malicious*
	Accept	20.1	-36.27
ad	*Deny*	0	0

The player Nature assigns a type to the subject s which the access control mechanism ad cannot be informed. But ad has trust evidences of s and calculates the trust value of s. By belief function B(t), we can get mechanism's belief in subject's types. For simplicity, supposing the maximum trust value $m_t = 100$, trust value Trust = 42.5, let B(t) = $\{p_1, p_2\}$ = $\{42.5/100, (100 - 42.5)/100\}$ = $\{0.425, 0.575\}$ where belief in normal $p_1 = 0.425$ and belief in malicious $p_2 = 0.575$.

Now that ad doesn't know the type of s, it has to choose its strategy by the expectation value. If ad's strategy is Accept, the expected reward will be $0.425 \cdot 20.1 + 0.575 \cdot (-36.27) = -12.31275$. If ad's strategy is Deny, the expected reward will be $0.425 \cdot 0.1 + 0.575 \cdot 0 = 0$. Because 0 is larger than -12.31275, ad may get more reward when it chooses strategy Deny. Thus strategy Deny is the optimal solution to the problem in this game. Since there is only one strategy download for s to choose, the strategy profile (Deny, download(normal)) (Deny, download(malicious)) is the Bayes-Nash equilibrium of this game. To describe the example more clearly, in Fig. 3, we give the graphical representation of this game from the access control mechanism's view.

According to the analysis by game model, our access control mechanism acquires the optimal strategy of the request from s. So it will decide to deny the request from s and give a negative response to the subject s.

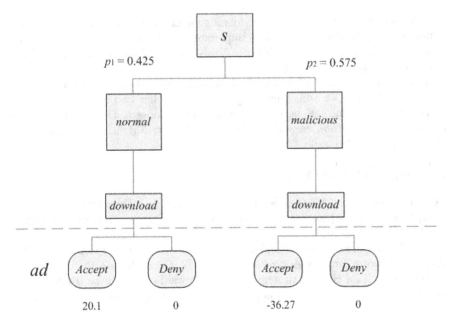

Fig. 3. Game from the access control mechanism's view

8 Future Work and Conclusions

Trust and risk are two facets of access control decision process through which we view events and make choice. Making decisions based on both trust and risk with assistance of game model will be flexible and considerate. In this paper, we proposed a novel access control mechanism taking both trust evaluation and risk assessment into account. With the introduction of static game model with incomplete information, the mechanism helps users make decision according to trust, risk and the other factors. Trust value is evaluated through the combination of direct trust and recommended trust. And the definition of risk is redefined so that it includes both reward and loss. Risk value is assessed according to the negative impact and positive impact caused by the particular event. The game model calculates the possible outcomes and concludes the optimal solution to indicate a decision result. In contrast to traditional access control models and mechanisms which make decisions according to single dimension (either trust or risk), this mechanism can depict the feasibility of a new transaction, based on binary dimensions.

As future work, some evaluation models can be introduced into the mechanism to refine the evaluation of trust and risk. First, how to make use of direct experience and recommendation to conclude a trust value is still a problem. Secondly, as risk evaluation is based on the amount of input, the amount of output, how to assess the amount more accurately remains a difficult problem. In the game model, it is also very important but a little ambiguous that the probabilities of types can be acquired by the belief function according to trust value. So it is still difficult to implement the belief function so that this function can work in common situation. As a continuation of this work, research will be conducted to elaborate the formal game model.

Acknowledgement

Research works in this paper are partial supported by National High-Tech Research and Development Plan of China (No.2006AA01Z455).

References

1. Adabala, S., Butt, A.R., Figueiredo, R.J., Kapadia, N.H., Fortes, J.A.B.: Security implications of making computing resources available via computational grids. Technical Resport TR-ECE01-2, Purdue University, West Lafayettc, IN (September 2001)
2. Samuelson, P.A., Nordhaus, W.D.: Microeconomics, 18th edn., p. 84. McGraw-Hill Irwin, New York (2005)
3. Foster, I., Kesselman, C.: Globus: ametacomputing infrastructure toolkit. The Int. J. Supercomputer Appl. High Performance Compute. 11(2), 115–128 (1997)
4. Foster, I., Kesselman, C., Tuecke, S.: The Anatomy of the Grid: Enabling Scalable Virtual Organizations. International Journal of High Performance Computing Applications 15(3), 200–222 (2001)
5. Gambetta, D.: Can We Trust Trust? In: Gambetta, D. (ed.) Trust: Making and Breaking Cooperative Relations. Basil Blackwell, Oxford (1990)
6. Lin, C., Varadharajan, V., Wang, Y.: Enhancing Grid Security with Trust Management. In: Proceedings of the 2004 IEEE International Conference on Services Computing, pp. 303–310 (2004)
7. Quercia, D., Hailes, S., Capra, L.: B-trust: Bayesian Trust Framework for Pervasive Computing. In: Stølen, K., Winsborough, W.H., Martinelli, F., Massacci, F. (eds.) iTrust 2006. LNCS, vol. 3986, pp. 298–312. Springer, Heidelberg (2006)
8. Josan, A., Presti, S.L.: Analysing the Relationship Between Risk and Trust. In: Jensen, C., Poslad, S., Dimitrakos, T. (eds.) iTrust 2004. LNCS, vol. 2995, pp. 135–145. Springer, Heidelberg (2004)
9. Zouridaki, C., Mark, B.L., Hejmo, M., Thomas, R.K.: A Quantitative Trust Establishment Framework for Reliable Data Packet Delivery in MANETs. In: Proceedings of the 3rd ACM Workshop on Security of Ad Hoc and Sensor Networks (SASN 2005), November 2005, pp. 1–10 (2005)
10. Alfieri, R., Cecchini, R., Ciaschini, V., dell'Agnello, L., Frohner, A., Gianoli, A., Lörentey, K., Spataro, F.: VOMS, an Authorization System for Virtual Organizations, DataGrid Project (2003),
http://grid-auth.infn.it/docs/VOMS-Santiago.pdf
11. Abdul-Rahman, A., Hailes, S.: Supporting Trust in Virtual Communities. In: Proceedings of the 33rd Annual International Conference on System Sciences, Maui, Hawaii, January 2000, vol. 6, p. 6007 (2000)
12. Damiani, E., et al.: A Reputation-Based Approach for Choosing Reliable Resources in Peer-to-Peer Networks. In: Proceedings of the 9th ACM conference on Computer and Communications Security (CSS 2002), pp. 207–216. ACM, New York (2002)

13. Gupta, M., Judge, P., Ammar, M.: A reputation system for peer-to-peer networks. In: Proceedings of the 13th international workshop on Network and operating systems support for digital audio and video, NOSSDAV (2003)
14. Chadwick, D., Otenko, A.: The Permis X.509 Role Based Privilege Management Infrastructure. In: Proceedings of SACMAT 2002 Conference, pp. 135–140. ACM Press, New York (2002)
15. Liau, C.Y., et al.: Efficient Distributed Reputation Scheme for Peer-to-Peer Systems. In: Chung, C.-W., Kim, C.-k., Kim, W., Ling, T.-W., Song, K.-H. (eds.) HSI 2003. LNCS, vol. 2713, pp. 54–63. Springer, Heidelberg (2003)
16. Ngai, E.W.T., Wat, F.K.T.: Fuzzy decision support system for risk analysis in e-commerce development. Decision support systems 40(2), 235–255 (2005)
17. Gran, B.A., Fredriksen, R., Thunem, A.P.-J.: An Approach for Model-Based Risk Assessment. In: Heisel, M., Liggesmeyer, P., Wittmann, S. (eds.) SAFECOMP 2004. LNCS, vol. 3219, pp. 311–324. Springer, Heidelberg (2004)
18. Baiardi, F., Suin, S., Telmon, C., Pioli, M.: Assessing the Risk of an Information Infrastructure Through Security Dependencies. In: López, J. (ed.) CRITIS 2006. LNCS, vol. 4347, pp. 42–54. Springer, Heidelberg (2006)
19. Wawrzyniak, D.: Information Security Risk Assessment Model for Risk Management. In: Fischer-Hübner, S., Furnell, S., Lambrinoudakis, C. (eds.) TrustBus 2006. LNCS, vol. 4083, pp. 21–30. Springer, Heidelberg (2006)
20. Quercia, D., Hailes, S.: Risk Aware Decision Framework for Trusted Mobile Interactions. In: Proceedings of the 1st IEEE/CreateNet International Workshop on The Value of Security through Collaboration, Athens, Greece (September 2005)
21. Dimmock, N., Bacon, J., Ingram, D., Moody, K.: Risk Models for Trust-Based Access Control(TBAC). In: Herrmann, P., Issarny, V., Shiu, S.C.K. (eds.) iTrust 2005. LNCS, vol. 3477, pp. 364–371. Springer, Heidelberg (2005)
22. Cahill, V., Gray, E., Seigneur, J.-M., Jensen, C., Chen, Y., Shand, B., Dimmock, N., Twigg, A., Bacon, J., English, C., Wagealla, W., Terzis, S., Nixon, P., Serugendo, G., Bryce, C., Carbone, M., Krukow, K., Nielsen, M.: Using Trust for Secure Collaboration in Uncertain Environments. IEEE Pervasive Computing Mobile and Ubiquitous Computing 2(3), 52–61 (2003)
23. Cvrcaronek, D., Moody, K.: Combining Trust and Risk to Reduce the Cost of Attacks. In: Herrmann, P., Issarny, V., Shiu, S.C.K. (eds.) iTrust 2005. LNCS, vol. 3477, pp. 372–383. Springer, Heidelberg (2005)
24. Thompson, M., Johnston, W., Mudumbai, S., Hoo, G., Jackson, K., Essiari, A.: Certificate-based Access Control for Widely Distributed Resources. In: Proceedings of the Eighth Usenix Security Symposium (August 1999)
25. Brandeland, G., Stolen, K.: Using Risk Analysis to Assess User Trust. In: Jensen, C., Poslad, S., Dimitrakos, T. (eds.) iTrust 2004. LNCS, vol. 2995, pp. 146–160. Springer, Heidelberg (2004)
26. Butt, A.R., Adabala, S., Kapadia, N.H., Figueiredo, R.J., Fortes, J.A.B.: Grid-computing portals and security issues. Journal of Parallel and Distributed Computing 63(10), 1006–1014 (2003)
27. Rasmusen, E.: Games and Information: An Introduction to Game Theory, p. 52. Blackwell Publishing, Malden (2007)

Impossible Differential Characteristics of Extended Feistel Networks with Provable Security against Differential Cryptanalysis

Huihui Yap

DSO National Laboratories
20 Science Park Drive, Singapore 118230
yhuihui@dso.org.sg

Abstract. The design of block ciphers with provable security against differential and linear cryptanalysis has always been an important consideration. However, it is also vital to evaluate the security of block ciphers against other forms of cryptanalysis, for example, impossible differential cryptanalysis, a variant of differential cryptanalysis (DC). In impossible differential cryptanalysis, impossible differential characteristics are used to retrive a subkey material for the first or the last several rounds of block ciphers. Thus the security of a block cipher against impossible differential cryptanalysis can be evaluated by impossible differential characteristics [1]. In this paper, we will first examine the security of Extended Feistel Networks (EFN) against DC and then use the U-method introduced in [1] to find impossible differential characteristics of EFN.

Keywords: Differential Cryptanalysis, Extended Feistel Networks, Impossible Differential Characteristics.

1 Introduction

Differential and linear cryptanalysis are the most common cryptanalyzing tools against block ciphers. Provable security against differential and linear cryptanalysis has been an important consideration in the design of block ciphers. However, this is not sufficient to guarantee the security of the block ciphers because they may be vulnerable to other types of cryptanalysis. Impossible differential cryptanalysis, a variant of differential cryptanalysis, is a method that was applied against Skipjack to reject wrong key candidates by using input difference and output difference pairs whose probabilities are zero. It can also be used to attack a 5-round Feistel structure even though the 3-round Feistel structure whose round functions are bijective has a provable security against differential and linear attacks [5].

In [1], a general tool, called U-method was introduced to find various impossible differential characteristics of block cipher structures in which the round functions are bijective. An algorithm was also provided to compute the maximum length of impossible differential characteristics that can be found in the

T.-k. Kim, T.-h. Kim, and A. Kiumi (Eds.): SecTech 2008, CCIS 29, pp. 103–121, 2009.

U-method. By modifying the algorithm, various impossible differential characteristics of the block cipher structures could be determined.

This paper is organized as follows. Section 2 briefly illustrates three types of Extended Feistel Network (EFN) and states some definitions and known results regarding differential probability and impossible differential cryptanalysis. Section 3 discusses and compares the the security of the three types of EFN against differential cryptanalysis. In Section 4, the *U*-method is applied to the three types of EFN to find the maximum number of rounds for impossible differential cryptanalysis.

2   Preliminaries

2.1   Notations

Throughout the rest of the paper, we will consider a round bijective function $F : GF(2)^m \rightarrow GF(2)^m$. We assume that round keys are independent and uniformly random. Furthermore, input data are also independent and uniformly random.

Let $X = (X_1, \cdots X_n)$ be the input data block comprising n sub-blocks. Similarly we use $Y = (Y_1, \cdots Y_n)$ to denote the output block of a round. Hence each sub-block comprises m bits. In addition, we use ΔX to denote a difference block. Note that we will always take n to be greater than or equal to 4.

With an input difference $\alpha = (\alpha_1, \alpha_2, \cdots, \alpha_n)$ and an output difference $\beta = (\beta_1, \beta_2, \cdots, \beta_n)$, a differential (the set of all differential characteristics) is denoted by $\alpha \xrightarrow{F} \beta$ or simply just $\alpha \rightarrow \beta$ when the context is clear. On the other hand, we denote a r-round impossible differential characteristic by $\alpha \nrightarrow_r \beta$.

Finally, to simplify notation, the "+" symbol is always taken to mean the $\oplus$ operator unless stated otherwise.

2.2   Extended Feistel Network

As introduced by [2], EFN are examples of Unbalanced Feistel Networks [4] whereby their sub-blocks are mixed through repeated application of keyed, non-linear F-functions. As in [2], we focus on three types of EFN, namely, EFN Type-I, EFN Type-II and EFN Type-III. The structures for the three EFN transformations are depicted in Figure 1, Figure 2 and Figure 3 respectively. EFN Type-I uses only one F-function in a round and the transformation can be described by

$$(Y_1, Y_2, \cdots, Y_{n-1}, Y_n) = (X_n, X_1, \cdots, X_{n-2}, X_{n-1} + F(X_n)).$$

For EFN Type-II, one F-function is used for every two consecutive sub-blocks. For $1 \leq i \leq n$, the transformation is defined by

$$Y_i = \begin{cases} X_n, & \text{if } i = 1, \\ X_{i-1}, & \text{if } i \neq 1 \text{ is odd}, \\ X_{i-1} + F(X_i), & \text{if } i \text{ is even}. \end{cases}$$

In this paper, we only consider EFN Type-II where n is even. For EFN Type-III, one F-function is used for every sub-block and is defined as follows:

$$(Y_1, Y_2, \cdots, Y_n) = (X_n, X_1 + F(X_2), \cdots, X_{n-1} + F(X_n)).$$

2.3   Differential Cryptanalysis

Differential cryptanalysis (DC) uses the non-uniformity of the output differences given input differences. Block ciphers are usually constructed iteratively with the same round function. So in order to avoid DC, it needs to use the round functions which have the good properties against such attack with sufficient rounds.

Definition 1. *[3] For any given $\Delta X, \Delta Y \in GF(2)^m$, the differential probability of a round function F is defined by*

$$DP^F(\Delta X \to \Delta Y) = \frac{\#\{X \in GF(2)^m | F(X) + F(X + \Delta X) = \Delta Y\}}{2^m}.$$

In the above definition, the probability refers to the average probability for all the possible keys. To give the provable security against DC with the theoretical measure we need the following definition.

Definition 2. *The maximal differential probability of F is defined by*

$$DP^F_{max} = \max_{\Delta X \neq 0, \Delta Y} DP^F(\Delta X \to \Delta Y).$$

Theorem 1. *[3] Let F_1 and F_2 be consecutive and relatively independent round functions from $GF(2)^m$ to $GF(2)^m$. For any $\Delta X, \Delta Z \in GF(2)^m$,*

$$DP^{F_1, F_2}(\Delta X \to \Delta Z) = \sum_{\Delta Y} DP^{F_1}(\Delta X \to \Delta Y) \cdot DP^{F_2}(\Delta Y \to \Delta Z).$$

Theorem 2. *[3] For any bijective function F,*

$$\sum_{\Delta X} DP^F(\Delta X \to \Delta Y) = 1.$$

Throughout the rest of this paper, we will use $DP(\Delta X \to \Delta Y)$ instead of $DP^F(\Delta X \to \Delta Y)$.

2.4   Impossible Differential Characteristics

Definition 3. *[1] The $n \times n$ Encryption Characteristic Matrix $\mathbf{E} = (E_{ij})_{n \times n}$ and $n \times n$ Decryption Characteristic Matrix $\mathbf{D} = (D_{ij})_{n \times n}$ are defined as follows.*

$$E_{i,j} = \begin{cases} 0, & \text{if } Y_j \text{ is not affected by } X_i, \\ 1, & \text{if } Y_j \text{ is affected by } X_i, \\ 1_F, & \text{if } Y_j \text{ is affected by } F(X_i). \end{cases}$$

$$D_{i,j} = \begin{cases} 0, & \text{if } X_j \text{ is not affected by } Y_i, \\ 1, & \text{if } X_j \text{ is affected by } Y_i, \\ 1_F, & \text{if } X_j \text{ is affected by } F(Y_i) \text{ or } F^{-1}(Y_i). \end{cases}$$

Definition 4. *[1] A matrix is a* **1-property matrix** *if the number of entries* 1 ($\neq 1_F$) *in each column of the matrix is zero or one.*

Definition 5. *[1] Given an input difference* $\alpha = (\alpha_1, \alpha_2, \ldots, \alpha_n)$, *the* **input difference vector** $\mathbf{a} = (a_1, a_2, \ldots, a_n)$ *corresponding to* α *is defined as follows.*

$$a_i = \begin{cases} 0, & \text{if } \alpha_i = 0, \\ 1^*, & \text{otherwise.} \end{cases}$$

Given an input difference, the possible output differences of each subblock after r rounds are summarized in Table 1. Table 2 list all the possible cases of multiplication and addition between an entry of the difference vector $\mathbf{a}$ and an entry of the matrix $\mathbf{E}$.

Table 1. Entries of difference vectors and corresponding type of differences

Entry	Corresponding type of difference
0	zero difference, denoted by 0
1	nonzero nonfixed difference, denoted by δ
1^*	nonzero fixed difference, denoted by γ
2^*	nonzero fixed difference $\oplus$ nonzero nonfixed difference, denoted by $\gamma \oplus \delta$
$t(\geq 2)$	nonfixed difference, denoted by ?

Table 2. Multiplication and Addition ($k \in \{0, 1, 1^*, 2^*, t\}, t, t' \geq 2$)

Multiplication ($a_i \cdot E_{i,j}$)	Addition
$k \cdot 0 = 0$	$0 + k = k$
$k \cdot 1 = k$	$1 + 1 = 2$
$0 \cdot 1_F = 0$	$1 + 1^* = 2^*$
$1^* \cdot 1_F = 1$	$1 + 2^* = 3$
$1 \cdot 1_F = 1$	$1 + t = 1 + t$
$2^* \cdot 1_F = 2$	$1^* + t = 1 + t$
$t \cdot 1_F = t$	$2^* + t = 2 + t$
	$t + t' = t + t'$

To find the output difference vector of each round, we can use Table 2 and define the multiplication of $\mathbf{a}$ and $\mathbf{E}$ (similar for $\mathbf{b}$ and $\mathbf{D}$) as follows:

$$\mathbf{a} \cdot \mathbf{E} = (a_i)_{1 \times n} \cdot (E_{i,j})_{n \times n}$$
$$= \left(\sum_i a_i \cdot E_{i,j} \right)_{1 \times n}$$

According to Table 1, in the case of entry $t(\geq 2)$, we do not know the difference to which entry t does not correspond. However, we are able to deduce the differences to which 0, 1, 1^* and 2^* each does not correspond. Let $U = \{0, 1, 1^*, 2^*\}$. In addition, we need to define an auxillary set $\bar{m}$ which has the following two properties:

1. $\bar{m}$ is a subset of U.
2. The elements of $\bar{m}$ correspond to the differences which cannot be represented by the entry m.

Table 3 shows the corresponding differences to the entries $m \in U$ and the auxillary sets $\bar{m}$.

Table 3. Entries and corresponding auxillary sets

Entry, m	Auxillary set $\bar{m}$
0	$\bar{0} = \{1, 1^*\}$
1	$\bar{1} = \{0\}$
1^*	$\bar{1^*} = \{0, 1^*, 2^*\}$
2^*	$\bar{2^*} = \{1^*\}$

It can be checked that

1. if $a_i^r = m$ and $b_i^{r'} \in \bar{m}$, then there exists $\alpha \not\rightarrow_{r+r'} \beta$;
2. if $a_i^r \in \bar{m}$ and $b_i^{r'} = m$, then there exists $\alpha \not\rightarrow_{r+r'} \beta$.

J. Kim et al. [1] call this method that uses the elements of U to find impossible differential characteristics as U-**method**. An algorithm (Algorithm 1) was presented in [1] to compute the maximum number of rounds for the impossible differential differential characteristics which can be found in the U-method. By modifying Algorithm 1, we can get specific forms of various impossible differential characteristics of the block cipher structures S.

3   Provable Security for EFN against DC

In this section, results regarding the differential probability of each type of EFN are presented.

Theorem 3. *If $r = 2n - 1$ and the round function of the EFN Type-I is bijective, then the r-round differential probabilities are bounded by p^2 where p is the maximal average differential probability of a round function.*

Proof. Let the input difference and output difference be $\alpha = (\alpha_1, \cdots, \alpha_n) \neq 0$ and $\beta = (\beta_1, \cdots, \beta_n) \neq 0$ respectively. Also let the output differences of the round function in the first $(n-1)$ rounds be $\epsilon_1, \cdots, \epsilon_{n-1}$ respectively. Then in general, the input-output differences for all round functions are as follows:

$$\alpha_n \rightarrow \epsilon_1$$
$$\alpha_{n-1} + \epsilon_1 \rightarrow \epsilon_2$$
$$\alpha_{n-2} + \epsilon_2 \rightarrow \epsilon_3$$
$$\vdots$$
$$\alpha_2 + \epsilon_{n-2} \rightarrow \epsilon_{n-1}$$
$$\alpha_1 + \epsilon_{n-1} \rightarrow \alpha_n + \beta_{n-1}$$
$$\beta_{n-1} \rightarrow \alpha_{n-1} + \beta_{n-2} + \epsilon_1$$
$$\beta_{n-2} \rightarrow \alpha_{n-2} + \beta_{n-3} + \epsilon_2$$
$$\vdots$$
$$\beta_2 \rightarrow \alpha_2 + \beta_1 + \epsilon_{n-2}$$
$$\beta_1 \rightarrow \alpha_1 + \beta_n + \epsilon_{n-1}$$

So from Theorem 1, we have the following:

$$DP(\alpha \rightarrow \beta) = \sum_{\epsilon_i, 1 \leq i \leq n+1} DP(\alpha_n \rightarrow \epsilon_1) \cdot DP(\alpha_{n-1} + \epsilon_1 \rightarrow \epsilon_2) \cdots$$
$$\cdot DP(\alpha_2 + \epsilon_{n-2} \rightarrow \epsilon_{n-1}) \cdot DP(\alpha_1 + \epsilon_{n-1} \rightarrow \alpha_n + \beta_{n-1})$$
$$\cdot DP(\beta_{n-1} \rightarrow \alpha_{n-1} + \beta_{n-2} + \epsilon_1) \cdots \cdot DP(\beta_2 \rightarrow \alpha_2 + \beta_1 + \epsilon_{n-2})$$
$$\cdot DP(\beta_1 \rightarrow \alpha_1 + \beta_n + \epsilon_{n-1})$$

We shall show that at least two of the input differences in the above equation are non-zero. With Theorem 2, this will imply that $DP(\alpha \rightarrow \beta) \leq p^2$. Suppose for a contradiction that at most one of the input differences is non-zero. If all input differences to the F-functions are zero, then

$$\alpha_n = 0,$$

$$\epsilon_1 = \cdots = \epsilon_{n-1} = 0,$$

and

$$\alpha_{n-1} + \epsilon_1 = \cdots = \alpha_1 + \epsilon_{n-1} = 0$$

which will in turn imply that $\alpha_1 = \cdots = \alpha_{n-1} = 0$ which contradicts that $\alpha \neq 0$. Hence exactly one of the input differences is non-zero and we have the following cases.

1. Suppose that only $\alpha_n \neq 0$. Hence $\alpha_n + \beta_{n-1} = 0$ and $\beta_{n-1} = 0$. It follows that $\alpha_n = 0$ which is a contradiction.
2. Suppose that only $\alpha_{n-i} + \epsilon_i \neq 0$ for exactly one value of i where $i = 1, \cdots$, or $n - 2$. Then $\alpha_{n-i} + \beta_{n-i-1} + \epsilon_i = 0$ and $\beta_{n-i-1} = 0$. It follows that $\alpha_{n-i} + \epsilon_i = 0$, a contradiction.
3. Suppose that only $\alpha_1 + \epsilon_{n-1} \neq 0$. Then $\alpha_n + \beta_{n-1} \neq 0$. Also $\alpha_n = 0$ and $\beta_{n-1} = 0$. It follows that $\alpha_n + \beta_{n-1} = 0$, a contradiction.
4. Suppose that only $\beta_{n-1} \neq 0$. Also $\alpha_n = 0$ and $\alpha_n + \beta_{n-1} = 0$. It follows that $\beta_{n-1} = 0$, a contradiction.
5. Suppose that only $\beta_i \neq 0$ for exactly one value of i where $i = 1, \cdots$ or $n - 2$. Also $\alpha_{i+1} + \beta_i + \epsilon_{n-i-1} = 0$ and $\alpha_{i+1} + \epsilon_{n-i-1} = 0$. This implies that $\beta_i = 0$, again a contradiction.

Therefore at least two of the input differences are non-zero and $DP(\alpha \to \beta) \leq p^2$.

Theorem 4. *If $n = 2k$ and the round function of the EFN Type-II is bijective, then the 3-round differential probabilities are bounded by p^2 where p is the maximal average differential probability of a round function.*

Proof. Let the input difference and output difference be $\alpha = (\alpha_1, \cdots, \alpha_n) \neq 0$ and $\beta = (\beta_1, \cdots, \beta_n) \neq 0$ respectively. Also let the output differences of the first k F-functions be $\epsilon_1, \cdots, \epsilon_k$ respectively. Then in general, the input-output differences for all round functions are as follows:

$$\alpha_2 \to \epsilon_1$$
$$\alpha_4 \to \epsilon_2$$
$$\vdots$$
$$\alpha_{2k} \to \epsilon_k$$
$$\alpha_1 + \epsilon_1 \to \alpha_{2k} + \beta_3$$
$$\alpha_3 + \epsilon_2 \to \alpha_2 + \beta_5$$
$$\alpha_5 + \epsilon_3 \to \alpha_4 + \beta_7$$
$$\vdots$$
$$\alpha_{2k-3} + \epsilon_{k-1} \to \alpha_{2k-4} + \beta_{2k-1}$$
$$\alpha_{2k-1} + \epsilon_k \to \alpha_{2k-2} + \beta_1$$
$$\beta_3 \to \alpha_{2k-1} + \beta_2 + \epsilon_k$$
$$\beta_5 \to \alpha_1 + \beta_4 + \epsilon_1$$
$$\beta_7 \to \alpha_3 + \beta_6 + \epsilon_2$$
$$\vdots$$
$$\beta_{2k-1} \to \alpha_{2k-5} + \beta_{2k-2} + \epsilon_{k-2}$$
$$\beta_1 \to \alpha_{2k-3} + \beta_{2k} + \epsilon_{k-1}$$

So from Theorem 1, we have the following:

$$DP(\alpha \rightarrow \beta) = \sum_{\epsilon_i, 1 \leq i \leq k} DP(\alpha_2 \rightarrow \epsilon_1) \cdot DP(\alpha_4 \rightarrow \epsilon_2) \cdots DP(\alpha_{2k} \rightarrow \epsilon_k)$$

$$\cdot DP(\alpha_1 + \epsilon_1 \rightarrow \alpha_{2k} + \beta_3) \cdot DP(\alpha_3 + \epsilon_2 \rightarrow \alpha_2 + \beta_5) \cdots$$

$$\cdot DP(\alpha_{2k-3} + \epsilon_{k-1} \rightarrow \alpha_{2k-4} + \beta_{2k-1})$$

$$\cdot DP(\alpha_{2k-1} + \epsilon_k \rightarrow \alpha_{2k-2} + \beta_1)$$

$$\cdot DP(\beta_3 \rightarrow \alpha_{2k-1} + \beta_2 + \epsilon_k)$$

$$\cdot DP(\beta_5 \rightarrow \alpha_1 + \beta_4 + \epsilon_1) \cdot DP(\beta_7 \rightarrow \alpha_3 + \beta_6 + \epsilon_2) \cdots$$

$$\cdot DP(\beta_{2k-1} \rightarrow \alpha_{2k-5} + \beta_{2k-2} + \epsilon_{k-2})$$

$$\cdot DP(\beta_1 \rightarrow \alpha_{2k-3} + \beta_{2k} + \epsilon_{k-1})$$

We shall show that at least two of the input differences in the above equation are non-zero. With Theorem 2, this will imply that $DP(\alpha \rightarrow \beta) \leq p^2$. Suppose for a contradiction that at most one of the input differences is non-zero. If all input differences are zero, then $\alpha_{2i} = 0$, $\epsilon_i = 0$ and $\alpha_{2i-1} + \epsilon_i = 0$ for all $1 \leq i \leq k$. This implies that $\alpha_{2i-1} = 0$ which contradicts that $\alpha \neq 0$. Hence exactly one of the input differences is non-zero and we have the following cases.

1. Suppose that only $\alpha_{2i} \neq 0$ for exactly one value of i where $i = 1, \cdots$, or $k-2$. Then $\alpha_{2i} + \beta_{2i+3} = 0$ and $\beta_{2i+3} = 0$. It follows that $\alpha_{2i} = 0$, a contradiction.
2. Suppose that only $\alpha_{2k-2} \neq 0$. Then $\alpha_{2k-2} + \beta_1 = 0$ and $\beta_1 = 0$. Hence $\alpha_{2k-2} = 0$, a contradiction.
3. Suppose that only $\alpha_{2k} \neq 0$. Also $\alpha_{2k} + \beta_3 = 0$ and $\beta_3 = 0$. It follows that $\alpha_{2k} = 0$ which is a contradiction.
4. Suppose that only $\alpha_1 + \epsilon_1 \neq 0$. Then $\alpha_{2k} + \beta_3 \neq 0$. But $\alpha_{2k} = 0$ and $\beta_3 = 0$ which imply that $\alpha_{2k} + \beta_3 = 0$, a contradiction.
5. Suppose that only $\alpha_{2i-1} + \epsilon_i \neq 0$ for exactly one value of i where $i = 2, \cdots$, or $k - 1$. Then $\alpha_{2i-2} + \beta_{2i+1} \neq 0$. But $\alpha_{2i-2} = 0$ and $\beta_{2i+1} = 0$. It follows that $\alpha_{2i-2} + \beta_{2i+1} = 0$, a contradiction.
6. Suppose that only $\alpha_{2k-1} + \epsilon_k \neq 0$. Then $\alpha_{2k-2} + \beta_1 \neq 0$. But $\alpha_{2k-2} = 0$ and $\beta_1 = 0$ which imply that $\alpha_{2k-2} + \beta_1 = 0$, a contradiction.
7. Suppose that only $\beta_3 \neq 0$. Also $\alpha_{2k} = 0$ and $\alpha_{2k} + \beta_3 = 0$ which imply that $\beta_3 = 0$, a contradiction.
8. Suppose that only $\beta_{2i-1} \neq 0$ for exactly one value of i where $i = 3, \cdots$, or k. Also $\alpha_{2i-4} = 0$ and $\alpha_{2i-4} + \beta_{2i-1} = 0$ which follows that $\beta_{2i-1} = 0$, a contradiction.
9. Suppose that only $\beta_1 \neq 0$. Then $\alpha_{2k-2} = 0$ and $\alpha_{2k-2} + \beta_1 = 0$. This results in $\beta_1 = 0$ which is a contradiction.

Therefore at least two of the input differences are non-zero and $DP(\alpha \rightarrow \beta) \leq p^2$.

Theorem 5. *There are at least two non-zero input differences to the F-functions in a 3-round differential of EFN Type-III.*

Proof. Let the input difference and output difference be $\alpha = (\alpha_1, \cdots, \alpha_n) \neq 0$ and $\beta = (\beta_1, \cdots, \beta_n) \neq 0$ respectively. Also let the output differences of the first $(2n - 3)$ F-functions be $\epsilon_1, \cdots, \epsilon_{2n-3}$ respectively. Then in general, the input-output differences for all round functions are as follows:

$$\alpha_2 \rightarrow \epsilon_1$$
$$\alpha_3 \rightarrow \epsilon_2$$
$$\vdots$$
$$\alpha_n \rightarrow \epsilon_{n-1}$$
$$\alpha_1 + \epsilon_1 \rightarrow \epsilon_n$$
$$\vdots$$
$$\alpha_{n-2} + \epsilon_{n-2} \rightarrow \epsilon_{2n-3}$$
$$\alpha_{n-1} + \epsilon_{n-1} \rightarrow \alpha_{n-2} + \beta_1 + \epsilon_{n-2}$$
$$\alpha_n + \epsilon_n \rightarrow \alpha_{n-1} + \beta_2 + \epsilon_{n-1}$$
$$\alpha_1 + \epsilon_1 + \epsilon_{n+1} \rightarrow \alpha_n + \beta_3 + \epsilon_n$$
$$\alpha_2 + \epsilon_2 + \epsilon_{n+2} \rightarrow \alpha_1 + \beta_4 + \epsilon_1 + \epsilon_{n+1}$$
$$\vdots$$
$$\alpha_{n-3} + \epsilon_{n-3} + \epsilon_{2n-3} \rightarrow \alpha_{n-4} + \beta_{n-1} + \epsilon_{n-4} + \epsilon_{2n-4}$$
$$\beta_1 \rightarrow \alpha_{n-3} + \beta_n + \epsilon_{n-3} + \epsilon_{2n-3}$$

Suppose for a contradiction that at most one of the input differences is non-zero. If all input differences are zero, then $\alpha_2 = \cdots = \alpha_n = 0$, $\epsilon_1 = 0$ and $\alpha_1 + \epsilon_1 = 0$. So α_1 also equals to 0 which contradicts that $\alpha \neq 0$. Hence exactly one of the input differences is non-zero and we have the following cases.

1. Suppose that only $\alpha_i \neq 0$ for exactly one value of i where $i = 2, \cdots$, or n. Then $\epsilon_i = 0$ and $\alpha_i + \epsilon_i = 0$. It follows that $\alpha_i = 0$, a contradiction.
2. Suppose that only $\alpha_1 + \epsilon_1 \neq 0$. Also $\epsilon_{n+1} = 0$ and $\alpha_1 + \epsilon_1 + \epsilon_{n+1} = 0$. It follows that $\alpha_1 + \epsilon_1 = 0$ which is a contradiction.
3. Suppose that only $\alpha_i + \epsilon_i \neq 0$ for exactly one value of i where $i = 2, \cdots$, or n. Then $\alpha_i = 0$ and $\epsilon_i = 0$. It follows that $\alpha_i + \epsilon_i = 0$, a contradiction.
4. Suppose that only $\alpha_i + \epsilon_i + \epsilon_{n+i} \neq 0$ for exactly one value of i where $i = 1, \cdots$, or $n - 3$. Also $\alpha_i + \epsilon_i = 0$ and $\epsilon_{n+i} = 0$ which follows that $\alpha_i + \epsilon_i + \epsilon_{n+i} = 0$, a contradiction.
5. Suppose that only $\beta_1 \neq 0$. Then $\alpha_{n-2} + \epsilon_{n-2} = 0$ and $\alpha_{n-2} + \beta_1 + \epsilon_{n-2} = 0$. This results in $\beta_1 = 0$ which is a contradiction.

Therefore at least two of the input differences are non-zero.

For provable security of EFN Type-III against differential cryptanalysis, we only consider $n = 4$.

Theorem 6. *For $n = 4$, if the round function of the EFN Type-III is bijective, then the 3-round differential probabilities are bounded by p^2 where p is the maximal average differential probability of a round function.*

Proof. Following the same notation in the previous proof, from Theorem 1, we have the following:

$$DP(\alpha \to \beta) = \sum_{\epsilon_i, 1 \leq i \leq 5} DP(\alpha_2 \to \epsilon_1) \cdot DP(\alpha_3 \to \epsilon_2) \cdot DP(\alpha_4 \to \epsilon_3)$$
$$\cdot DP(\alpha_1 + \epsilon_1 \to \epsilon_4) \cdot DP(\alpha_2 + \epsilon_2 \to \epsilon_5)$$
$$\cdot DP(\alpha_3 + \epsilon_3 \to \alpha_2 + \beta_1 + \epsilon_2)$$
$$\cdot DP(\alpha_4 + \epsilon_4 \to \alpha_3 + \beta_2 + \epsilon_3)$$
$$\cdot DP(\alpha_1 + \epsilon_1 + \epsilon_5 \to \alpha_4 + \beta_3 + \epsilon_4)$$
$$\cdot DP(\beta_1 \to \alpha_1 + \beta_4 + \epsilon_1 + \epsilon_5)$$

We shall consider all the 3-round differential probabilities classified by the conditions on the non-zero input differences α.

Case 1: $\alpha_2 = \alpha_3 = \alpha_4 = 0$, $\alpha_1 \neq 0$
$\Rightarrow \epsilon_1 = \epsilon_2 = \epsilon_3 = \epsilon_5 = 0$, $\epsilon_4 \neq 0$

$$DP(\alpha \to \beta) = \sum_{\epsilon_4} DP(\alpha_1 \to \epsilon_4) \cdot DP(\epsilon_4 \to \beta_2) \cdot DP(\alpha_1 \to \beta_3 + \epsilon_4)$$
$$\cdot DP(\beta_1 \to \alpha_1 + \beta_4)$$
$$\leq \sum_{\epsilon_4} DP(\alpha_1 \to \epsilon_4) \cdot p \cdot p \cdot 1$$
$$= p^2, \text{ by Theorem 2.}$$

Case 2: $\alpha_2 = \alpha_3 = 0$, $\alpha_4 \neq 0$
$\Rightarrow \epsilon_1 = \epsilon_2 = \epsilon_5 = 0$, $\epsilon_3 \neq 0$, $\beta_1 \neq 0$

$$DP(\alpha \to \beta) = \sum_{\epsilon_3, \epsilon_4} DP(\alpha_4 \to \epsilon_3) \cdot DP(\alpha_1 \to \epsilon_4) \cdot DP(\epsilon_3 \to \beta_1)$$
$$\cdot DP(\alpha_4 + \epsilon_4 \to \beta_2 + \epsilon_3) \cdot DP(\alpha_1 \to \alpha_4 + \beta_3 + \epsilon_4)$$
$$\cdot DP(\beta_1 \to \alpha_1 + \beta_4)$$
$$\leq p^3 \cdot \sum_{\epsilon_4} DP(\alpha_1 \to \epsilon_4) \cdot DP(\alpha_1 \to \alpha_4 + \beta_3 + \epsilon_4)$$
$$\cdot \sum_{\epsilon_3} DP(\alpha_4 + \epsilon_4 \to \beta_2 + \epsilon_3)$$
$$\leq p^3, \text{ by Theorem 2.}$$

Case 3: $\alpha_2 = 0$, $\alpha_3 \neq 0$
$\Rightarrow \epsilon_1 = 0$, $\epsilon_2 \neq 0$, $\epsilon_5 \neq 0$

$$DP(\alpha \to \beta) = \sum_{\epsilon_2,\epsilon_3,\epsilon_4,\epsilon_5} DP(\alpha_3 \to \epsilon_2) \cdot DP(\alpha_4 \to \epsilon_3) \cdot DP(\alpha_1 \to \epsilon_4)$$
$$\cdot DP(\epsilon_2 \to \epsilon_5) \cdot DP(\alpha_3 + \epsilon_3 \to \beta_1 + \epsilon_2)$$
$$\cdot DP(\alpha_4 + \epsilon_4 \to \alpha_3 + \beta_2 + \epsilon_3)$$
$$\cdot DP(\alpha_1 + \epsilon_5 \to \alpha_4 + \beta_3 + \epsilon_4)$$
$$\cdot DP(\beta_1 \to \alpha_1 + \beta_4 + \epsilon_5)$$
$$\leq p^2 \cdot \sum_{\epsilon_3} DP(\alpha_4 \to \epsilon_3) \cdot \sum_{\epsilon_2} DP(\alpha_3 + \epsilon_3 \to \beta_1 + \epsilon_2)$$
$$\cdot \sum_{\epsilon_4} DP(\alpha_1 \to \epsilon_4) \cdot (\alpha_4 + \epsilon_4 \to \alpha_3 + \beta_2 + \epsilon_3)$$
$$\cdot \sum_{\epsilon_5} DP(\beta_1 \to \alpha_1 + \beta_4 + \epsilon_5) \cdot DP(\alpha_1 + \epsilon_5 \to \alpha_4 + \beta_3 + \epsilon_4)$$
$$\leq p^2, \text{ by Theorem 2.}$$

Case 4: $\alpha_2 \neq 0$, $\alpha_3 = 0$
$\Rightarrow \epsilon_2 = 0$, $\epsilon_1 \neq 0$, $\epsilon_5 \neq 0$

$$DP(\alpha \to \beta) = \sum_{\epsilon_1,\epsilon_3,\epsilon_4,\epsilon_5} DP(\alpha_2 \to \epsilon_1) \cdot DP(\alpha_4 \to \epsilon_3) \cdot DP(\alpha_1 + \epsilon_1 \to \epsilon_4)$$
$$\cdot DP(\alpha_2 \to \epsilon_5) \cdot DP(\epsilon_3 \to \alpha_2 + \beta_1)$$
$$\cdot DP(\alpha_4 + \epsilon_4 \to \beta_2 + \epsilon_3) \cdot DP(\alpha_1 + \epsilon_1 + \epsilon_5 \to \alpha_4 + \beta_3 + \epsilon_4)$$
$$\cdot DP(\beta_1 \to \alpha_1 + \beta_4 + \epsilon_1 + \epsilon_5)$$
$$\leq p^2 \cdot \sum_{\epsilon_3} DP(\alpha_4 \to \epsilon_3) \cdot DP(\epsilon_3 \to \alpha_2 + \beta_1)$$
$$\cdot \sum_{\epsilon_4} DP(\alpha_4 + \epsilon_4 \to \beta_2 + \epsilon_3) \cdot \sum_{\epsilon_1} DP(\alpha_1 + \epsilon_1 \to \epsilon_4)$$
$$\cdot \sum_{\epsilon_5} DP(\alpha_1 + \epsilon_1 + \epsilon_5 \to \alpha_4 + \beta_3 + \epsilon_4)$$
$$\cdot DP(\beta_1 \to \alpha_1 + \beta_4 + \epsilon_1 + \epsilon_5)$$
$$\leq p^2, \text{ by Theorem 2.}$$

Case 5: $\alpha_2 \neq 0$, $\alpha_3 \neq 0$
$\Rightarrow \epsilon_1 \neq 0$, $\epsilon_2 \neq 0$

$$DP(\alpha \rightarrow \beta) \leq p^2 \cdot \sum_{\epsilon_3} DP(\alpha_4 \rightarrow \epsilon_3) \cdot \sum_{\epsilon_2} DP(\alpha_3 + \epsilon_3 \rightarrow \alpha_2 + \beta_1 + \epsilon_2)$$
$$\cdot \sum_{\epsilon_5} DP(\alpha_2 + \epsilon_2 \rightarrow \epsilon_5) \cdot \sum_{\epsilon_4} DP(\alpha_4 + \epsilon_4 \rightarrow \alpha_3 + \beta_2 + \epsilon_3)$$
$$\cdot \sum_{\epsilon_1} DP(\alpha_1 + \epsilon_1 \rightarrow \epsilon_4) \cdot DP(\alpha_1 + \epsilon_1 + \epsilon_5 \rightarrow \alpha_4 + \beta_3 + \epsilon_4)$$
$$\cdot DP(\beta_1 \rightarrow \alpha_1 + \beta_4 + \epsilon_1 + \epsilon_5)$$
$$\leq p^2, \text{ by Theorem 2.}$$

This completes the proof of the theorem.

From the results, we see that EFN Type-I requires a much larger number of rounds to be secure against differential cryptanalysis as compared to EFN Type-II and EFN Type-III. The results for EFN Type-II and Type-III are comparable with the main results of [6] whereby the average differential probabilities over at least 2 rounds of Feistel-variant A structure and 1 round of Feistel-variant B structure are both upperbounded by p^2. On the other hand, the average differential probabilities over at least 5 rounds of CLEFIA, MISTY-FO-variant A, B, C and D structures are upperbounded by $p^4 + 2p^5$, p^4, p^4, $2p^4$ and $2p^4$ respectively.

4   Impossible Differential Characteristics of EFN

We denote the Encryption and Decryption Characteristics Matrices of EFN Type-I, Type-II and Type-III by E_1 and D_1, E_2 and D_2, and, E_3 and D_3 respectively.

$$E_1 = \begin{pmatrix} 0 & 1 & 0 & \cdots & 0 \\ 0 & 0 & 1 & \ddots & \vdots \\ \vdots & \vdots & 0 & \ddots & 0 \\ 0 & \cdots & \cdots & 0 & 1 \\ 1 & 0 & \cdots & 0 & 1_F \end{pmatrix}_{n \times n}, D_1 = \begin{pmatrix} 0 & \cdots & 0 & 1_F & 1 \\ 1 & \ddots & \vdots & 0 & 0 \\ 0 & \ddots & 0 & \vdots & \vdots \\ \vdots & \ddots & 1 & 0 & 0 \\ 0 & \cdots & 0 & 1 & 0 \end{pmatrix}_{n \times n}$$

$$E_2 = \begin{pmatrix} 0 & 1 & 0 & \cdots & 0 \\ 0 & 1_F & 1 & \ddots & \vdots \\ \vdots & 0 & 0 & \ddots & 0 \\ 0 & \vdots & \vdots & \ddots & 1 \\ 1 & 0 & \cdots & 0 & 1_F \end{pmatrix}_{n \times n}, D_2 = \begin{pmatrix} 0 & 0 & \cdots & \cdots & 0 & 1_F & 1 \\ 1 & 0 & \cdots & \cdots & \cdots & 0 & 0 \\ 1_F & 1 & 0 & \cdots & \cdots & 0 & 0 \\ 0 & 0 & \ddots & \ddots & & \vdots & \vdots \\ \vdots & \ddots & 1_F & \ddots & \ddots & \vdots & \vdots \\ \vdots & \vdots & \ddots & \ddots & \ddots & 0 & \vdots \\ 0 & 0 & \cdots & 0 & 0 & 1 & 0 \end{pmatrix}_{n \times n}$$

$$\mathbf{E}_3 = \begin{pmatrix} 0 & 1 & 0 & \cdots & 0 \\ 0 & 1_F & 1 & \ddots & \vdots \\ \vdots & 0 & 1_F & \ddots & 0 \\ 0 & \cdots & \ddots & \ddots & 1 \\ 1 & 0 & \cdots & 0 & 1_F \end{pmatrix}_{n \times n} , \mathbf{D}_3 = \begin{pmatrix} 1_F & 1_F & \cdots & 1_F & 1 \\ 1 & 0 & \cdots & 0 & 0 \\ 1_F & 1 & \ddots & \vdots & \vdots \\ \vdots & \ddots & \ddots & 0 & 0 \\ 1_F & \cdots & 1_F & 1 & 0 \end{pmatrix}_{n \times n}$$

Since all the matrices are 1-property matrices, we can apply the corresponding networks to Algorithm 1 in [1]. The following results are based on the stimulation. Here $\alpha_i \neq 0$ and $\beta_i \neq 0$.

Proposition 1. *The maximum number of rounds for impossible differential characteristics that can be found by the U-method for EFN Type-I is $n^2 + n - 1$. The generalized impossible differential characteristics is*

$$(\alpha_1, 0, \cdots, 0) \nrightarrow_{n^2+n-1} (0, \cdots, 0, \beta_n).$$

Proposition 2. *For n even, the maximum number of rounds for impossible differential characteristics that can be found by the U-method for EFN Type-II is $2n + 1$. The generalized impossible differential characteristics are*

$$(\alpha_1, 0, \cdots, 0) \nrightarrow_{2n+1} (0, \beta_2, 0, \cdots, 0),$$

$$(0, 0, \alpha_3, 0, \cdots, 0) \nrightarrow_{2n+1} (0, 0, 0, \beta_4, 0, \cdots, 0),$$

$$\vdots$$

$$(0, \cdots, 0, \alpha_{n-1}, 0) \nrightarrow_{2n+1} (0, \cdots, 0, \beta_n).$$

Proposition 3. *The maximum number of rounds for impossible differential characteristics that can be found by the U-method for EFN Type-III is $n + 2$. An generalized impossible differential characteristics is*

$$(0, \cdots, 0, \alpha_n) \nrightarrow_{n+2} (0, \beta_2, 0, \cdots, 0).$$

In particular, we consider the case when $n = 4$. Readers may refer to the appendix for the tables which depict an impossible differential characteristics for each EFN.

For EFN Type-I, the matrices are

$$\mathbf{E}_1 = \begin{pmatrix} 0 & 1 & 0 & 0 \\ 0 & 0 & 1 & 0 \\ 0 & 0 & 0 & 1 \\ 1 & 0 & 0 & 1_F \end{pmatrix}, \mathbf{D}_1 = \begin{pmatrix} 0 & 0 & 1_F & 1 \\ 1 & 0 & 0 & 0 \\ 0 & 1 & 0 & 0 \\ 0 & 0 & 1 & 0 \end{pmatrix},$$

and an impossible differential characteristics is $(\gamma, 0, 0, 0) \nrightarrow_{19} (0, 0, 0, \gamma)$.

For EFN Type-II, the matrices are

$$\mathbf{E}_2 = \begin{pmatrix} 0 & 1 & 0 & 0 \\ 0 & 1_F & 1 & 0 \\ 0 & 0 & 0 & 1 \\ 1 & 0 & 0 & 1_F \end{pmatrix}, \mathbf{D}_2 = \begin{pmatrix} 0 & 0 & 1_F & 1 \\ 1 & 0 & 0 & 0 \\ 1_F & 1 & 0 & 0 \\ 0 & 0 & 1 & 0 \end{pmatrix},$$

and an impossible differential characteristics is $(\gamma, 0, 0, 0) \not\rightarrow_9 (0, \gamma, 0, 0)$.

For EFN Type-III, the matrices are

$$\mathbf{E}_3 = \begin{pmatrix} 0 & 1 & 0 & 0 \\ 0 & 1_F & 1 & 0 \\ 0 & 0 & 1_F & 1 \\ 1 & 0 & 0 & 1_F \end{pmatrix}, \mathbf{D}_3 = \begin{pmatrix} 1_F & 1_F & 1_F & 1 \\ 1 & 0 & 0 & 0 \\ 1_F & 1 & 0 & 0 \\ 1_F & 1_F & 1 & 0 \end{pmatrix},$$

and an impossible differential characteristics is $(0, 0, 0, \gamma) \not\rightarrow_6 (0, \gamma, 0, 0)$.

As in the case of differential cryptanalysis, we see that EFN Type-I is the most vulunerable to impossible differential cryptanalysis, as compared to EFN Type-II and EFN Type-III.

5   Conclusion

This paper presented some results regarding the security of three types of EFN against differential cryptanalysis. We also used the U-method to find the maximum number of rounds for impossible differential characteristics and generalized impossible differential characteristics for the various EFNs. Note that the results hold for all EFNs with bijective F-functions. The security against differential cryptanalysis and impossible differential cryptanalysis improve with more F-functions in each round. For future work, we will analyze the security of the EFNs against impossible differential cryptanalysis by taking into account the model for the F-function.

Acknowlegements. The author would like to thank Dr Khoongming Khoo for his invaluable suggestions with this paper.

References

1. Kim, J., Hong, S., Sung, J., Lee, S., Lim, J., Sung, S.: Impossible Differential Cryptanalysis fir Block Cipher Structures. In: Johansson, T., Maitra, S. (eds.) INDOCRYPT 2003. LNCS, vol. 2904, pp. 82–96. Springer, Heidelberg (2003)
2. Ibrahim, S., Maarof, M.A., Ngadiman, M.S.: Practical Security against Differential Cryptanalysis for Extended Feistel Network. Universiti Teknologi Malaysia
3. Sung, J., Lee, A., Lim, J., Hong, S., Park, S.: Provable Security for the Skipjack-like Structure against Differential Cryptanalyis and Linear Cryptanalysis. In: Okamoto, T. (ed.) ASIACRYPT 2000. LNCS, vol. 1976, pp. 274–288. Springer, Heidelberg (2000)
4. Schneier, B., Kelsey, J.: Unbalanced Feistel Networks and Block-Cipher Design. In: Gollmann, D. (ed.) FSE 1996. LNCS, vol. 1039, pp. 121–144. Springer, Heidelberg (1996)

5. Aoki, K., Ohta, K.: Strict evaluation of the maximum average of differential probability and the maximum average of linear probability. IEICE Transactions fundamentals of Electronics, Communications and Computer Sciences 1, 2–8 (1997)
6. Kim, J., Lee, C., Sung, J., Hong, S., Lee, S., Lim, J.: Seven New Block Cipher Structures with Provable Security against Differential Cryptanalysis. IEICE Transactions fundamentals of Electronics, Communications and Computer Sciences 10, 3047–3058 (2008)

A   Tables and Diagrams

Table 4. A 19-round impossible differential characteristics of EFN Type-I

Round (r)	Difference vector	α^r
$\downarrow$0	$(1^*, 0, 0, 0)$	$(\gamma, 0, 0, 0)$
1	$(0, 1^*, 0, 0)$	$(0, \gamma, 0, 0)$
2	$(0, 0, 1^*, 0)$	$(0, 0, \gamma, 0)$
3	$(0, 0, 0, 1^*)$	$(0, 0, 0, \gamma)$
4	$(1^*, 0, 0, 1)$	$(\gamma, 0, 0, \delta)$
5	$(1, 1^*, 0, 1)$	$(\delta, \gamma, 0, \delta)$
6	$(1, 1, 1^*, 1)$	$(\delta, \delta, \gamma, \delta)$
7	$(1, 1, 1, 2^*)$	$(\delta, \delta, \delta, \gamma \oplus \delta)$
8	$(2^*, 1, 1, 3)$	$(\gamma \oplus \delta, \delta, \delta, ?)$
9	$(3, 2^*, 1, 4)$	$(?, \gamma \oplus \delta, \delta, ?)$
	$(2, 1^*, 1, 1)$	$(?, \gamma, \delta, \delta)$
10	$(1, 2, 1^*, 0)$	$(\delta, ?, \gamma, 0)$
11	$(0, 1, 2, 1^*)$	$(0, \delta, ?, \gamma)$
12	$(1^*, 0, 1, 1)$	$(\gamma, 0, \delta, \delta)$
13	$(1, 1^*, 0, 0)$	$(\delta, \gamma, 0, 0)$
14	$(0, 1, 1^*, 0)$	$(0, \delta, \gamma, 0)$
15	$(0, 0, 1, 1^*)$	$(0, 0, \delta, \gamma)$
16	$(1^*, 0, 0, 0)$	$(\gamma, 0, 0, 0)$
17	$(0, 1^*, 0, 0)$	$(0, \gamma, 0, 0)$
18	$(0, 0, 1^*, 0)$	$(0, 0, \gamma, 0)$
$\uparrow$19	$(0, 0, 0, 1^*)$	$(0, 0, 0, \gamma)$

Table 5. A 9-round impossible differential characteristics of EFN Type-II

Round (r)	Difference vector	α^r
$\downarrow 0$	$(1^*,0,0,0)$	$(\gamma,0,0,0)$
1	$(0,1^*,0,0)$	$(0,\gamma,0,0)$
2	$(0,1,1^*,0)$	$(0,\delta,\gamma,0)$
3	$(0,1,1,1^*)$	$(0,\delta,\delta,\gamma)$
4	$(1^*,1,1,2)$	$(\gamma,\delta,\delta,?)$
5	$(2,2^*,1,3)$	$(?,\gamma\oplus\delta,\delta,?)$
6	$(3,4,2^*,4)$	$(?,?,\gamma\oplus\delta,?)$
	$(1,1,1^*,0)$	$(\delta,\delta,\gamma,0)$
7	$(0,0,1,1^*)$	$(0,0,\delta,\gamma)$
8	$(1^*,0,0,0)$	$(\gamma,0,0,0)$
$\uparrow 9$	$(0,1^*,0,0)$	$(0,\gamma,0,0)$

Table 6. A 6-round impossible differential characteristics of EFN Type-III

Round (r)	Difference vector	α^r
$\downarrow 0$	$(0,0,0,1^*)$	$(0,0,0,\gamma)$
1	$(1^*,0,0,1)$	$(\gamma,0,0,\delta)$
2	$(1,1^*,0,1)$	$(\delta,\gamma,0,\delta)$
3	$(1,2,1^*,1)$	$(\delta,?,\gamma,\delta)$
4	$(1,3,3,2^*)$	$(\delta,?,?,\gamma\oplus\delta)$
5	$(2^*,4,6,5)$	$(\gamma\oplus\delta,?,?,?)$
	$(1^*,0,0,0)$	$(\gamma,0,0,0)$
$\uparrow 6$	$(0,1^*,0,0)$	$(0,\gamma,0,0)$

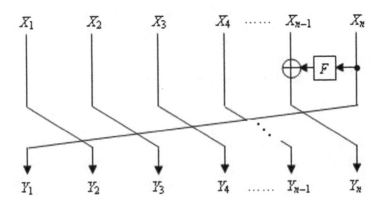

Fig. 1. EFN Type-I transformation structure

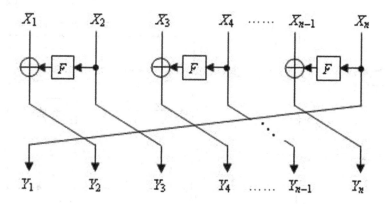

Fig. 2. EFN Type-II transformation structure

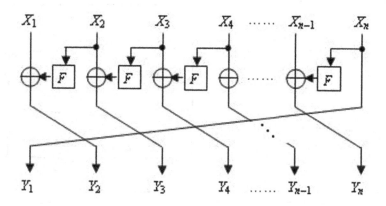

Fig. 3. EFN Type-III transformation structure

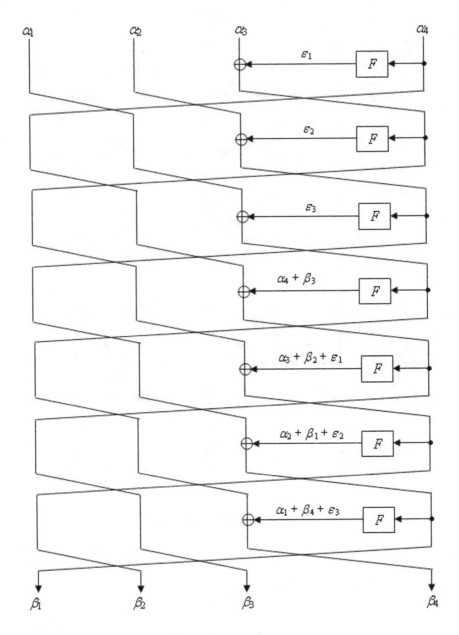

Fig. 4. 7-round differential for EFN Type-I when $n = 4$

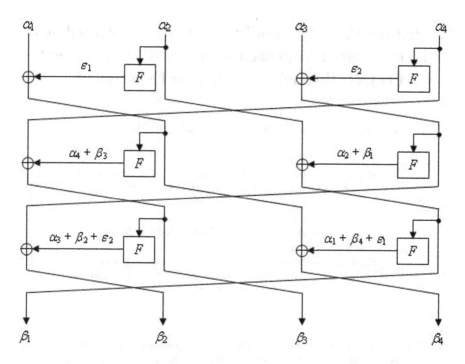

Fig. 5. 3-round differential for EFN Type-II when $n = 4$

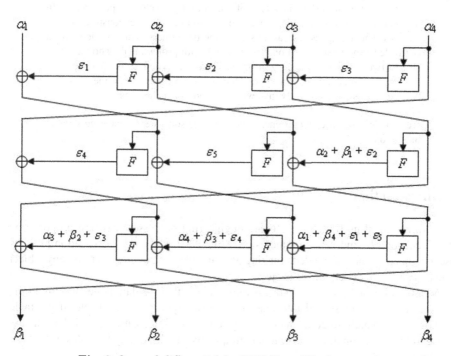

Fig. 6. 3-round differential for EFN Type-III when $n = 4$

Evaluating the Applicability of a Use Case Precedence Diagram Based Approach in Software Development Projects through a Controlled Experiment

José Antonio Pow-Sang[1,3], Arturo Nakasone[2], Ana María Moreno[3], and Ricardo Imbert[3]

[1] Departamento de Ingeniería, Pontificia Universidad Católica del Perú,
Av. Universitaria 1801, San Miguel, Lima 32, Peru
japowsang@pucp.edu.pe
[2] National Institute of Informatics
2-1-2 Hitotsubashi, Chiyoda Ku, Tokyo 101-8430, Japan
arturonakasone@nii.ac.jp
[3] Facultad de Informática, Universidad Politécnica de Madrid,
Campus de Montegancedo, 28660 Boadilla del Monte (Madrid), Spain
{rimbert,ammoreno}@fi.upm.es

Abstract. Use Cases are the most utilized technique to specify software requirements. Currently, there are several proposals based on this technique to address the problem of determining the scope and construction sequence of a software, but most of them lack ease of use from the developer's perspective. In this paper, we present an approach to determine software construction sequences which emphasizes easiness from the developers' point of view and a controlled experiment based on this approach with professionals who have had at least two years of experience in software projects. The results obtained from this experiment show that our approach enables developers to define construction sequences more precisely than with other ad-hoc techniques.

Keywords: use case, requirements precedence, software engineering experimentation.

1 Introduction

The utilization of use cases in software engineering processes was first proposed by Ivar Jacobson [7], and, since its inclusion in the UML standard specification [13], its use has been greatly extended, making it a mandatory requirement for any object oriented software development project.

As an established practical fact, it is quite known that the data tables for any information system are classified into one of these two types: Master Table, if the table contains data which seldom changes (e.g. customer information), and Transaction Table, if the table contains data which is frequently modified (e.g. the sales order for a customer).

T.-k. Kim, T.-h. Kim, and A. Kiumi (Eds.): SecTech 2008, CCIS 29, pp. 122–137, 2009.

Based on this table classification, we identified three types of use cases: (1) use cases that deal with master table maintenance, (2) use cases that deal with transaction table maintenance, and (3) use cases that deal with data reporting.

Even though there are several approaches to determine software construction sequences that consider which requirement must be constructed first based on a simple requirements prioritization scheme, most of them do not take into consideration the developer's perspective in terms of ease of construction to define such priorities. As an example, we applied a survey among sixty undergraduate students at our university and we obtained the following requirements sequence based on their construction easiness: use cases that maintain master tables, use cases that maintain transaction tables and, finally, use cases that present reports. In spite of the fact that these poll results cannot be applied to every software project, taking into consideration the valuable opinion of developers during the analysis phase can improve considerably the project's chance of success in the end.

Our paper presents a novel technique to determine software construction sequences based on use cases precedence diagrams and the developer's point of view regarding requirements prioritization based on their ease of construction.

The rest of the paper is organized as follows: Section 2 describes the related work in the area, Section 3 details our proposed technique to define software requirements construction sequences, Section 4 presents the background scenario for the empirical study; Section 5 shows the obtained results for the experimental study; Section 6 discusses those results. Finally, a summary and our plans for future research will conclude our paper.

2 Related Work

In order to deal with the problem of construction sequence definition, there are several proposals that establish guidelines to prioritize software requirement construction by considering criteria that do not take into consideration the easiness from the developer's point of view. Denne et al. [3] propose a method called "Incremental Funding Method", which defines construction increments based on financial decisions. Evolve, a technique proposed by Rühe et al. [4][5][12][17], determines the construction sequence by using questionnaires among the stakeholders. Firesmith [6] presents general guidelines in which different perspectives from stakeholders are included, but without defining a specific technique. All these proposals, excepting the one made by Firesmith, do not utilize use cases at all and only make mention of the concept of requirements.

Moisiadis [11] proposes the realization of a use case prioritization only considering their dependencies based on existing pre and post conditions and the stakeholders' opinions. Moisiadis [10] and Kundu [9] proposed the elaboration of dependency diagrams for use cases scenarios in order to establish their priority. Some [20] utilizes activity diagrams to show the dependency between use cases. Nevertheless, none of these techniques indicates how they can be used to define construction sequences. Ryser presents the SCENT-Method technique [18] which makes use of diagrams that show all the different types of dependencies between use cases to generate test cases, although it does not properly define a technique for sequence determination.

In summary, the techniques that mainly consider the stakeholders' perspective do not include the construction of diagrams for dependency between requirements. And those ones that do consider them do not deliver guidelines on how they can be utilized to determine construction sequences. Moreover, some of them include too many relation dependency types which make the diagrams overly complex to determine an appropriate construction sequence.

3 Use Case Precedence Diagrams and the Construction Sequence

According to UML, the relations that can exist between use cases are: include, extend, and generalization. In addition to the standard, we propose the inclusion of a new relation: precedence; and all these relations will be shown in the use case precedence diagram (UCPD). The concept of this diagram was taken from Doug Rosenberg [16], who proposed the use of a similar diagram, specifying the relations "precedes" and "invoke" to determine user requirements. Fig. 1 shows an example of a UCPD.

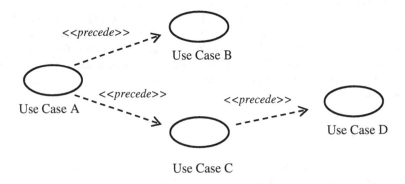

Fig. 1. Use Case Precedence Diagram

In order to obtain precedence relations between use cases, the following rules must be considered:

Rule 1. A use case U1 precedes another use case U2 if there is a precondition that corresponds to the execution of a scenario in U1 that must be fulfilled before executing a scenario of U2.

For instance, to execute a scenario from the "Make Reservation" use case, the actor must have been validated by the system (i.e. execute a login). Hence, the "Login" use case precedes the "Make Reservation" use case. This is shown in Fig. 2.

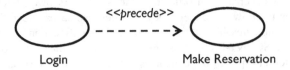

Fig. 2. Precedence rule 1 - diagram example

Rule 2. A use case U1 precedes another use case U2 if a U2 needs information that is registered by U1. For instance, to perform the payment for a reservation, this reservation must have been made. Having two use cases "Make Reservation" and "Pay Reservation", the former precedes the later. This is shown in Fig. 3.

Make Reservation   Pay Reservation

Fig. 3. Precedence rule 2 - diagram example

It is important to note that in the UCPD, Included and Extended Use Cases have not been considered since they can be part of other use cases that refer to them. Based on this UCPD, a construction sequence is defined. The use cases that are on the left side of the diagram will be implemented before the ones that are on the right side. For instance, in Fig. 1, "Use case A" will be implemented before "Use case C".

4   Experimental Design

The UCPD has been utilized in projects with students in a class to define construction increments, giving very good results. In those projects, students made use of the Rational Unified Process methodology [15] (the details of this experience are documented in [14]). Even though the advantages of using students in experiments are well known [2], our controlled experiment was performed with practitioners to determine the viability of our approach in real world projects.

For the experiment design, we considered the experimental software engineering suggestions made by Juristo & Moreno [8]. The goal of the experiment was to empirically corroborate if our approach provides more accurate results than informal techniques to determine the sequence use case construction.

Using the Goal/Question/Metric (GQM) template for goal-oriented software measurement [1], we defined this experiment as follows:

Analyze: Ad-hoc construction planning versus precedence diagram based construction planning
For the purpose of: Compare
With respect to: their accuracy
From the point of view of: the researcher
In the context of: practitioners with at least 2 years of experience in software development projects and considering that the developer is free to select the sequence to construct use cases (there are no user's constraints).

The research question was: Does our approach provide more accurate results than informal approaches when determining the sequence to construct use cases?

4.1 Variables Selection

The independent variable was the method used by subjects to define the construction sequence of use cases. The dependent variable was accuracy: the agreement between the measurement results and the true value.

For this experiment, it was considered as "true value" the fact that the easiest construction sequence for use cases is "master-transaction-reports", as identified in the introduction of this paper.

4.2 Subjects

In this experiment, we had 34 practitioners with at least 2 years in software development projects as participants. Many of the practitioners work in companies that are improving their software processes in order to obtain CMMi level 3 [19] or to obtain this certification.

Before the experiment session, we delivered a use case training class in order to standardize the knowledge of all participants. The training class was delivered four days before the experiment day.

4.3 Materials and Case Studies

The materials used in the experiment were two case studies and four questionnaires. The first case study corresponds to the elaboration of a sales system for a restaurant, and the second corresponds to the elaboration of an enrollment registration system for a high school. Both case studies are information systems.

For each case study, the following documentation was delivered: the use case diagram, the description for each use case along with its preconditions, and the information, in terms of classes or entities, that is needed by each use case.

Three questionnaires (1, 2 & 3) corresponds to questions in which subjects have to decide between two use cases and answer which one they would construct first. For instance, for the first case study, one of the questions included was:

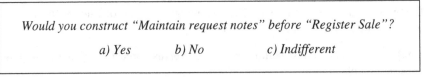

Would you construct "Maintain request notes" before "Register Sale"?

     a) Yes   *b) No*   *c) Indifferent*

Fig. 4. First case study – question sample

There are also other types of questions that allow the selection among the following use case type pairs: master-transaction, transaction-transaction, master-reports, and transaction-reports.

The fourth questionnaire was to know a practitioner's opinion regarding the easiness and usefulness of our technique, and the easiest way to construct software between master, transaction and report use cases.

In addition, in questionnaires 1, 2, and 3, we included questions regarding the sequence of tests, which were not included in this paper.

Further details of the case studies and used instruments can be found at:

http://macareo.pucp.edu.pe/japowsang/precedence/usecase.html

4.4 Tasks Performed during the Experiment

The practitioners had to apply the first case study with their ad-hoc techniques and the second one with our technique. We applied two different case studies with similar characteristics (both are information systems) in order to mitigate the learning effects. Table 1 shows the tasks carried out in the session by the practitioners.

Table 1. Tasks carried out by the practitioners

Task N°	Description
1	Receive case study 1 and questionnaire 1
2	Fill in questionnaire 1
3	Receive case study 2 and questionnaire 2
4	Elaborate use case precedence diagram for case study 2
5	Fill in questionnaire 2
6	Elaborate use case precedence diagram for case study 1
7	Fill in questionnaire 3
8	Fill in questionnaire 4

The session lasted approximately one hour and the practitioners performed 45 minutes on average to complete all the tasks. Even though it was not part of this study to know which technique demanded less time, we could observe that they spent less than 10 minutes to elaborate our proposed UCPD.

5 Results

Fig. 5 shows the answers of practitioners in terms of percentage to the question "Select the sequence to construct use cases that you normally follow if you do not have user's constraints: maintain master tables, maintain transaction tables and reports". This question was included in questionnaire 4.

In this figure, we only included the sequences with one or more answers. The sequences that nobody selected were *report-master-transaction* and *report-transaction-master*.

For the next results, we did not considered the questionnaires of subjects that answered a sequence different from *master-transaction-report* (8 participants) and one participant that did not understand how to elaborate the use case precedence diagram. We could observe that for some people who selected a different sequence, their answered options in questionnaires 2 and 3 were in disagreement with the UCPD that they themselves elaborated.

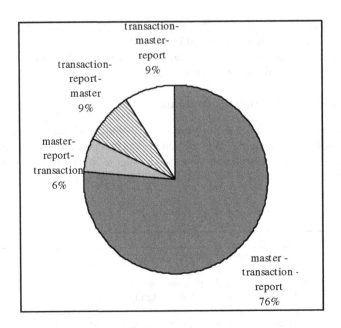

Fig. 5. Sequence of construction selected by the practitioners

5.1 Comparison between Ad-hoc and UCPD

Table 2 presents the results obtained from the case studies. We established a significance level of 0.05 to statistically test the obtained results. In order to compare these results, we have tested the percentage of correct answers.

Table 2. Descriptive statistics - Sequence of use case construction

Variable	Ad-hoc (Case Study 1)	UCPD (Case Study 2)
Observations	25	25
Minimum	0.0%	40.0%
Maximum	100.00%	100.00%
Mean	77.33%	90.40%
Std. Deviation	23.014	17.436

In order to determine if the grades obtained with each technique followed a normal distribution, we applied the Shapiro-Wilk test. Table 3 shows the results obtained with this test.

Since the computed p-value was lower than the significance level alpha=0.05, we rejected the normal distribution hypothesis for all techniques and accepted the non-normal distribution hypothesis. Due to these results, we could not use the paired sample t-test and we had to select a non-parametric alternative. The Wilkoxon signed rank test was chosen for this purpose.

Table 3. Results obtained to test normality with the Shapiro-Wilk test

Variable	Ad-hoc (Case Study 1)	UCPD (Case Study 2)
W	0.785	0.616
p-value	0.000	<0.0001
Alpha	0.05	0.05

The statistical hypotheses formulated to test both techniques were:

- H0: The distributions of the ad-hoc and UCPD-Case Study 2 are not significantly different.
- Ha: The distribution of the ad-hoc sample is shifted to the left of the distribution of the UCPD-Case Study 2.

Table 4. Wilkoxon signed rank test results ad-hoc vs. UCPD-Case Study 2

Variable	Result
V	76.000
Expected value	157.500
Variante (V)	1356.125
p-value (one-tailed)	0.014
Alpha	0.05

Since the computed p-value was lower than the significance level alpha=0.05, we rejected the null hypothesis H0 and accepted the alternative hypothesis Ha. It means that we can empirically corroborate that our proposal produces more accurate assessments than ad-hoc techniques.

5.2 Comparison between Ad-hoc and UCPD in the Same Case Study

Even though the previous results were more than enough to determine the benefits of our approach in lieu of the ad-hoc techniques, we elaborated a third questionnaire in which the practitioners had to solve case study 1 using UCPD. The next table presents the normality test for Case Study 1 using UCPD.

Table 5. Descriptive statistics sequence of use case construction

Variable	UCPD (Case Study 1)
Observations	25
Minimum	66.67%
Maximum	100.00%
Mean	87.33%
Std. Deviation	9.954

In order to determine if the grades obtained with each technique followed a normal distribution, we applied the Shapiro-Wilk test. **Table 6** shows the results obtained with this test.

Table 6. Results obtained to test normality distribution with the Shapiro-Wilk test

Variable	UCPD (Case Study 1)
W	0.757
p-value	<0.0001
Alpha	0.05

Since the computed p-value was lower than the significance level alpha=0.05, we rejected the normal distribution hypothesis for this case and accepted the non-normal distribution hypothesis. Because of these results, we could not use the paired samples t-test and we had to select a non-parametric alternative. The Wilkoxon signed rank test was chosen for this purpose.

The statistical hypotheses formulated to test both techniques were:

- H0: The distributions of the ad-hoc and UCPD using the same case study (Case Study 1) are not significantly different.
- Ha: The distribution of the ad-hoc sample is shifted to the left of the distribution of the UCPD.

Table 7. Wilkoxon signed rank test results ad-hoc vs UCPD (Case Study 1)

Variable	Result
V	63.500
Expected value	129.500
Variante (V)	1220.375
p-value (one-tailed)	0.030
Alpha	0.05

Since the computed p-value is lower than the significance level alpha=0.05, we rejected the null hypothesis H0 and accepted the alternative hypothesis Ha. With these additional results, we can truly and empirically corroborate that our proposal produces more accurate assessments than ad-hoc techniques.

5.3   Comparison between Case Studies Using UCPD

Similarly to the previous section and based on questionnaire 3, we conducted a hypothesis test to determine if the results that made use of the UCPD are significantly similar between the different case studies.

The statistical hypotheses formulated to test both scenarios were:

- H0: The distributions of the UCPD-Case Study 2 and UCPD-Case Study 1 are not significantly different.

- Ha: The distributions of the UCPD-Case Study 2 and UCPD-Case Study 1 are significantly different.

Table 8. Wilkoxon signed rank test results with UCPD for Case Studies 1 and 2

Variable	Result
V	191.000
Expected value	155.000
Variante (V)	1329.125
p-value (one-tailed)	0.330
Alpha	0.05

Since the computed p-value is greater than the significance level alpha=0.05, we did not reject the null hypothesis H0 and rejected the alternative hypothesis Ha. It means that we can empirically corroborate that our proposal produces the same accurate assessments despite the differences in both case studies.

5.4 Qualitative Results

In questionnaire 3, we included three questions about the precedence diagram. The practitioners had to evaluate the following criteria from 0 (less) to 4 (more): ease to elaborate the UCPD, usefulness of UCPD to determine the construction sequence and if he or she would utilize UCPD in his or her own software development projects.

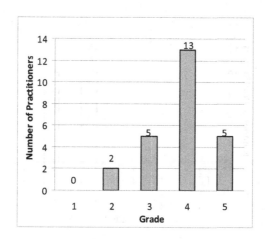

Fig. 6. Results of the question about ease to elaborate precedence diagram

From Fig. 6, it can be noted that in the question about ease to elaborate the UCPD, most of the practitioners considered that the diagram is easy to prepare. Two practitioners thought that the diagram was, in a way, difficult to prepare (grade 1). The average grade for this question was 2.84.

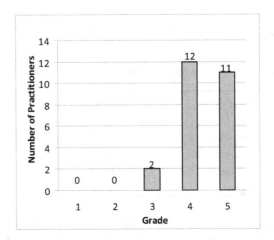

Fig. 7. Results of the question about utility of use case precedence diagram to determine sequence of construction

From Fig. 7, we noticed that in the question about usefulness of use case precedence diagram to determine the construction sequence, most of the practitioners considered that the diagram was useful to a degree in order to determine the sequence of construction. Nobody thought technique was useless (grade 0 or 1). The average grade for this question was 3.36.

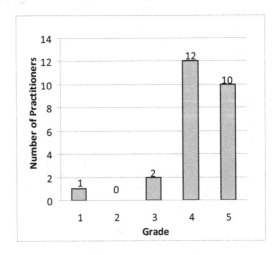

Fig. 8. Results of the question if he or she would use the diagram in software development projects

From Fig. 8, we could observe that in the question regarding if he or she would use the UCPD in his or her own projects, most of the practitioners considered that they would use the diagram. Only one practitioner would not utilize the technique (grade 0) and two were undecided. The average grade for this question was 3.2.

Finally, as it can be observed from Figures 6, 7 and 8, the questionnaire results do not disagree with the results obtained when practitioners applied the UCPD.

6   Discussion

In this section, we discuss various threats to validity of the empirical study and the way we attempted to alleviate them.

6.1   Threats to Construct Validity

The construct validity is the degree to which the independent and the dependent variables are accurately measured by the measurement instruments used in the study. Our questionnaires allowed us to quantitatively measure the precision of the ad-hoc and UCPD techniques through correct answer percentage calculations. In addition, our questions considered the construction selection among a fixed set of use case type pairs: master-transaction, transaction-transaction, master-reports, and transaction-reports. This allowed us to compare the obtained results for both case studies.

6.2   Threats to Internal Validity

The internal validity is the degree to which conclusions can be drawn about cause - effect of independent variables on the dependent variables, and, seeing the results of the experiment, we could conclude that an empirical evidence of the existing relationship between the independent and the dependent variables exists. We have tackled different aspects that could threaten the internal validity of the study.

Differences among subjects. The subjects had different background and some of them did not utilize use cases at work, but everybody knew about requirements management. To minimize this problem, we performed a training session regarding use cases previous to the execution of the experiment.

Learning effects. The application of two different case studies cancelled the learning effect due to similarities.

Knowledge of the universe of discourse. We used the same case studies (with the same type of information system) for all subjects.

Fatigue effects. Each practitioner took one hour on average per session to apply both case studies and answer questionnaires. So, fatigue was not relevant.

Persistence effects. The practitioners had never done a similar experiment before.

Subject motivation. The practitioners were motivated because they wanted to know about new techniques to improve their work. Some of them are working in companies that are preparing to obtain CMMi level 3.

6.3   Threats to External Validity

One threat to external validity was identified which limited the ability to apply any such generalization: the materials. In the experiment, we tried to utilize case studies which can be good representations of real life cases. Although the subjects came from a business environment, more empirical studies with real life cases from software companies must be performed.

Another aspect that could limit generalization is the fact that some practitioners considered that the easiest construction sequence from the developer's perspective was different from the master-transaction-report sequence. From the point of view of these practitioners, use cases regarding master maintenance are not important, and the technique could be useful if only use cases regarding transactions and reports were considered.

7 Conclusions and Future Work

This paper presents our approach to determine software requirement construction sequences based on use case precedence diagrams from the developer's perspective. This technique has been used previously in projects with students that used the Rational Unified Process model to determine the use cases to be constructed for each stage of the development process, with very good results and good comments from the students themselves.

We also included a controlled experiment in which UCPD is applied in case studies by practitioners and the obtained results show that our approach has more significant advantages over the utilization of ad-hoc techniques. And, even though polls among students indicated that the easiest way to construct use cases was through the master-transaction-reports sequence, for some practitioners, that was not the case. As a future work, we plan to adapt our technique, so it will be able to consider other developers' and other stakeholders' perspectives.

Acknowledgments

We are indebted to Natalia Juristo from Technical University of Madrid, for her valuable comments for the preparation of the experiment included in this paper. We would like to thank to all of the participants of the experiment.

This research work has been performed with the support of Dirección Académica de Investigación of Pontificia Universidad Católica del Perú, under projects DAI-E039 and DAI-4051.

References

1. Basili, V.R., Caldiera, G., Rombach, H.D.: Goal Question Metric Paradigm. In: Marciniak, J.J. (ed.) Encyclopedia of Software Engineering. Wiley, Chichester (1994)
2. Carver, J., Jaccheri, L., Morasca, S.: Issues in Using Students in Empirical Studies in Software Engineering Education. In: METRICS 2003, p. 239. IEEE Computer Society, Los Alamitos (2003)
3. Denne, M., Cleland-Huang, J.: The Incremental Funding Method: Data-Driven Software Development. IEEE Software 21(1) (2004)

4. Du, G., McElroy, J., Ruhe, G.: Ad Hoc Versus Systematic Planning of Software Releases - A Three-Staged Experiment. In: Münch, J., Vierimaa, M. (eds.) PROFES 2006. LNCS, vol. 4034, pp. 435–440. Springer, Heidelberg (2006)
5. Du, G., McElroy, J., Ruhe, G.: A family of empirical studies to compare informal and optimization-based planning of software releases. In: ISESE 2006, pp. 212–221. IEEE Computer Society, Los Alamitos (2006)
6. Firesmith, D.: Prioritizing Requirements. Journal of Object Technology 3(8) (2004), http://www.jot.fm
7. Jacobson, I.: Object-Oriented Software Engineering. In: A Use Case Driven Approach. Addison-Wesley, Reading (1992)
8. Juristo, N., Moreno, A.M.: Basics of Software Engineering Experimentation. Kluwer Academic Publishers, Boston (2001)
9. Kundu, D., Samanta, D.: A Novel Approach of Prioritizing Use Case Scenarios. In: APSEC 2007, pp. 542–549. IEEE Computer Society, Los Alamitos (2007)
10. Moisiadis, F.: Prioritizing Scenario Evolution. In: ICRE 2000, pp. 85–94. IEEE Computer Society, Los Alamitos (2000)
11. Moisiadis, F.: Prioritising Use Cases and Scenarios. In: TOOLS'37-2000, pp. 108–119. IEEE Computer Society, Los Alamitos (2000)
12. Ngo-The, A., Ruhe, G.: A systematic approach for solving the wicked problem of software release planning. In: Soft Computing, vol. 12, pp. 95–108. Springer, Heidelberg (2008)
13. Object Management Group, OMG Unified Modeling Language USA (2008), http://www.uml.org
14. Pow-Sang, J.A., Jolay-Vasquez, E.: An Approach of a Technique for Effort Estimation of Iterations in Software Projects. In: APSEC 2006, pp. 367–376. IEEE Computer Society, Los Alamitos (2006)
15. Rational Software, Rational Unified Process version 2001A.04.00.13, USA (2001)
16. Rosenberg, D., Scott, K.: Use Case Driven Object Modeling with UML. Addison-Wesley, Massachusets (1999)
17. Ruhe, G., Omolade, M.: The Art and Science of Software Release Planning. IEEE Software 22(1), 47–53 (2005)
18. Ryser, J., Glinz, M.: Using Dependency Charts to Improve Scenario-Based Testing. In: 17th International Conference on Testing Computer Software TCS 2000, Washington D.C., USA (2000)
19. Software Engineering Institute (SEI), Capability Maturity Model® Integration, http://www.sei.cmu.edu/cmmi/
20. Some, S.: Specifying Use Case Sequencing Constraints using Description Elements. In: Sixth International Workshop on Scenarios and State Machines (SCESM 2007), vol. 4. IEEE Computer Society, Los Alamitos (2007)

Appendix: Results from Questionnaires

Tables 9, 10, 11 and 12 show the results from questionnaire 1, 2 and 3. We have not included in the results the questionnaires of subjects that answered a sequence different from master-transaction-report (8 participants) and one participant that did not understand how to elaborate the use case precedence diagram.

Table 9. Results from Questionnarie 1 (0 is incorrect answer an 1 is correct answer)

Participant	Question						% of Correct Answers
	1	2	3	4	5	6	
1	0	0	0	0	0	0	0.00
2	1	0	0	1	0	0	33.33
3	1	1	1	1	1	1	100.00
4	1	1	1	1	1	1	100.00
5	1	1	1	0	1	1	83.33
6	1	0	1	1	1	1	83.33
7	1	0	1	1	1	1	83.33
8	1	0	1	1	1	1	83.33
9	1	1	0	1	1	1	83.33
10	1	0	1	1	1	1	83.33
11	1	0	1	1	1	0	66.67
12	1	1	0	1	0	0	50.00
13	1	1	1	1	1	1	100.00
14	1	0	1	0	1	1	66.67
15	1	1	1	1	1	1	100.00
16	1	1	1	1	0	1	83.33
17	1	1	1	1	1	1	100.00
18	1	1	1	1	1	0	83.33
19	1	0	1	1	1	1	83.33

Table 10. Results from Questionnarie 1 (cont.)

Participant	Question						% of Correct Answers
	1	2	3	4	5	6	
20	1	0	1	1	0	1	66.67
21	1	1	1	1	1	0	83.33
22	1	1	1	1	1	1	100.00
23	1	0	1	1	1	1	83.33
24	1	0	1	1	1	0	66.67
25	1	1	1	1	0	0	66.67

Table 11. Results from Questionnarie 2 (0 is incorrect answer an 1 is correct answer)

Participant	Question					% of Correct Answers
	1	2	3	4	5	
1	1	1	1	0	1	80.00
2	1	1	0	1	1	80.00
3	1	1	0	0	1	60.00
4	0	1	0	0	1	40.00
5	1	1	1	1	1	100.00
6	1	1	1	1	1	100.00
7	0	1	1	0	1	60.00
8	1	1	1	1	1	100.00
9	1	1	1	1	1	100.00
10	1	1	1	1	1	100.00

Table 11. (*Continued*)

11	1	1	1	1	1	100.00
12	1	1	1	1	1	100.00
13	1	1	1	1	1	100.00
14	1	1	1	1	1	100.00
15	1	1	1	1	1	100.00
16	1	1	1	1	1	100.00
17	1	1	1	1	1	100.00
18	1	1	1	1	1	100.00
19	1	1	0	0	1	60.00
20	1	1	1	1	1	100.00
21	1	1	1	1	1	100.00
22	1	1	1	1	1	100.00
23	1	1	1	1	1	100.00
24	1	1	1	1	1	100.00
25	1	0	1	1	1	80.00

Table 12. Results from Questionnarie 3 (0 is incorrect answer an 1 is correct answer)

Participant	Question						% of Correct Answers
	1	2	3	4	5	6	
1	1	1	1	0	1	1	83.33
2	1	1	1	1	1	1	100.00
3	1	1	1	1	1	1	100.00
4	1	1	1	1	0	1	83.33
5	1	1	0	1	1	1	83.33
6	1	0	1	1	1	0	66.67
7	1	0	1	1	1	1	83.33
8	1	1	0	1	1	1	83.33
9	1	1	1	1	1	1	100.00
10	1	1	1	1	0	1	83.33
11	1	1	1	1	1	0	83.33
12	1	1	1	1	1	1	100.00
13	1	1	1	1	1	1	100.00
14	1	1	1	1	0	1	83.33
15	1	1	0	1	1	1	83.33
16	1	1	1	1	1	1	100.00
17	1	1	1	1	1	1	100.00
18	1	1	1	1	0	1	83.33
19	1	1	1	1	1	1	100.00
20	1	1	1	1	0	1	83.33
21	1	1	1	1	0	1	83.33
22	1	1	0	1	1	1	83.33
23	1	1	0	1	1	1	83.33
24	1	1	1	1	0	1	83.33
25	1	1	1	1	0	0	66.67

Software Project Profitability Analysis Using Temporal Probabilistic Reasoning; An Empirical Study with the CASSE Framework

Joseph K. Balikuddembe, Isaac O. Osunmakinde, and Antoine Bagula

Department of Computer Science, University of Cape Town
Private Bag Rondebosch 7701, South Africa
{jbalikud,segun,bagula}@cs.uct.ac.za

Abstract. Undertaking adequate risk management by understanding project requirements and ensuring that viable estimates are made on software projects require extensive application and sophisticated techniques of analysis and interpretation. Informative techniques and feedback mechanisms that help to assess how well and efficiently a specific development methodology is performing are still scanty. Analyzing project tasks would enhance how well individual tasks are estimated, how well they are defined, and whether items are completed on-time and on-budget. In this paper, we propose a temporal probabilistic model that addresses feedback control mechanisms in project planning using the Complex Adaptive Systems Software Engineering framework (CASSE). We have tested our approach in industry with a software development company in South Africa on two commercial project evaluations. Our preliminary results show that the temporal probabilistic model of the framework demonstrably enhances practitioners' understanding in managing software projects profitably - hence increasing business sustainability and management.

Keywords: Requirement Engineering, Project Management, Project Profitability, Probabilistic Modeling, CASSE Framework.

1 Introduction

Many projects fail in their expected scope, benefits, cost and time targets due to inadequate technical skills or management quality [1]. Conventionally, a project should deliver agreed-upon functionality on time and within budget, governed by the overall objective of maximizing the net present value of all cash flows of that project. However, in the practice of software engineering today, it is still a central issue that total budget and human resources are frequently not managed optimally to bring about successful project completion and optimal production [2].

Recent studies show that most developments are more expensive than projected, with processes rendered more difficult through series of problems including poor project management, cost and schedule overruns, poor quality software and under-motivated developers [3]. Failure to anticipate these uncertainties and to link the planning capabilities of different sections of project management, particularly with

T.-k. Kim, T.-h. Kim, and A. Kiumi (Eds.): SecTech 2008, CCIS 29, pp. 138–150, 2009.

budget optimization while analyzing profitability, leads to disconnected silos of information which may limit the potential benefits of the whole project.

Our approach aims at establishing a link between management capabilities. It examines the strategic, process and organizational issues that enterprises need to address in order to implement world-class development strategies that generate value. We have perceived a compelling need for organizations to link their projects to their corporate strategies and to train advanced project management skills, which will better enable projects to survive shifting organizational priorities. Accordingly, and to meet this need, our framework is based on the notion that economic concepts, models and tools can help to advance understanding and improvement of the development of software and the processes that produce it.

2 Rationale

The planning decision is essentially a strategic process which requires planning for requirements of varied resources and types relating to every time period of the planning horizon [4]. Inevitably, failure to interpret different complexities within the planning process results in huge project bottlenecks. Misunderstanding and management of software project risks lead to a variety of problems, including cost and schedule overruns, unmet user requirements, and the production of systems that are unused or do not deliver business value [5]. In some instances, projects have been characterized by project estimates being made to appear lower than they would be in reality, with a hope of getting final project approval. Such a predicament affects the overall development portfolio.

How can we therefore integrate value-based methods into project planning and control for strategic business valuation so as to ensure that software projects are successful and profitable? Can such feedback arising out of project evaluation assist in re-aligning our development process so as to produce profitability in our engineering processes? In this work, we aim at answering these questions so as to facilitate the realignment and optimization of software development processes.

3 Coordination and Management

3.1 Project Coordination in the Agile Environment

In this paradigm shift of agile software development, software engineering project work is increasingly becoming a highly cooperative activity, and promises to continue in this way. Coordinating projects demands managerial control over time and resources. The more complex the project is, the more expensive and time consuming it becomes [6]. Project planning should consider the availability of good resources along with commitments to customers and the organization. A well-defined plan where all facts and practical aspects have been determined is the key to success.

Planning and executing are two different functions. Planning requires that consultations be held with those who are actually going to execute the plans, cross-checking facts and calculating risks using a good dose of practicality. If commitments to customers are broken, whatever the reason may be, it becomes one cause for the client to drift away from the project. Cost factors should be considered and balanced, and previous experience and best practices taken into account so as to refine the development approach.

Tracking tasks, compiling costs and expenses, and managing people involved in business projects are all made more manageable when using a project scheduling technique that views requirements as value-generating tasks with complex interdependencies. The way we schedule our resources on the project, mandated with various tasks, determines their productivity and overall performance and ultimately, the success of the project [7]. The objective of the agile development process is to create software development and maintenance processes that maximize the agility of application development. Project failure directly impacts upon customers by lowering customer satisfaction, while giving competitive advantage to our competitors. A collective and systematic project management approach is required to substantially increase the project's success rate and help to minimize the loss of benefits.

Projects are often driven and defined by customers. Management needs to review all existing projects in relation to strategy and if they are not contributing to strategy, they should be dropped. Benefits management which applies project profitability analysis as well as business strategic evaluation is therefore important. Organizations need to make the business case for the benefits that each project can bring. Benefits analysis and evaluation need to be part of the metrics that senior management use to measure the business. Success of any project must be the objective for those individuals who are making decisions for the business.

3.2 Deriving Project Value Tasks

Projects can be driven off the Use-case list and every step in the life cycle derives benefit from this list. If a project is approached from this perspective, Use-case offers rewards for each group, including analysts, project managers, clients, testers, designers, estimators and programmers. What drives all scheduling are the project requirements. Requirements play a vital role in enhancing value creation in the properties and value attributes of an entire project. The way we allocate time to these requirements must derive value in order to mitigate the unforeseen challenges on the project. [8]. If a project is likely to operate within the break-even space, without necessarily making profit, it is imperative that experienced programmers are scheduled while the inexperienced ones undertake the testing. If the project is likely to make a profit, it is essential that a combination of experienced programmers with a juniors peer program so as to disseminate knowledge and build human capital development on the project.

It is easier to quantify work done per functionality – which may occasionally be synonymous with requirements – than entire components at a time. Analyzing and achieving functionality in a bottom-up, micro value to macro system value approach, derives value for all stakeholders on the project and usually accelerates functional acceptability and project signoff [9]. By using this approach you can gauge how productive the resources on the project are and how the project is progressing. Equally, milestones can be evaluated and attained easily and issues that usually cause IT projects to fail, like inability to deliver products on time, would be mitigated.

Most researchers, in particular Nagappan [10] and Kan [11], agree that poor requirements are the biggest single source of defects in software projects. Poor requirements lead to weak estimates and over-ambitious project plans. There is enough evidence to suggest that during the early stages of the development process, most software projects are already in trouble, that project managers are overly optimistic in their perceptions, and that executives receive status reports very different from reality, depending on the risk level of the project and the amount of bias applied by the project manager [12]. Key findings suggest that executives should be skeptical of favorable status reports. Rather, they should concentrate on decreasing bias if they are to improve the accuracy of project management and reporting [13].

The software business is surely about satisfying and sustaining our clients. We can only achieve this if we firstly understand project requirements and secondly improve our reporting techniques and mechanisms on each project. However, many questions still arise as we turn our endeavours to realizing this. If we understand the client requirements well, how can we selectively implement requirements that generate value to us as a business and the clients we serve on the project? How can we analytically verify those requirements that increase our clientele commitment to the project while accelerating milestone acceptance? How can our scheduling and resource allocation mechanism help us realize value on the project throughout the project lifecycle? Our approach aims at addressing these issues using temporal probabilistic modeling and reasoning as a guiding factor in the project design space.

4   Temporal Probabilistic Reasoning

4.1   The Fundamental Theory

A Bayesian belief network is formally defined as a directed acyclic graph (DAG) represented as G = {X(G), A(G)}, where X(G) = {X_1,...,X_n}, vertices (variables) of the graph G and $A(G) \subseteq X(G) \times X(G)$, set of arcs of G. The network requires discrete random values such that if there exists random variables $X_1, \ldots, X_n$ with each having a set of some values $x_1, \ldots, x_n$ then, their joint probability density distribution can be defined as shown in equation 1 but not over time. Suppose the variable X is represented as variable V then, $\pi(V_i)$ represents a set of probabilistic parent(s) of child V_i [14]. A parent variable otherwise refers to as *cause* has a dependency with a child variable known as *effect*. Every variable V with a combination of parent(s) values on the graph G captures probabilistic knowledge as conditional probability table (CPT). A variable without a parent encodes a marginal probability. Having a Bayesian network model in place, a probabilistic inference is required for reasoning about any software project situations using the Bayes' theorem [14].

We base our modelling on the Dynamic Bayesian Networks theory defined in various works [15]. We specifically utilise this model to evaluate project performance over time by examining acceptance signoff of the various tasks on the project and how this acceptance pattern affects the overall profitability curve of the development process.

As literature suggests, Dynamic Bayesian Networks (DBN) can be understood to be interconnections of ordinary Bayesian networks over finite time steps as temporal measurements [15]. Temporal probabilistic modelling is an extension of ordinary Bayesian Networks, as defined by Bayesian Network proponents such as Muphy [16] and Choudhury [17]. Modelling is applied on key variables of interest in any domain of assessment.

Variables of a time step, usually referred to as frames, can have various impacts on the variables of the subsequent frames through temporality links across the frames. According to Russel [14], construction of the temporal model requires prior matrix, Pr (V_0); transition matrix, Pr ($V_t | V_{t-1}$); and sensor matrix, Pr ($E_t | V_t$) of state variables V and E. The three matrices can be estimated during the intra- or inter-frame learning of the model using parameter learning algorithms such as maximum likelihood estimate (MLE). The intra-frame learning estimates the conditional probability distributions (CPDs) for every time step t, while the inter-frame learns the CPDs over time. We describe these required matrices in equations 1 and 2 below.

The joint probability distribution for any frame of random variables V_1 to V_n at time t is given as:

$$Pr(V_1,...,V_n) = \prod_{i=1}^{n} Pr(V_i | \pi(V_i)) \tag{1}$$

The combined joint probability distribution for any temporal model to a finite time t is also described as:

$$Pr(V_0, V_1,...,V_t, E_1,...,E_t)$$
$$= Pr(V_0) \prod_{i=1}^{t} Pr(V_i | V_{i-1}) Pr(E_i | V_i) \tag{2}$$

These two foundational steps result in Emergent Situation Awareness (ESA) techniques used in this study.

4.2 The Emergent Situation Awareness Technology

The temporal modelling technique adopted in this work is the ESA initially proposed and developed by Osunmakinde [18]. ESA is an innovative technology, which realistically evolves temporal models and reveals what is currently happening over time in any domain of interest. One of its powerful features is its evolvement from Multivariate Time Series (MTS) data in the absence of domain experts.

ESA advances the algorithms of ordinary Bayesian Networks to evolve dynamically as it changes its network and the probabilistic distributions with time. It has 3 notable components: the learning algorithms, the probabilistic reasoner and the trend analyzer.

The learning component uses genetic algorithms to produce temporal Bayesian Networks, called frames, over the time steps from the MTS environments. The probabilistic reasoner is the Bayesian inference engine, which executes the necessary forward and backward propagations through the links of the frames and generates probable results. The trend analyzer is an interface that generates n-dimensional transition matrices of knowledge, where n corresponds to the pieces of knowledge to be revealed, e.g. a transition matrix of target probabilities, a transition matrix of target parameter values, etc.

We utilized this approach in our study to answer the following questions on the software projects: [i] What is happening on the project(s)? [ii] Why is it happening? [iii] What will happen next? [iv] What can one do about it? The experimental results discussed in the next section detail the characteristics of the projects analyzed using this technique, while fostering managerial answers to the above questions.

5   Experimental Analysis and Interpretation

5.1   The ESA as Applied to Software Projects

The case study was carried out with one of the software development houses in South Africa. In this analysis, two commercial projects were selected. Project 1 started in November 2007 and was scheduled to end in March 2008, while Project 2 was scheduled to start in February 2008 and end in April 2008. We specifically wanted to understand project progress complexities and how they impact on the overall company revenue. In our study, profitability analysis implied evaluation of the amount of time taken to complete a given task. This implementation time determines the overall cost for that project since resource inputs are valued and paid for on an hourly basis. For example, if a task was scheduled to take 40 hours, and it overlaps to 60 hours, this implies that the company is incurring more time on completing this task than earlier on anticipated, thus eroding project profits or even setting the project into loss levels. If this task implementation time has overran and worse still it has not reached acceptance standards for the client, more time would be added to satisfy client acceptance standards. More time added would imply more cost to company and less on profit. If this pattern applies to various tasks on the project and there are mechanisms of detecting such performances (such as our model) behavior, we can already detect such complexities on even ongoing projects.

Given this background therefore, we looked at one project which was complete and another ongoing one. For the completed project, we were interested in understanding how tasks were quickly completed and how best they met client requirements to be acceptable for signoff. For the ongoing project, we wanted to analyze the possible risks that were slowing the project either in terms of task completion or acceptance bottlenecks. This was for the purpose of evaluating whether there was a need to re-align the development process or optimize on resource allocation. Our model would help capture these evolving properties of the project.

Both projects selected were utilizing requirements of the same product-line, that is, utilizing core components of the development house. They only differed in visualization requirements and data-handling types. Both projects had inelastic budgets. Project schedule requirements differed depending on a number of externalities affecting the projects. Both projects were developed in agility using eXtrem Programming and had to be executed in parallel from the point of project period intersection. All projects went through the requirements analysis phase where key project requirements and milestones were agreed upon. There was a 60% allocation rate of the resources assigned to execute tasks on both projects.

We looked at a 3-dimensional variable analysis of the results. For both projects, the key variables of interest examined entailed: requirement or task acceptance patterns, task completion patterns throughout the project duration and profitability analysis.

5.2 Task Acceptance Patterns

5.2.1 Project 1 Acceptance Analysis

Using our model, we analyzed how each project milestone was accepted by the client throughout the project duration. In order to increase client participation and commitment to the project, an incremental functional delivery and signoff development approach was utilized. In measuring the task acceptance pattern, we examined how each project performed on a monthly basis. Figure 1 below shows the results obtained on Project 1 in this dimension of acceptance criteria evaluation and validation pattern analysis. The X-Axis measure observation period while the Y-Axis measure project acceptance percentages.

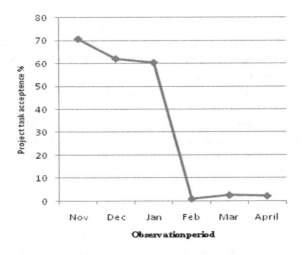

Fig. 1. Project 1 acceptance pattern

The graph above shows that for Project 1 in November, there was a 70.72% likelihood that task acceptance would not suffice in the first frame of the project. The 29.28% difference implied that earlier milestones in the project were accepted, such as project inception deliverables which were derived in the earlier part of the month. Given that requirement analysis, documentation and validation had to precede implementation, functional acceptance would therefore have a higher completion failure in that time frame. As the project progressed in December, the validation failure decreased by 8.59% of the overall tasks in that time frame. This implies that as development started, project delivery maximization was being delayed at a rate of 8.59%. An optimal validation rate would be targeted to being higher than 37.87% since functionality required was mostly from the existing core components. In January, the delivery rate was not very significant either; it only increased by 1.67% from the previous time frame. However, as the February time frame set in, the validation rate increased to 98.99%. This shows that a great deal of effort was expended to ensure that the March deadline would be reached while all tasks were completed and signed off. The remaining 1.01% would only be for bug fixes while more attention was directed to Project 2.

5.2.2 Project 2 Acceptance Analysis

Figure 2 below shows the acceptance pattern evaluation of Project 2 in the study.

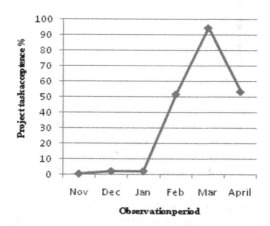

Fig. 2. Project 2 acceptance

At the start of Project 2 in February, the acceptance targets were improved to 48.25%. Perhaps lessons learned on Project 1 led to this improvement, or components development completed in Project 1 which were required by Project 2 led to this accelerated increase in performance. The March time frame reveals that the acceptance rate was improved by 42.94%, leading to a 94.69% likelihood of overall project acceptance in that time frame. However, in the April time frame, this performance seems to have dropped by 41.21%, leading to a 53.48% likelihood of project acceptance in this time frame.

These findings show that there is a strong need to manage the acceptance rate over and above 60% in each project time frame if a given project is to be signed off gracefully at completion, if all requirements will be accepted at signoff and if resources need to take up other roles on other projects that may begin before the present project is completed. Maintaining the project acceptance rates at the rate of 40% in a given time frame would increase the likelihood of a project being delayed due to unaccepted tasks. Therefore, project managers need to evaluate project time frames with keen interest so as to mitigate project delays that may arise due to relative acceptance rate targets.

5.3 Task Completion Patterns

5.3.1 Project 1 Completion Analysis

In this measurement, we analyzed the task completion rate of each project in a given time frame. As shown in Figure 3 below, for Project 1 there was 40.88% likelihood that tasks would be completed over and above 70% at project inception in November. In December the completion rate likelihood seems to have decreased by 2.02%, with tasks only being completed between 31 – 45% on average.

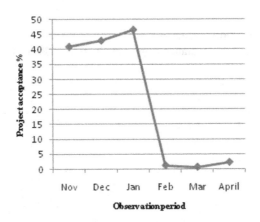

Fig. 3. Completion rate analysis for project 1

In January the completion rate dropped by 3.61%, leading to a 46.51% likelihood of tasks being completed with a progress level of 31% on average, perhaps due to the festive and holiday season around the previous time frame. As the project tended towards completion in February, the task completion rate improved significantly at a rate of 1.1% per task, leading to 98.9% increment in task completion with a task progress average of 69%. In March the completion average dropped to 38%. This was the time for bug fixes and resources were executing other tasks on the next project in parallel.

The findings indicate that as the project tends towards completion, the task completion rate reduces considerably. This could be due to other project externalities on the project, such as delayed customer feedback on the deliverables. Although the acceptance rates rise in the last time frames, other project externalities affect the completion rate on final tasks preceding project signoff, hence impacting on our average profitability margins.

5.3.2 Project 2 Completion Analysis

Figure 4 below shows the results of the completion rate analysis done on Project 2 in this study.

Although Project 2 started in March, our model shows that should the project have started in November, there would have been an average of 1.12% likelihood of task completion through till January. This can be attributed to the fact that since the same resources were working on both projects, they would not achieve higher completion margins on competing projects; hence completing one at a higher acceptance rate before embarking on the next one. At project inception in February, the project completion rate increased by 55.27% leading to a 69% completion progress rate on average. This can be explained perhaps with the fact that both projects required similar components. Given that Project 1's acceptance rate had already reached 97.37% around this time frame and that the functional baseline had already been realized, the

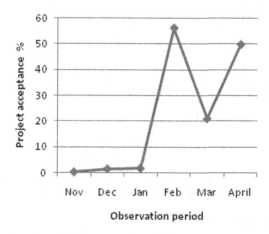

Fig. 4. Completion analysis for project 2

acceleration of project completion for Project 2 tasks was invariably enhanced. In March, however, the completion rate dropped by almost 78.98% leading to an average task completion rate of 38%. This is perhaps due to the fact that resources were divided between both projects; as they fixed bugs on the other, they would also try to work on tasks on Project 2. The pattern seems to have changed in April after Project 1 was completed. The completion rate rose to 50%; implying that resources were now redirected to Project 2.

5.4 Profitability Analysis Patterns

5.4.1 Project 1 Analysis
We examined how profitability fluctuated over time in the various time frames. Figure 5 below shows the results obtained on Project 1 under this evaluation. In the November time frame, there was a 67.04% chance that profits would be realized in that time frame given the number of tasks and resources available. The 32.96% difference implies that profits on the tasks would be realized at such a threshold. In December, however, the profitability likelihood increased by 1.52%, leading to a 34.48% chance that maximum profit of R1600 would be realized on each task.

In January, however, the likelihood of making some profit on project tasks increased by 7.83% from the previous time frame. This led to an overall 42.31% profit realization likelihood. From February until the end of the project in March, the likelihood that profit margins would increase dropped significantly. In February for instance, there was a 99.1% chance that profits would be realized on tasks executed in that time frame but zero profits were attained. In March, the profitability likelihood dropped to 98.97%, implying that there was only a 1.03% chance of making R1 600 on each task in this time frame.

Although the tasks were being accepted as the project was progressing in the last three months, the profitability pattern seems to have been dropping considerably. This implies that more time was invested in completing the tasks to acceptance standards while compromising profit on this project.

Fig. 5. Profitability on project 1

5.4.2 Project 2 Analysis

For Project 2, the profitability pattern seems to have been different, as shown in Figure 6 below.

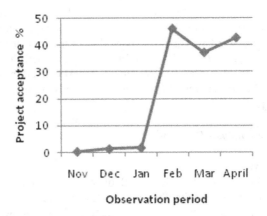

Fig. 6. Project 2 profitability analysis

As the project started in February, there was a 46% chance that some profits would be realized in that time frame. However, the threshold was too low to realize any profit. In March, the likelihood of realizing R1600 profit per task executed in this time frame decreased by 8.86% to 37.13%. In April the pattern seems to have improved significantly, by 5.47% from the previous time frame, implying that there was a 42.61% chance that a profit margin of R1600 would be realized.

As the task acceptance rates increased in February and March, the profitability margins seem to have fluctuated considerably, with a 3.39% drop rate on the average R1600 task profitability projection.

Therefore, as we increase the acceptance rates in each time frame, we ought to take our profit margins into consideration. The likelihood that we can win customer trust in the first two time frames after project inception, by delivering validated tasks, implies that we are likely to decrease our average profitability rates by 3.39% in the subsequent time frames.

6 Implications and Future Work

The area of post project review as a key project management competence is still in its infancy requiring rigorous techniques of analysis. We have demonstrated that we can look at various aspects of the project, including profitability analysis using our technique. Our approach however, is an alternative solution that has been tested in the commercial environment on real life projects specifically embracing key business project values such as project profitability. Our technique is developed in such a way that it is extensive and pluggable, thus it can be generalized to other areas of Software Engineering and other disciplines.

Project variants including requirement or task acceptance, task completion throughout the project duration and profitability analysis patterns impact considerably, on development processes in the first place, and on resource allocation and management capabilities in the second. The order in which selected tasks are prioritized, executed, completed and validated is very important. Our results show that if we use such modeling techniques for ongoing project review processes, we can enhance project portfolio management in the following ways: by determining proper project estimation, by delivering projects on-time and on-budget, and by properly identifying key project requirements and risks.

The benefit of this approach is that measurement of overall project success is improved, thus enhancing a company's ability to handle project portfolio significantly, as it compels the company to consider the magnitude or complexity of software projects taken on. Consequently, if we extend our representation model to address changing tasks and requirements on a project, we can overcome some of the problems that arise under multi-project environments such as resource allocation, coordination or communications. The final goal of our work therefore is not only the improvement of software engineering as a discipline, but also the improvement in management of projects in order to derive value in development of IT projects.

Managers will be able to prioritize activities for the effective management of project completion, and shorten the planned critical path of projects by pruning critical path activities, by performing more activities in parallel, and/or by shortening the durations of critical path activities through adding resources, hence preparing for scheduling and resource planning effectively. The identification of the critical chain of events would make it possible to mitigate their negative effects since risk lists of projects can be generated as a result of sensitivity analysis.

Acknowledgment

Great thanks to Complex Adaptive Systems (Pty) Ltd for their support both technically and academically.

References

1. Zafra-Cabeza, A., Ridao, M.A., Camacho, E.F.: Using a Risk-based Approach to Project Scheduling: A Case Illustration from Semiconductor Manufacturing. EJOR 190, 708–723 (2008)

2. Alba, E., Chicano, J.F.: Software Project Management with GAs. Info. Scie. 177, 2380–2401 (2007)
3. Verner, J.M.: Quality Software Development: What do we Need to Improve in the Software Development Process? In: WoSQ 2008 (2008)
4. Gonçalves, J.F., Mendes, J.J.M., Resende, M.G.C.: A Genetic Algorithm for the Resource Constrained Multi-project Scheduling Problem. EJOR 189, 1171–1190 (2008)
5. Wallacea, L., Keilb, M., Raic, A.: Understanding Software Project Risk: a Cluster Analysis. Information & Management 42, 115–125 (2004)
6. Wateridge, J.: The Role of Configuration Management in the Development and Management of Information Systems/Technology (IS/IT) Projects. Int. J. Proj. Manag. 17(4), 237–241 (1999)
7. Zhang, H., Li, H., Tam, C.: Particle Swarm Optimization for Resource-constrained Project Scheduling. Int. J. Proj. Manag. 24(1), 83–92 (2006)
8. Fidel, R., Scholl, H.J., Liu, S., Unsworth, K.: Mobile Government Fieldwork: A Preliminary Study of Technological, Organizational, and Social Challenges. In: 8th AICPS: dg.o 2007, pp. 131–139 (2007)
9. Morales, A., Barra, L.: System Development Techniques for Small and Medium Size Installations. In: 15th SIGCPR, pp. 241–247 (1977)
10. Nagappan, N., Ball, T.: Use of Relative Code Churn Measures to Predict System Defect Density. In: 27th ICSE 2005, pp. 284–292 (2005)
11. Kan, S.H.: Metrics and Models in Software Quality Engineering, 2nd edn. Longman, Boston (2002)
12. Snow, A.P., Keil, M.: The Challenge of Accurate Software Project Status Reporting: a Two-stage Model Incorporating Status Errors and Reporting Bias. IEEE Trans. on Eng. Manag. 49(4), 491–504 (2002)
13. Snow, A.P., Keil, M.: The Challenges of Accurate Project Status Reporting. In: HICSS 2001, vol. 8, p. 8043 (2001)
14. Russell, S., Norvig, P.: Artificial Intelligence, A Modern Approach, 2nd edn. Prentice Hall Series, New Jersey (2003)
15. An, X., Jutla, D., Cercone, N.: Privacy Intrusion Detection Using Dynamic Bayesian Networks. In: ICEC 2006, pp. 208–215. ACM, New York (2006)
16. Murphy, K.: Dynamic Bayesian Networks Representation, Inference and Learning. PhD thesis, UC Berkeley (2002)
17. Choudhury, T., Rehg, J.M., Pavlovic, V., Pentland, A.: Boosting and Structure Learning in Dynamic Bayesian Networks for Audio-visual Speaker Detection. In: ICPR 2002, vol. 3, pp. 789–794 (2002)
18. Osunmakinde, I.O., Potgieter, A.: Astute Decision. In: Business Intelligence Using Temporal Probabilistic Reasoning. SAIMS (2008)

A Secured Technique for Image Data Hiding

Debnath Bhattacharyya[1], Poulami Das[1], Swarnendu Mukherjee[1],
Debashis Ganguly[1], Samir Kumar Bandyopadhyay[2], and Tai-hoon Kim[3]

[1] Computer Science and Engineering Department, Heritage Institute of Technology,
Kolkata-700107, India
{debnathb,dasp88,mukherjee.swarnendu,DebashisGanguly}@gmail.com
[2] Department of Computer Science and Engineering, University of Calcutta,
Kolkata-700009, India
skb1@vsnl.com
[3] Hannam University, Daejeon – 306791, Korea
taihoonn@empal.com

Abstract. In this paper, a new technique for hiding the data of images has been proposed. This method is invented to hide an image file entirely with in another image file keeping two considerations in mind which are Size and Degree of Security. At the source, the image which is to be hidden (target image) is encoded at the end of another image (cover image). Double layer security of the hidden image can be achieved (over the untrusted network) by; firstly, the starting point of encoding the image data is depended on the size of the images and it is stored within the encoded image at the end of its header information as a cipher text.; secondly, the target image is hidden behind the cover image by following our encrypted image hiding technique.

Keywords: Data, image, Hiding, security, encryption.

1 Introduction

Data hiding can be defined as the process by which any message signal or image is imperceptibly embedded into a host or cover to get a composite signal. Steganography is the art and science of writing hidden messages in such a way that no one apart from the sender and intended recipient even realizes there is a hidden message. Here, the message may present in any format and based on its format we use a particular steganographic technique to hide it. Normally, the actual information is not maintained in its original format and thereby it is converted into an alternative equivalent multimedia file like image, video or audio which in turn is being hidden within another object. This final message (known as stego-object in usual terms) is sent through the network to the recipient, where the actual message is seperated from it.

In this paper, we have considered some important features of data hiding. Our first consideration is that of embedding information into image, which could survive attacks on the network. Next, a hybrid digital embedding technique is proposed for hiding an image into another image in such a way that the quality of the recovered image remains unaltered. Also to make the proposed scheme to run free of size constraints, we have introduced the concept of Padding before doing the actual hiding.

T.-k. Kim, T.-h. Kim, and A. Kiumi (Eds.): SecTech 2008, CCIS 29, pp. 151–159, 2009.

Another important feature, conceived in the encryption process of the images is Multilayered Security. Here, firstly the size difference of the two considered images (target and cover image) is hidden in an encrypted format with in the cover image. After that the entire target image is hidden at the end of the cover image by following our encryption technique which is described in the section-III.C. The stated encryption technique is also different from the existings. Here, based on the pixel value of the target image the cover image is encrypted. Thus if the ultimate object to be transferred gets snooped from the information channel, then also from it no way the information can be retrieved.

Lastly, in most of the algorithms designed based on the principle of Steganography, requires the sending original cover image along with the encoded cover image to the receiver. This approach makes the designed algorithm weaker as it conveys some idea of data hiding to the eavesdropper. But our method covers this lack as here only the final encoded image will be sent to the receiver.

To the best of our knowledge, this work is specifically focused on protection of any information which is in the form of image. The design of this technique is based on extensive analytical as well as experimental modeling of the data-hiding process.

2 Related Works

The majority of today's steganographic systems uses images as cover media because people often transmit digital pictures over email and other Internet communication. Several methods exist to employ the concept of Steganography as well as plenty algorithms have been proposed in this regard. To gather knowledge regarding our approach, we have concentrated on some techniques and methods which are described below.

Least significant bit (LSB) insertion is a common and simple approach to embed information in a cover file. In this method the LSB of a pixel is replaced with an M's bit. If we choose a 24-bit image as cover, we can store 3 bits in each pixel. To the human eye, the resulting stego image will look identical to the cover image.

In the field of image security, Miroslav Dobsicek [1] has developed an interesting application of steganography where the content is encrypted with one key and can be decrypted with several other keys, the relative entropy between encrypt and one specific decrypt key corresponds to the amount of information.

Yusuk Lim, Changsheng Xu and David Dagan Feng, 2001, described the web-based authentication system consists of two parts: one is a watermark embedding system and the other is authentication system. In case of watermark embedding system, it is installed in the server as application software that any authorized user, who has access to server, can generate watermarked image. The distribution can use any kind of network transmission such as FTP, email etc. Once image is distributed to externally, client can access to authentication web page to get verification of image [2].

Min Wu and Bede Liu, June, 2003, proposed [3] a new method to embed data in binary images, including scanned text, figures, and signatures. The method manipulates "flippable" pixels to enforce specific block based relationship in order to embed a significant amount of data without causing noticeable artifacts. They have applied Shuffling before embedding to equalize the uneven embedding capacity from region to region. The hidden data can then be extracted without using the original image, and can also be accurately extracted after high quality printing and scanning with the help of a few registration marks.

Rehab H. Alwan, Fadhil J. Kadhim, and Ahmad T. Al- Taani, 2005, have explained a method with three main steps. First, the edge of the image is detected using Sobel mask filters. Second, the least significant bit LSB of each pixel is used. Finally, a gray level connectivity is applied using a fuzzy approach and the ASCII code is used for information hiding. The prior bit of the LSB represents the edged image after gray level connectivity, and the remaining six bits represent the original image with very little difference in contrast. The given method embeds three images in one image and includes, as a special case of data embedding, information hiding, identifying and authenticating text embedded within the digital images [4].

In 2007, Nameer N. EL-Emam proposed an algorithmic approach to obtain data security using LSB insertion steganographic method. In this approach, high security layers have been proposed through three layers to make it difficult to break through the encryption of the input data and confuse steganalysis too [5].

S. K. Bandyopadhyay, Debnath Bhattacharyya, Swarnendu Mukherjee, Debashis Ganguly, Poulami Das in 2008 has proposed a heuristic approach to hide huge amount of data using LSB steganography technique. In their method, they have first encoded the data and afterwards the encoded data is hidden behind a cover image by modifying the least significant bits of each pixel of the cover image. The resultant stego-image was distortion less. Also, they have given much emphasis on space complexity of the data hiding technique [6].

There is also a good method proposed by G. Sahoo and R. K. Tiwari in 2008. Their proposed method works on more than one image using the concept of file hybridization. This particular method implements the cryptographic technique to embed two information files using steganography. And due to this reason they have used a stego key for the embedding process [7].

F. Bartolini, A. Tefas, M. Barni and I. Pitas discussed the problem of authenticating video surveillance image. After an introduction used to stimulate the need for a watermark-based authentication of VS (Video Surveillance) sequences, a brief survey of the main watermark-based authentication techniques has been presented and the requirements that an authentication algorithm should satisfy for VS applications are discussed. A novel heuristic approach which is suitable for VS visual data authentication has been proposed [8].

Mark A. Masry, 2005, proposed a novel blind watermarking algorithm designed for map and chart images. The algorithm segments the image into homogeneous regions and adds multiple watermark signals to the locations of the pixels on the boundary of several regions. The presence of these signals in the watermarked image is determined using a correlation based detector. The watermarks can be detected in the presence of synchronization errors such as those incurred by cropping the image, or shifting by several columns or rows, and in the presence of noise. The algorithm is designed to efficiently process typical map images [9].

S. K. Bandyopadhyay, Debnath Bhattacharyya, Swarnendu Mukherjee, Debashis Ganguly, Poulami Das in 2008 has also proposed a new algorithmic approach to hide image data using image watermarking technique. In their method, an image is hidden behind another image after zone wise replacement of pixels. The thought behind their work comes from the classical problem of designing a mosaic pattern of tiles in a rectangular floor which indeed is to be cost effective [10].

Generally, modification of any image changes its statistical properties, so eavesdroppers can detect the distortions in the resulting stego-image's statistical properties. In fact, the embedding of high-entropy data (often due to encryption) changes the histogram of colour frequencies in a predictable way. So, in order to obtain more security in our prescribed method, we have embedded an entire image behind another image by modifying discrete zone of pixels. By selecting discrete zone, we have tried to avoid any remarkable change in the cover image.

3 Our Work

Before discussing the details of the algorithm proposed here for invisible watermark of the information behind the cover object, it is better to mention about the selection of the images and information which are to be steganographed. Here in this paper, the algorithm is basically implemented over normal bitmap image file, but it should be clarified that the same scheme can be extended to operate over other file formats also. The image file which is to be hidden is here referred as TargetImage and the image behind which it is to be hidden is termed as CoverImage. The selection of neither the TargetImage nor the CoverImage is constrained by any size limit.

After selecting the pictures, we have to pad the CoverImage with required white spaces, i.e., addition of extra white pixels if the size of it is less than the TargetImage. The padding will be done in such a way that after padding the size of the CoverImage will be equal to the size of the TargetImage in addition with 57. In the CoverImage, apart from the header information (54 bytes) three extra bytes are taken to store the size difference of the padded CoverImage and the TargetImage in an encoded format. In next attempt, the entire TargetImage will be hidden in the CoverImage starting from byte position whose value will be equal to size by following our data hiding technique.

It is better to be confessed that the method for encryption can be personalized, i.e., can be selected according to the user needs. But, the authors specifically suggests this specialized scheme, proposed in this paper, as because here the information are no longer being merged or masked with another and instead of that keeping the TargetImage as a key the information in the carrier, i.e., the CoverImage is altered to obtain resultant image which is taken as FinalImage. Thus no essence of the actual information is retrained in the FinalImage, whereas in usual methods of the mostly done bitwise merging; the information belongs in encrypted way directly merged into final object obtained.

3.1 SIDH_MAIN (TargetImage, CoverImage)

This is the main function in our algorithm. This function will be used in the sender side and will call other modules of our algorithm like Padding and Encryption.

Arguments: This function will take TargetImage and CoverImage as argument and finally it will output the encoded stego-image.

1. Obtain the size of the TargetImage and store it as TargetImageSize.
2. Now choose the CoverImage and obtain its size and store it in CoverImageSize.

3. Now check the TargetImageSize and the CoverImageSize. If the TargetImageSize is greater than the CoverImageSize then call the PAD module with argument CoverImage and newSize where newSize is equal to the sum of TargetImageSize and 57.

4. Next obtain the difference of CoverImageSize and TargetImageSize and store it in Size.

5. Now call the SIDH_ENC module to hide the TargetImage behind the CoverImage with arguments CoverImage, TargetImage and size and thereby obtain the finalImage.

6. Send only the finalImage over the network to reach the intended destination.

3.2 PAD (PICTURE, SIZE)

This function is used in the algorithm to pad an image to obtain an image of the desired size from the input image.

Arguments: This function will take the image, which has to be padded along with the desired image size which is to be obtained after padding.

1. Obtain the width, length of the pixel matrix of the PICTURE (say R_P and C_P).

2. Fill pixels with white color until $R_P * C_P * DPI >= SIZE$.
    Here DPI stands for Depth per Index.

3. Return the PICTURE.

3.3 SIDH_ENC (PICTURE_1, PICTURE_2, SIZE)

This function is used in the algorithm to encrypt an image with the help of either same image (self encryption) or another image to obtain an encrypted image of the desired size.

Arguments: This function will take the cover image (PICTURE_1) in which another image will be hidden; the target image (PICTURE_2), which will be hidden, and finally it will output the stego-image as final image.

1. Read the bytes from starting of the PICTURE_1.

2. Repeat step 1 if numbers of bytes read is not equal to 54 (header size for a BMP image).

3. Obtain the octal format of SIZE and count the number of digits present in that format and store it in a variable say key.

4. Read the next byte of PICTURE_1 and replace it with key.

5. Next read key number of bytes of PICTURE_1 and replace each of them with the digits present in the octal format of SIZE staring from Left.

6. Read the first byte of the PICTURE_2.

7. If the value of the read byte is 0 then replace the current byte of the PICTURE_1 with 255 and read the next byte of PICTURE_1 and PICTURE_2. Otherwise go to the next step.

8. If the value of the read byte is 255 then replace the current byte of the PICTURE_1 with 0 and read the next byte of PICTURE_1 and PICTURE_2. Otherwise go to the next step.

9. If the value of the read pixel is greater than 0 and less than 255 then do the following operations. byte'' = byte' + SPN where byte' is the corresponding byte of the PICTURE_1 and SPN is the sum of prime numbers starting from 0 to SIZE.

10. Now if the calculated byte'' is greater than 255 then calculate: byte''' = byte'' − 255 and replace the current byte of PICTURE_1 with byte'''. Read the next byte of PICTURE_1.

11. Read the next byte of PICTURE_2 and go to step 4.

12. Now if the condition of the step 10 is false then replace the current byte of PICTURE_1 with byte'' and read the next byte of PICTURE_1 and go to step 11.

13. Repeat the above steps from 7 to 12 until the end of any image is reached.

14. Return PICTURE_1 as final image.

3.4 SIDH_DEC (PICTURE_1, PICTURE_2, SIZE)

This function is used in the algorithm to decrypt an image with the help the original image to obtain a hidden image. This module will be executed in the receiver's side.

Arguments: This function will take only the source image (PICTURE_1) which has to be decrypted as this algorithm only requires the final stego-image to obtain the image behind it.

1. Read the bytes from starting of the PICTURE_1.

2. Repeat step 1 if numbers of bytes read is not equal to 54 (header size for a BMP image).

3. Read the next byte of PICTURE_1 and store it in a variable say key'.

4. Next read key' number of bytes of PICTURE_1 and store each of them in an array of bytes.

5. Obtain the entire array from the above step. Now perform the following operation :
    SIZE' = $\sum$ array[i] * 8^i where i varies from 0 to (key' − 1). This step is performed to locate the starting position of the hidden image within PICTURE_1.

6. Go to the byte number SIZE' of PICTURE_1.

7. Open a new image file say PICTURE_2.

8. If the value of the read byte from PICTURE_1 is 0 then store 255 in the PICTURE_2.

9. If the value of Pixel' is 255 then store 0 in the PICTURE_2.

10. Now if the value of read byte is greater than 0 and less than 255 then calculate: byte1 = byte - SPN and store byte1 in the PICTURE_2. Here SPN determines Sum of Prime Numbers in between 0 and SIZE'.

11. Now if the calculated byte1 is greater than 255 then calculate: byte11 = byte1 + 255 and store it in PICTURE_2.

12. If the condition of the above step is false then simply store byte1 in PICTURE_2.

13. Read the next byte of PICTURE_1 and go to step 8.

14. Return PICTURE_2.

4 Result and Discussion

The stated Algorithm has got five distinct divisions, a. main function which calls next three sections; b. Arrange: to calculate desired row and column of pictures; c. Pad: to pad the images as per row-column given by previous sections; d. Encryption; e. Decryption.

4.1 Complexity Analysis of the Stated Algorithm

For Padding (Section III.B): To pad an image row wise, then we $O(n^2)$ is incurred. Again to pad an image column wise, complexity of $O(n^2)$ has incurred. So, overall time complexity becomes $O(2*n^2)$.

For Encryption and Decryption (Section III.C and Section III.D): For each row wise and column wise scan is being done. So, each one requires time of $O(rowsize*columnsize) \equiv O(n^2)$.

In this algorithm, operation is being done byte wise. So, no need of remembering whole pixel matrix is required. Thus amount of space required to run this algorithm comes under $O(\log n)$ and thereby it becomes an inplace algorithm.

4.2 Test Results

To test the algorithm, we have chosen one cover image having size 350000 Bytes and one target image having size 97300 Bytes and they are shown in Figure 1. After selecting the images, we need to perform the size comparison in between them. Now clearly size of the cover image is greater than the size of the target image. So, calling of the PAD module of our algorithm is not required. But, if any user chooses the target image which is having greater size than the selected cover image then PAD module should be invoked to efface the size constraint which is stated in our algorithm. Next, we have calculated the size parameter of our algorithm and here it is 253700 Bytes. So, according to the algorithm the value of key is 6 and the octal representation of the parameter size is 757404. That means 55th no. byte will be modified with key and stating from 56th no. byte to (key+55) no. byte will be modified by the digits present in the octal format of size starting from left.

Cover Image [351000 Bytes]   Target Image [97300 Bytes]

Fig. 1. Cover Image and Target Image

Final Image [351000 Bytes]   Retrieved Target Image [97300 Bytes]

Fig. 2. Final Image and Retrieved Target Image

In next, we have to move to the byte position size of the cover image and then we have to modify the successive bytes depending on the target image. Here, all the header information of the target image is itself encoded within the cover image. Thus at the time of recovery, entire hidden data has to be retained to get the original target image back.

The resultant output Image shown in Fig. 2 after the execution of Encryption algorithm; in our case it is SIDH_ENC Algorithm. Only Final Image will be sent to the receiver.

The resultant output Image shown in Fig. 3 after the execution of Decryption algorithm; in our case it is SIDH_DEC Algorithm. From the output image it can be easily inferred that the quality of the target image is not getting modified after the execution of our proposed scheme. So, our technique is not introducing any noise at the time of performing either encryption or decryption. But, the Final image may suffer some distortion due to the channel noise. So, in that case, noise filters have to be used prior to the application of the proposed scheme.

This algorithm is tested using different type of images. We have also observed that this work is well applicable for grayscale images. Also, at the time of implementation the functioning of padding module is checked by violating the size constraints of our algorithm.

5   Conclusion

In this paper the major emphasis is given on the size and computational complexity, which incurs at the time of doing any operation in Steganographic approach. Most of the steganographic algorithms deal with two images at the receiver side in order to retrieve the original message. But, here only a single image will be sent to the receiver. Thus we can say that this proposed technique is helpful in reducing network traffic. Again use of single encrypted image over the untrusted network, led the intruders to route in a different direction.

In this paper, the authors implemented the basic algorithm through bitmap pictures, but there is no such constraint over selection of file format, i.e., the same procedure can be realized through any of available multimedia file formats. It is thereby expected that any kind of future endeavor in this field will definitely route it a path to design a secure system using the proposed algorithm for both Internet and Mobile Communication Technology.

References

1. Dobsicek, M.: Extended steganographic system. In: 8th Intl. Student Conf. on Electrical Engineering, FEE CTU 2004, Poster (2004)
2. Lim, Y., Xu, C., Feng, D.D.: Web based Image Authentication Using Invisible Fragile Watermark. In: Pan-Sydney Area Workshop on Visual Information Processing (VIP 2001), Sydney, Australia, pp. 31–34 (2001)
3. Wu, M., Liu, B.: Data Hiding in Binary Image for Authentication and Annotation. IEEE Trans. Image Processing 6(4), 528–538 (2004)
4. Alwan, R.H., Kadhim, F.J., Al-Taani, A.T.: Data Embedding Based on Better Use of Bits in Image Pixels. International Journal of Signal Processing 2(2), 104–107 (2005)
5. EL-Emam, N.N.: Hiding a large amount of data with high security using steganography algorithm. Journal of Computer Science, 223–232 (April 2007)
6. Bandyopadhyay, S.K., Bhattacharyya, D., Mukherjee, S., Ganguly, D., Das, P.: A Secure Scheme for Image Transformation. IEEE SNPD, 490–493 (August 2008)
7. Sahoo, G., Tiwari, R.K.: Designing an Embedded Algorithm for Data Hiding using Steganographic Technique by File Hybridization. IJCSNS 8(1), 228–233 (2008)
8. Masry, M.A.: A Watermarking Algorithm for Map and Chart Images. In: Proceedings of the SPIE Conference on Security, Steganography and Watermarking of Multimedia Contents VII, January 2005, pp. 495–504 (2005)
9. Bartolini, F., Tefas, A., Barni, M., Pitas, I.: Image Authentication Techniques for Surveillance Applications. In: IEEE Proceedings, October 2001, vol. 89(10), pp. 1403–1418 (2001)
10. Bandyopadhyay, S.K., Bhattacharyya, D., Mukherjee, S., Ganguly, D., Das, P.: Padding and Zonal Substitution Scheme for Image Watermarking. In: International Conference on Contemporary Computing (IC3 Noida), August 2008, pp. 122–127 (2008)

Author Index